THE MOST DANGEROUS MAN

AND THE RAPE OF DELAWARE COUNTY

E. H. TURLINGTON II, SSG USA (RETIRED)

Southron Press

Jay, Oklahoma

Southron Press, LLC
68901 East County Road 370
Jay, Oklahoma 74346
www.RapeofDelco.com
Documentation Information:
This site may contain copyrighted material the use of which has not always been specifically authorized by the copyright owner. Southron Press states that any such material is used as part of their efforts to advance the understanding of its readers regarding significant cultural, historical, political and legal issues, and that Southron Press believes this constitutes a "fair use" of the material in accordance with Title 17 U.S.C. Section 107.
Some of the documents in this book have been cropped (fax header information, etc.) to increase text size. Complete court transcripts, police interview recordings, police wiretap recordings, official police photographs, medical reports and other documentation are online at www.RapeOfDelco.com.

The Most Dangerous Man: The Rape of Delaware County/
E.H. Turlington SSG USA (Retired). —1st ed.
ISBN 978-0-578-54335-2

This book is dedicated to the victims of physical and sexual assault and torture in Delaware County jails, to those denied medical treatment while in the custody of Delaware County jails; to those who have been arrested on the basis of unsubstantiated "snitch" testimony given by informants in exchange for lighter sentences; to those who have had their property seized and sold by Delaware County authorities without a conviction; to those who have been victimized by the rampant property crimes perpetrated by meth addicts; and to the victims of offenders who appear to be immune from prosecution due to connections or informant status.

No dedication would be complete without acknowledging the patriots in our community, including the honest and diligent law enforcement officers such as Detective Frank Miller and Deputy Chris Hardison (both formerly employed by the Delaware County Sheriff's Office), Ottawa County Sheriff Jeremy Floyd, principled and benevolent attorneys like Jason David Smith and former Assistant District Attorney David Anderson, old veterans like Robert Lawson, the commander of the Jay American Legion hall, who not only volunteer their time and resources ensuring our community's fallen patriots are never forgotten, but who also lend their voices and authority for the patriots still among us. I would also like to thank the individual members of the NRA and other gun rights groups, but in particular, the Gun Owners of America, and the GOA's Oklahoma affiliate, the Oklahoma 2nd Amendment Association. Vietnam Veteran and fellow All American Doug Dollar mentored me with much needed advice on authoring, printing, and publishing. Finally, this book is dedicated to all patriots everywhere, like activists Tanya Hathaway and Rita De Castro, who stand in defense for victims of government abuse and oppression wherever those victims may be.

- Ed "Hoss" Turlington, SSG USA (Retired)

The most dangerous man
to any government
is the man who is able to
think things out for himself

—H. L. Menken

Government is that organisation in
society which attempts to maintain
a monopoly on the use of force
and violence in a given territory

—Murray Rothbard

Contents

Complete Court Transcripts, Audio Recordings of Police Interviews and Police Wiretaps, Police Videos, Investigation Photographs and Documents, Philpott's Criminal Records, etc. can be found at www.RapeOfDelco.com

A disabled veteran and former law enforcement officer catches a violent career felon with multiple warrants for his arrest, trespassing and burning something. The felon attacks; the veteran shoots; the Sheriff arrests the veteran. The veteran learns the felon is a protected police informant.

Probable Cause *(15) The felon turns out to be a convicted drug dealer with active warrants for his arrest, but the local Sheriff protects the felon. The lead investigator decides Turlington is the aggressor* **before the investigation starts.** *(28) The Sheriff's Department* **withholds evidence** *(18) and* **alters evidence** *(27) submitted to the public and to the Court.* **The felon tells the Investigator, "I'll never give you the same answer twice".** *(56)* **The investigator admits to the felon, "I am just trying to help you"** *(37)*

A brief history of Turlington's family ties to the area from his ancestors who pioneered Delaware District, Indian Territory, to growing up in Delaware and Ottawa Counties and raising the 7th generation of his family here.

Long after Turlington's charges should have been dismissed due to the lack of a speedy trial, the prosecution finally conducts the Preliminary Hearing. The State's sole witness is unable to identify Turlington, the prosecutor offers evidence into the record he knows to be false (three times) (149), and Turlington's attorney (who has since been shown to have ties to the leader of a local drug ring) fails to make even the simplest motions (169)

Philpott's decades long relationship with Delaware County Law Enforcement begins with his first known "deal" 1991. (234) Philpott, the violent career criminal, turns 18, begins 40 year crime spree. (181) Convicted for felony theft and felony robbery. 8 days later charged with felony drug dealing (later convicted) Beats wife during and after marriage, assaults her daughter, threatens to burn their house while brandishing a firearm (179)

*Turlington retains prominent defense attorney Winston Connor. Authorities then wiretap Connor soliciting murder and conspiring with a convicted cop killer and drug ring leader. (184) **Winston threatens to kill his adversary's boyfriend**, according to testimony by a local attorney and former 13th Judicial District Assistant District Attorney. (198) According to court records, Connor trades legal services for sex with prostitutes and is able to get "deferred deals" for women charged with prostitution. (204)*

Turlington waives his right to an attorney and presents his own case to the prosecutor. (213) The prosecutor violates his oath and responsibilities as an attorney by allowing falsehoods in the record to go uncorrected. (211) Ed goes public with evidence of police crimes, the criminal record of Philpot (the felon/star witness), and the prosecution's misconduct. Turlington goes to the Oklahoma Bar Association with claims of prosecutorial misconduct. (225)

After more than five years of looking at a life sentence in prison for something he didn't do, Turlington posts to social media that he would post "true and accurate, documented and very embarrassing videos" of the prosecution team if his case wasn't "dropped soon". (250) After more than five years of trying to imprison Turlington, the District Attorney finally drops Turlington's charges, misleading the public one last time. (253)

Foreword

I have been friends with Ed Turlington and his family for nearly forty years. During this time, I have known Ed in a variety of capacities. I first trained with Ed in Tai Koshi Do in the early eighties under Mr. Wayne L. Davis. After Ed served in the Army with the 82d Airborne Division, and at NATO Headquarters as a member of General James P. McCarthy's security detachment, he joined the 45th Infantry Brigade. In the 45th, I was the Platoon Sergeant of Company C, 1st Battalion 279th Infantry in Tulsa, Oklahoma, and Ed was one of my Soldiers. I continued to mentor Ed in his military career when I was the Command Sergeant Major of the 45th Infantry Brigade Combat Team.

In 2011, the US Army Reserve Command selected Ed and his wife Julie to represent the state of Kansas at the Army Reserve's 106th Birthday Ceremony in Washington DC. The Commanding General of the US Army Reserves reenlisted Ed under the Declaration of Independence and the Constitution. Ed retired from the 45th Infantry Brigade in 2017.

Ed and his wife are certified Private Investigators as well as certified teachers. Ed is certified to teach Oklahoma History, US History, Government, Economics, World Geography, World History, Health, PE and is qualified to coach High School sports. He is currently working on his master's degree in Education Administration. This is relevant, because when I read that Philpott accused Ed of screaming "I ain't afraid to bust a cap in a motherf*cker", or words to that effect, I knew Philpott was liar. Ed is an educated, intelligent man, and he hasn't used street slang like that in the 4 decades I have known him. However, I know that **is** how drug addicts talk, and that's how a drug addict would imagine someone else talking during a confrontation.

I have been friends with Ed and his family for a long time.

Ed is morally and physically strong, maybe even bullheaded. No matter where he has lived, he always tries to make his community a better place. As long as I have known him Ed has always done what he believed was right, regardless of the consequence.

In closing I should say something about Deputy Gayle Wells. I was ordained as a minister during my military career and now am the pastor at Bar None Cowboy Church in Afton. I'm also a reserve Nowata County K9 Officer in my personal time, so I can help support law enforcement. As part of my law enforcement certification, Gayle Wells taught one of my classes. My personal experience was that Wells neither respects nor appreciates veterans. When I took the class from Wells, I was already a combat veteran, and experienced in detainee operations, the use of force, and firearms. As the proprietor of Team Phoenix Instructions, LLC, I had instructed hundreds of people, including law enforcement officers, in personal defense and firearms tactics. In other words, I had already done everything a small-town police officer like Wells would ever do in a career and then some. Still, I went to his training with humility, ready to learn, and I didn't brag about what I had done. I was not looking for special treatment but did expect to be treated with at least a nominal amount of professional courtesy. Instead, I found Wells to be an insufferable braggart, who was condescending to me, and to his students in general. Wells doesn't treat veterans with any respect because he has not gone through what veterans go through; he doesn't understand their experiences or their character.

Alderman Dean Bridges,
CSM USA (retired)
Pastor, Bar None Cowboy Church
former Nowata County Commissioner

Preface

What follows is not an angry rant, or an editorial piece. I will cite facts and back them up with government documents. The bottom line is that the system had an informant to protect, so the Sheriff abused his power to get the result he wanted. He protected a violent criminal at the expense of a veteran.

The prosecutor seemed unconcerned that his star witness was a multiple felon when I shot him, had active arrest warrants at the time of the shooting, was convicted for a meth felony after I shot him, or that he committed perjury regarding his felonies. Neither did the prosecutor seem concerned that the lead investigator withheld exculpatory evidence or tampered with witness testimony.

Understanding all of this, I believed I was just collateral damage to protect an informant. My own defense attorney wouldn't even enter the evidence into court that would impeach the government witness, and then my attorney got caught soliciting murder and conspiring with a drug dealer, proving that the local legal system and drug rings are working together in some cases. What chances of a fair trial did I have against a local drug ring that was raking in a million dollars a week from my judicial district? When drug dealing felons are protected as informants, and my own attorney is part of the criminal control of the countyside, what could I do? I could take my case to the public and hope someone would listen. This is my story.

-   E. H. "Hoss" Turlington II, 15 June 2019,
    Delaware County, Oklahoma

Introduction

Although I wrote this book as a means to clear my name, its purpose is much further reaching than my own experience. Readers should also understand the consequences of having people of one culture rule over another. In particular, this is an example of city people ruling over country people.

Oklahoma's 13th Judicial District is composed of Ottawa and Delaware Counties. Almost all of Delaware County and the eastern half of Ottawa County are in the Ozark Mountains. Ottawa County borders Missouri and Delaware County borders both Missouri and Arkansas.

I am directly descended from 8 Indian Territory pioneers[1] who settled in Delaware District. My cousin, Indian Territory pioneer Sam Fullerton sr,[i] was the first Presiding Judge of the 13th. This area is a product of my people, and my people are a product of this area.

However, this cannot be said for the people running this area. It should be noted that every single person involved in my false arrest, the biased investigation that led to it, and the five-year prosecution are carpetbaggers. They are outsider city people whose priority is to enrich themselves with power over our community rather than to represent the values of our community.

The District Attorney at the time of my arrest, Eddie Wyant, is a feminine marshmallow of a man who now defends admitted pedophiles at his hometown of Enid. In a

---

[1] www.rapeofdelco.com/fftt.htm

recent child pornography case in which the children being raped were between the ages of 5 and 10, and for which the penalty was punishable up to 20 years in prison. Wyant fought for probation. (see Appendix W).

His replacement, Kenny Wright, grew up in a wealthy Tulsa suburb. The prosecutor in my case, who violated his oath multiple times throughout my case, is a second generation American raised in Boston and educated in Connecticut. The dirty cop is an old draft dodger from Missouri who has a history of harassing veterans and women. Winston Connor, the criminal defense attorney (and former Delaware County prosecutor) is an East Coast liberal. He was unwilling to get my charges dropped. Not long after I discharged Connor, authorities wiretapped him soliciting murder to a convicted Delaware County cop killer and leader of a local drug ring. Last is the dirty Sheriff Harlan Moore, who had Wells summoned from home at night to take over the investigation from the experienced detectives at the scene, so it could be molded to fit the Sheriff's narrative: that their snitch, the violent triple felon with active warrants for his arrest, was somehow the innocent victim and the disabled veteran family man was the aggressor. Neither Wyant, Wright, Lelecas, Connor, Moore, nor Wells are from here. [ii]

Jay, Oklahoma, the Delaware County seat, has a per capita income of $13,045. The only thing the men in the preceding paragraph understand about poverty is that poor people are easy targets. That is why these outsiders are here. This doesn't only apply to cops and lawyers. Corruption begets corruption. As explained in chapter 3 below, street criminals (like the one Turlington shot on his farm) are drawn here for the police protection they receive.

Not only do the above outsiders not share our values, they are just not tough people. None of the above people has ever been in a fist fight. None of the above people has ever taken a physical risk for another person, much less for a notion or value. To a man, they are physical and moral cowards.

Kenny Wright recites his part in the talent show.

Cameron Carlson and Brad Boyle are acting their parts in "The Rimers of Eldritch."

"Country Kenny" Wright's talent: pretending to be from the country, Broken Arrow High School Talent Show, circa 1987

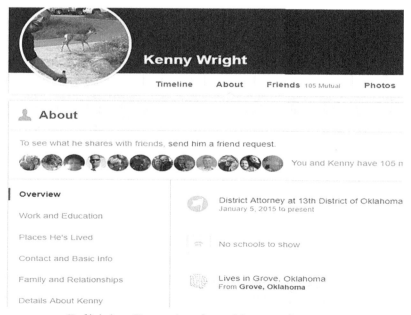

Politician Kenny's talent 30 years later:
pretending he's not a city boy

The natives of our area, like the Indians and Pioneers who established it, are very tough people. Jay is the hometown of former world boxing champion Tommy Morrison.[2]

The real estate agent who sold us our farm, Brian Elder, grew up with Morrison in Jay. Brian is a former regional Toughman Champion.[3] Brian really is a tough man, but that is not unusual here.

---

[2] Tommy's 3rd Great Grandfather, William Morrison, was a corporal in Company K, 49th regiment, Kentucky Infantry. William's grandfather, North Carolinian Thomas Morrison, was a sergeant in the American Revolution and fought in Virginia, where he stayed after the war.

[3] Toughman contests are amateur boxing matches consisting of three, two-minute bouts. Sixteen people have died in Toughman or Toughman style tournaments since the first one in 1979. including Oklahoman Shannon Sizemore in 1996. The Labor Commission outlawed Toughman Competitions in January 97, but six months later the contests were reinstated. Oklahoma leads the country in number of Toughman contests. Tommy Morrison, "Mr. T", and "Butterbean" all began their careers in Toughman competitions.

Baddest Realtor in Delaware County: Toughman Brian Elder on ESPN[4] discussing his friend Tommy Morrison

Neighboring Grove is the hometown of our State Representative Josh West.[5] Josh earned the Bronze Star for valor while saving his Battalion Commander's life in Iraq. Josh's abdomen and legs were shot up by AK47 fire in the process. Josh has seen the photographs of Philpott's gun shot wounds, and he concurs that the bullet entered the front of Philpott's leg and exited the rear. The entry and exit wounds are covered in Chapter 2.

Josh descends from Indian Territory pioneers John West and Nora Mosby. John West's father, Thomas Rankin West,

---

[4] "Tommy - ESPN Films: 30 for 30," ESPN (ESPN Internet Ventures), accessed October 19, 2019,

http://www.espn.com/30for30/film/_/page/Tommy.

[5] Joshua Kelly West > Kelly Ray West & Darlene Griffith > Henry Lee West & Alice May Greer > John Richard West & Nora E Mosby > Thomas Rankin West & Arminda Elenor Crawford > Reverend Major Samuel West & Ann Dinwiddie Rankin

Documentation at www.rapeofdelco.com/joshwest.htm

was a Confederate soldier in Company A, 32nd Tennessee Infantry. Thomas West's grandfather, Virginian Edward West, was granted land in Tennesse from the newly formed United Stated government for fighting against the Chickamauga Indians during the Revolutionary War.

Former National Champion Cody Springsguth
with son Cody jr

Grove Fit is one of two martial arts gyms in Grove. Owner Cody Springsguth is a national TKD sparring champion and was the senior coach for Team USA at the International Tae Kwon Do Federation World Championship Tournament when his son Cody jr placed 8th. Cody jr played quarterback at Kansas Wesleyan University and now coaches Northwest Louisiana State. Cody sr and both his brothers, Troy and Sean, served in the military. My first coon hunt was with Cody sr on his Grandfather Earl Kelly's ranch in Zena in the 70s.

Jim Roach is descended from Miami, Indian Territory pioneer Isaiah Newton Swan Roach. Isaiah's father, James Harrison Roach, was a Confederate in Company B., Tennessee Artillery Corps.[6] I went to school in Afton with Jim and learned martial arts with his big brother Mark.[7] Mark was a Grove cop in the 80s and now is an Oklahoma Highway Patrol. Jim, who won several Oklahoma Golden Gloves championships in the 80s, now runs the Grove Boxing Club from his gym. In 2016, Jim won his professional boxing debut at 48 years old. His opponent was 29 years his junior.

---

[6] James Joseph Roach > John Robert Roach & Bettie Jean Matthews > Sherman Roach & Bertha Greiner > William John Roach & Nancy Chastain > Isaiah Newton Swan Roach & Lucy Ann Bailey

Documentation at www.rapeofdelco.com/roach.htm

[7] See photo page 87

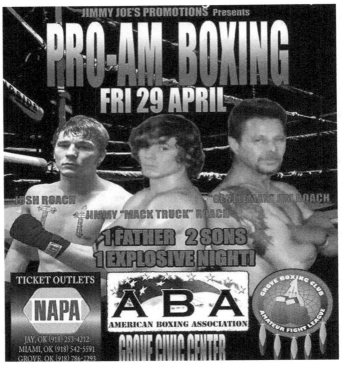

2016 Fight advertisement for 48 year old Gentleman Jim Roach and sons Jimmy jr and Josh. It was Jim sr's professional boxing debut. Jim won the match. His opponent was half his age.

Afton is also the home of my first real hero, Doug Gibson. My father was the school superintendent at Afton when Doug went to high school. Doug was a big polite farm boy and one of my father's favorite students. In 1994, Ottawa county suffered a wave of cattle rustling. Doug lost 4 head in two weeks that March. On March 30 Doug laid in wait with a shotgun, caught the thieves trespassing, and shot one with double ought buckshot.[8] Our community was elated. Doug

---

[8] Appendix X, "Doug Gibson Becomes a Hero by Murdering a Cattle Rustler", and Scott Parks, "Rancher Becomes Hero By

plead to a manslaughter charge and 18 months unsupervised probation. Afterwards, the conviction was removed from his record. If your'e thinking Doug must've been a wealthy rancher to get away with it, he was not. At the time, Doug was a tree trimmer and lived in a house with no air conditioning. He had less than 50 head of cattle. His community supported him and the District Attorney knew it. As a younger man I was in more than one situation when I asked myself, "What would Doug Gibson do?"

Early in my case, my brother Lance and I tried to understand why the District Attorney was taking so long to dismiss the charges. We understood why I was arrested the night I shot a violent trespasser; because he was a protected police informant, and the Sheriff, not being from around here, didn't know the veteran from the felon. But once the DA understood the situation, why didn't he give the benefit of the doubt to the disabled veteran, rather than the violent felon with active warrants for his arrest? Because the DA, like everyone else involved in my prosecution, is not from here and they don't share our values.

During the same conversation with Lance, he remarked that were he a judge, and a man was charged for assault for defending his wife's honor, he would consider every possible angle from the vantage point of giving the husband the

---

Killing Apparent Cattle Rustler," | Seattle Times Newspaper, June 26, 1994, accessed August 05, 2019, and

http://community.seat-
tletimes.nwsource.com/achive/?date=19940626&slug=1917390.

benefit of the doubt, and would personally consider that sometimes "direct action" is adequate justice served. Sometimes, a man has it coming. While readers not from here may think Lance sounds like an uneducated redneck, they would only be half right. Lance is a full bird Colonel in the Army JAG Corps, has multiple graduate degrees, and is a member of the Oklahoma Bar. He has fifty lawyers and paralegals working for him. The prosecutors who work for him have supervisors *who have supervisors* who report to Lance. He actually does understand the nuances of the law, but his values are still those of someone from rural Oklahoma.

When Lance was a new lawyer in the Army, he once asked an instructor if Army defense attorneys had the right to refuse cases, when they found the crime (or the defendant) so morally repugnant that the attorney would be unable to provide a zealous defense. The instructor, a northeastern liberal, was shocked that Lance could even ask such a question (the Oklahoma Code of Ethics for Attorneys states that lawyers have not only the right, but the obligation, to refuse the case in such a situation). The instructor then asked Lance if he actually believed in the Constitution, and the right of Due Process. Lance replied that if any framers of the Constitution were approached by a potential client who had confessed to raping a toddler, that framer would be more likely to participate in a lynching than to defend the rapist in court. I think Lance was right about that, but the instructor was a product of a different culture.

The point again, is that country people have different values than city people, regardless of education or occupation. Country people understand that some men need their asses kicked, some men need shot, and sometimes, a man just has it coming to him.

Louisana Justice: Gary Plauchet executes the man that molested Plauchet's 11 year old son. Plauchet plead no contest and received a suspended sentence.

Prologue

April 7, 2014: the bank closed on the sale of a remote, foreclosed property in Delaware County, Oklahoma, and this was the beginning of a project to build the Turlington family farm. It is also the beginning of a true story about crime, corruption, and the perversion of the legal system in rural Oklahoma.

The property sat in the foothills of the Ozarks, in a clearing in the woods at the bottom of a holler. The house, barn, chicken coop and workshop had suffered extensive damage while it sat in foreclosure the preceding years. Thieves had stripped the house of all removable objects, including the hot water heater and even the toilet. I am convinced this was the work of meth addicts because they had gone so far as to rip out all of the electrical wiring, which only has value as copper scrap. Stealing wire for scrap is not a very profitable criminal venture, so typically, only the most desperate drug addicts even bother with it.

Electrical wire torn out of walls in Turlington's future home.
Thieves also stole the hot water heater and toilet.

For the next few days, I camped at the house with my firstborn son, "Hardee", who was about to turn five. We didn't have electricity or running water, but we were cleaning it up and making repairs. My wife Julie, four months pregnant with our daughter Audrey Maxine, stayed with our second born son, Hoss, at my mother's house in Miami, Oklahoma. Julie was and is a Biology Teacher at Miami Public Schools.

Our property sits in the extreme Northeast Corner of Oklahoma, so even though it has a Jay, Oklahoma address, it is actually much closer to Southwest City, Missouri and Maysville, Arkansas. I started calling it "the farm" from day one, because I saw it for its potential, not its run-down condition. I made a supply run into town, and on my way back, I saw something very suspicious on the edge of the property near the dirt road. What happened next changed my life and my family's lives. What follows is my story, in my words.

Spring 2014. Turlington and his firstborn, Hardee, taking a break from making repairs to their new home

Hardee on his 5th birthday with sheep, May 2014

Sheep and chickens on farm, June 2014

House with electricity and wood stove, October 2014

E. H. Turlington II, SSG USA (Retired)

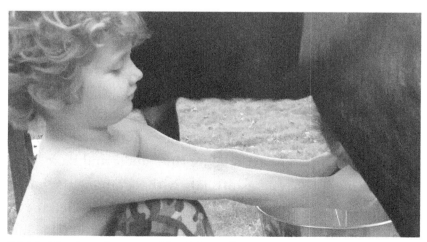

2014. Hardee, 5 years old with snake caught from chicken coop, checking bees, and milking his goat, Caprina

[1]

STAND YOUR GROUND

EXACTLY ONE WEEK after the real estate closing on my family's new home, I was driving on a dirt road on my return from a supply-run. Right before I got to my driveway, I found three local drug addicts trespassing on the farm. They were huddled around a small fire, with a pallet set up, doing something with plastic sheeting and a can of Coleman camp fuel. I am a former law enforcement officer, and I had been recently certified as a Private Investigator (P.I.). The instructor for my P.I. Course was NEO A&M Chief of Police Mark Wall. Mark is a former Delaware County Sheriff's Deputy, and former Mayor of Jay. So, not only am I familiar with the law and detecting violations of the law, but I had also been trained in citizen's arrest, use of force, and self-defense.

I immediately recognized that the trespassers were engaged in criminal activity. I knew that at a minimum, the men were trespassing and burning something. I also thought they were cooking meth, using the "shake and bake" method of setting up a makeshift lab with components including camp fuel. Knowing that meth addicts had robbed my house in the past, I was alarmed. I would have called 911, but the farm is so remote, there is no cell phone coverage.

I also noticed that they had taken the license plate off their truck, so they couldn't be identified if anyone spotted them trespassing, cooking meth, or robbing local houses. Based on my law enforcement and private investigation training and experience, I executed a citizen's arrest in accordance with Title 22 section 187 of the Oklahoma Statutes, for the crimes of trespassing, starting the fire, and suspicion of drug manufacturing.[9]

I told the group that they were under arrest, and I later reported this to police. I was lawfully carrying a pistol, and one of the men, Darrell Philpott, saw that he was dealing with an armed man. Nonetheless, Philpott picked up a glass bottle, which he later admitted in court,[10] challenged me, and repeatedly called me "motherfucker", which he also admitted to law enforcement.[11]

Imagine what any police officer in America would do if a suspect came at the officer with a glass bottle in hand, while calling the officer a "punk motherfucker". This is sufficient aggression for any police officer in America to shoot someone

---

[9] 22 OK Stat § 22-202 Arrest by Private Person. A private person may arrest another: 1. For a public offense committed or attempted in his presence. 2. When the person arrested has committed a felony although not in his presence. 3. When a felony has been in fact committed, and he has reasonable cause for believing the person arrested to have committed it.

[10] Appendix F, Preliminary Hearing Transcripts, pp 21-22 Philpott Arms Himself with a Bottle

[11] Appendix G, PC Affidavit, page 6/17, para.1

dead. When later asked at the preliminary hearing why he picked up the glass bottle, Philpott claimed it was to see if it had collected enough rainwater to put out the fire that he started.[12]

But back in reality, Philpott rushed me, and in fear for my life, I fired **one shot** in self-defense. As a former law enforcement officer, I used extreme restraint. My one shot was aimed at the lower leg, from about an arm's length away. Philpott and his accomplices fled the scene but did not go directly to the nearest hospital. Instead, they *stopped to change clothes*, (Philpott reeked of meth) and *then* went to a hospital in Arkansas where Philpott's cousin worked. This all a matter of record.

I immediately drove close enough to town to get cell phone reception, and then made two phone calls. The first was to my brother, Army Colonel and Member of the Oklahoma Bar Lance Turlington. The other call, made within minutes of getting cell phone reception, was to 911 to report the shooting, call an ambulance for Philpott, and notify the authorities that I was coming into town to make a statement.[13] In contrast, **Darryl Philpott NEVER called the police, and neither did any of his accomplices.** They just fled the scene. The only reason the police knew to find Philpott in the Arkansas

---

[12] Appendix F, Preliminary Hearing Transcripts, "Philpott Arms Himself with a Bottle"

[13] Appendix G Radio Log Record, lines 5 and 12

emergency room, was that a female relative reported the shooting[14] after the men went home to change clothes.

Meanwhile, back in Jay, city police officer Bill "Nerves of Steel"[15] Hobbs pulled me over within view of the Sheriff's Department, preventing me from walking in voluntarily, as I had told the 911 dispatcher I was going to do. Hobbs screamed at me to exit my truck and lay on the ground, while sticking his gun in my face.

According to his police report, Jay Police Chief Mike Shambaugh had been advised that "the suspect was supposedly on his way to the sheriff's office to turn himself in."[16] By reporting that I was going to turn myself in, DCSO implied that I had admitted guilt. By clarifying it was the *supposed* reason, DCSO implied perhaps I had a sinister motivation for going into town. Actually, I was the one who called the shooting in as the victim and said I was coming in to make a statement. The implication that I had already admitted guilt put the police officer on edge and could've gotten me killed.

As the Army veteran who actually reported the incident and was trying to make a statement to the police, I was handcuffed and treated like garbage. At the same time, over in Gravette Arkansas, Philpott (then a *triple* felon), with active warrants for his arrest, was with Deputy Wells, laughing

---

[14] Ibid, line 1

[15] Appendix U Jay Police Officer Bill "Nerves of Steel" Hobbs Police Report

[16] Appendix V Jay Police Chief Mike Shambaugh Police Report

about his drinking whiskey[17], and being coached through his interview. I say "then" triple felon, because since this incident, Philpott has been convicted of his 4ᵗʰ felony, *and* has threatened to kill a police officer at least four times, but more on that later.

Shambaugh, a big Jay Indian ("Big Chief" Shambaugh) and former collegiate athlete, immediately told Hobbs to put his gun away and helped me to my feet. He asked for permission to move my pickup from the road and escorted me to the Sheriff's Office. Whether or not I gave Shambaugh permission to move my truck wouldn't have mattered, what mattered is that he treated me with respect, when he didn't have to. He's just a decent man. Shambaugh was calm and level-headed and polite. He reminded me of Sheriff Andy Taylor.

While the initial arrest was much more hostile than necessary, once I got to the station, I received a very warm welcome from the deputies who had been working the case. I made a statement to Detective Frank Miller, who seemed very sympathetic to my situation. However, Sheriff Harlan Moore ordered Miller, by telephone, to arrest me. **Interestingly, Detective Miller recorded this phone call with his own Sheriff, in front of me.**[18]

---

[17] E. H. Turlington, II, "Career Felon Philpott Police Interview," April 14, 2014, accessed July 28, 2019, http://RapeOfDelco.com/philpott.mp3. (33:00)

[18] This recording can be heard in its entirety at www.rapeofdelco.com/turlington.mp3

When Harlan Moore ordered my arrest, he had to specify to Detective Miller, who had almost thirty years law enforcement experience at the time, to charge me with felony assault with a firearm. Keep in mind that Detective Miller already knew all about the shooting, but he believed me. The following December, at the Preliminary hearing, Detective Miller felt so bad about the situation he hugged my elderly mother who was there to watch.

Thankfully, Detective Miller (who is no longer employed by Delaware County Sheriff's Office) went to the scene of the trespass the following day, while I was in jail, to gather more evidence. On his own time, in his personal vehicle, Detective Miller took pictures of exculpatory evidence that I mentioned during the interview, including the "No Trespassing" sign right next to the pallet and fire site. Miller made sure it was entered into the investigation record, for which I am grateful.

Despite my report to the police, and Detective Miller's initial objection to charging me, Harlan Moore was determined to portray Darryl Philpott as an innocent victim. The Sheriff's first move in shaping this narrative was to summon Delaware County Deputy Gayle Wells, at his home, to go handle the investigation, even though experienced detectives were already at the scene.

> **Before Deputy Wells even left his house, he declared Phil-**
> **pott the "victim"** *(thus Turlington was the guilty party).*
> *This was **prior** to hearing any testimony or seeing any ev-*
> *idence.*[19] *The Sheriff's Office then proceeded to mold the*
> *narrative by making conclusory statements to local report-*
> *ers, and in the PC Affidavit, telling half-truths, and mis-*
> *representing the testimony of the witnesses.*

VETERANS AND GAYLE WELLS

Most locals are either veterans, or have veterans in their family, or at least appreciate traditional American values, and respect the service of others. **Deputy Gayle Wells,** however, is not from here, **and is infamous for being hostile to veterans.**

I am a member of the American Legion and belong to the Jay chapter. The Post Commander of the Jay American Legion at the time of my arrest, who earned a Bronze Star for Valor in Vietnam, wasted no time expressing his disgust for the "coward draft dodger" Gayle Wells. He went on to explain Well's apparent jealousy and mistreatment of veterans, to include a personal story of Wells lying about him. He noted the only reason Wells didn't get away with it was that the Commander was considered an important person in the community.

On 4 January 2017, the Grand Lake News reported that 20 veterans and patriots filed into Delaware County

---

[19] Appendix G, PC Affidavit, page 3/17, paras. 8-9

Commissioners meeting to protest Gayle Wells' flagrant disrespect and lack of professionalism.[20] This protest was, in part, to **Wells insulting a veteran to his face by telling him "I don't give a g--ddamn about your PTSD shit."** This quote accurately reflects Gayle Well's condescending personality and absolute lack of professionalism.

Bobbi spoke on behalf of the veterans regarding this particular incident. Bobbi Bonebrake is a veteran, a nationally appointed VFW Auxiliary officer and a past VFW State President. Her husband is a disabled Vietnam Veteran. The veteran Wells attacked in the above story is Bobbi's grandson.

Jack Hazelwood reported other incidents, and said this particular time was just one example in a pattern of Well's misconduct.

Sheriff Harlan Moore offered a "no comment" response, but neither Moore nor Wells would offer an apology. They are above reproach or accountability.

---

[20] Collums, Zach. "Commissioners Hear Public Complaints Regarding Investigator." *Grand Lake News*, January 5, 2017, www.grandlakenews.com/news/20170104/commissioners-hear-public-complaints-regarding-investigator .

A local TV station profiles Turlington as a "4-State Hero".

Outsiders like those involved in Turlington's prosecution may not have any respect for military service, but people from around here do.

This photo was published on News Channel 6, and The Tulsa World, both in Tulsa, The Daily Oklahoman in Oklahoma City, and all of the local news outlets. Unless a suspect is a threat to society and a mugshot is the only photograph available, there is no legitimate reason for the police to have the media publish a mugshot. The functional purpose for this is that it helps the prosecution paint the worst possible picture of the person accused.

A simple "Edwin Hardee Turlington Facebook" internet query would have shown my Facebook page and dozens of photographs that do not portray me as a criminal. That same search turns up a newspaper article with my photo titled, "Turlington Honored" about a 3 star General honoring Turlington as "the fabric of our nation" at Washington, D.C.

Private Turlington, 82d Airborne Division,
Fort Bragg, North Carolina, 1988

[2]

"ALL I'M TRYING TO DO IS HELP YOU"

- THE CRIMINAL COP TO THE CAREER FELON

Police throughout the United States have been caught fabricating, planting, and manipulating evidence to obtain convictions where cases would otherwise be very weak. Some authorities regard police perjury as so rampant that it can be considered a "subcultural norm rather than an individual aberration" of police officers. Large-scale investigations of police units in almost every major American city have documented **massive evidence of tampering, abuse of the arresting power, and discriminatory enforcement of laws.** *There also appears to be widespread police perjury in the preparation of reports because police know these reports will be used in plea bargaining. Officers often justify false and embellished reports on the grounds that it metes out a rough justice to defendants who are guilty of wrongdoing but may be exonerated on technicalities.*

-Dale Carpenter, Flagrant Conduct: The Story of Lawrence v. Texas

"Knowingly or recklessly made false statements in the Probable Cause Affidavit... violates the Fourth Amendment. ...(W)hen the **lies are taken out and the exculpatory evidence is added in, (the) Probable Cause Affidavit fails to show Probable Cause...** *(b)ecause it is clearly established that it violates the Fourth Amendment "to use deliberately falsified allegations to demonstrate probable cause" – Franks v. Delaware, 438 US 154, 168 (1978)"*
-Rainsberger v. Benner, 2019 (7th Cir. 2019)

The test for determining whether an affiant's statements were made with reckless disregard for the truth is ...whether, viewing all of the evidence, the affiant must have entertained serious doubts as to the truth of his statements or had obvious reasons to doubt the accuracy of the information he reported. -U.S. v. Clapp 46 F.3d 795 (1995)

A CRIMINAL INVESTIGATION must do a couple things to ensure the integrity of the process. The first imperative is to protect the integrity of the evidence, which includes testimony. The second imperative is to ensure that the Probable Cause (PC) Affidavit captures a fair, complete picture of the facts and circumstances of the case, as this is the file that a District Attorney will use to make charging decisions. If either of these principles is violated, the process that follows will be flawed, and the accused will be denied his Constitutional "Due Process" rights.   Evidence tampering includes altering or concealing evidence with the intent to interfere with an investigation by a law enforcer. Sworn testimony is evidence. This is why it is important that investigators refrain from altering, coaching, or suggesting testimony to witnesses. In this chapter, you will see that **Deputy Wells repeatedly altered the testimony of Darrell Philpott** and **misrepresented the testimony of another witness in the PC Affidavit.**

PROBABLE CAUSE

> **probable cause.** A reasonable ground to suspect that a person has committed or is committing a crime or that a place contains specific items connected with a crime. Under the Fourth Amendment, probable cause – which amounts to more than a bare suspicion but less than evidence that would justify a conviction – must be shown before an arrest warrant or search warrant may be issued.
>
> – Black's Law Dictionary, 7th Edition

"Probable Cause" is the standard of proof that drives the Criminal Justice system and is a constitutional requirement for an arrest. The Supreme Court has extended the 4th Amendment requirement for Probable Cause to warrantless arrests.

In Oklahoma, arresting agencies send a report to the DA after every arrest based on Probable Cause. This report shows why it is likely that a crime was committed. It can include sworn statements by police and/or witnesses, and photographic or other evidence, but it *must* include any evidence that is favorable to the arrested individual. This report is called a "Probable Cause Affidavit" (PC Affidavit) . The District Attorney reads the PC Affidavit and decides which charges will be formally filed by the state, if any.

In this chapter, you will see that **Deputy Wells withheld exculpatory evidence in multiple instances in his PC Affidavit**, in addition to altering witness testimony.

It is important to understand how serious this problem is. For comparison, in a previous federal court case, in which the arresting officer withheld exculpatory evidence from the PC Affidavit, the court ruled that it is a 4th Amendment violation to knowingly include false statements in the PC Affidavit if those statements are material to probable cause. Whether a matter is material or not "depends on whether the affidavit demonstrates probable cause when the lies are taken out and **the exculpatory evidence is added in.**" Rainsberger v. Benner, 2019 (7th Cir. 2019)

Read the following, and after you add the exculpatory evidence that Deputy Wells omitted, and take out Wells' misrepresentations, then ask yourself – Is it more probable that the aggressor was the disabled veteran with a background in law enforcement, who retired after 20 years of military service, and is a certified private investigator, or, is it more probable that the aggressor was the convicted drug dealer with multiple active arrest warrants at the time of the shooting, and a RAP sheet of dangerous and violent crime spanning nearly FOUR decades, including four felony convictions, who at the time of the shooting had active Missouri warrants for his arrest, and is currently wanted by police on Benton County, Arkansas Arrest Warrant #51052018?

THE STATE'S CONSTITUTIONAL DUTY TO DISCLOSE EVIDENCE

evidence, *n.* **1.** Something (including testimony, documents, and tangible objects) that tends to prove or disprove the existence of an alleged fact

- Black's Law Dictionary, 7th Edition

Due Process Clause. The constitutional provision that prohibits the government from unfairly or arbitrarily depriving a person of life, liberty, or property.

– Black's Law Dictionary, 7th Edition

WITHHOLDING EVIDENCE

The convicted felon Philpott claimed that I "shot him from the rear, in the back of the leg" and Wells then made the conclusory statement that the "wound appeared to be a through and through... gunshot... from rear to front".[21] In contrast, I reported that I shot Philpott as he approached with a glass bottle in his hand, calling me a "punk mother-fucker", and challenging me to "settle it" like a man. **Philpott admitted to the glass bottle and name calling**, so the main question left in dispute is whether Philpott was shot in the front or the back. There was significant evidence to support me and contradict Philpott, but Deputy Wells withheld this evidence from the PC Affidavit.

Specifically, **Wells withheld the clearest photos from the PC Affidavit**; namely the large, color, high resolution wound photographs that show an obvious depiction of an entry wound in the front and an exit wound in the back. As any hunter, lawman or Soldier knows, an entry wound is the smaller wound, and the exit is the larger wound. The photos below show a tiny entrance wound in the front of the leg, with a single drop of blood, contrasted to the much larger exit wound toward the rear of the leg, that is bleeding profusely, even at the Emergency Room. (see photos)

---

[21] Appendix G, PC Affidavit, Page 6/17, para. 6

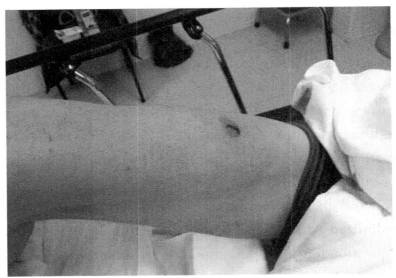

Emergency room photograph taken by Deputy Gayle Wells on 14 April 2014. This smaller wound, with a single drop of blood running back towards the crotch, must be compared to the larger wound in the next photo in order to determine which was the entry and which was the exit. This clearly shows the smaller entry wound was at the FRONT of Philpott's leg, which corroborates my statement that Philpott was advancing toward me, not walking away from me. Note this wound was not wiped clean, so the bloodspot is much larger than the wound itself. If Wells wanted to show the relative sizes of the wounds (entrance versus exit), he would have wiped the blood off for the photo and measured the wound. He did neither. High resolution photo available for closer inspection at: www.RapeOfDelco.com/entry.png. Photo courtesy DCSO.

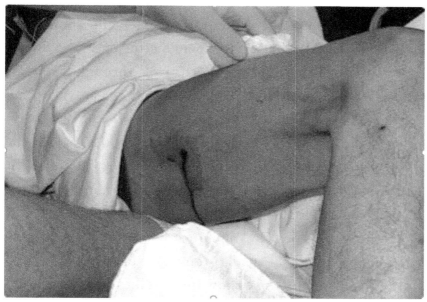

Emergency room photograph taken by Deputy Gayle Wells on 14 April 2014. This photo clearly shows the larger exit wound at the back of Darrell Philpott's leg. This photo proves that Philpott was advancing toward me, not running away from me as he claimed. A closer examination of this photo reveals a second, smaller exit wound just to the rear of the large one, indicating that a fragment of the bullet splintered off and exited toward the rear. It is IMPOSSIBLE for an entry wound to have such a fragment exit, because **bullets fragment and expand after impact, not before**, *and anyone familiar with firearms knows this to be true. This wound had to be cleaned, because it was still gushing blood two hours after the shooting, as is typical of an exit wound. High resolution photo available inspection at: www.RapeOfDelco.com/exit.png. Photo courtesy DCSO.*

The reason that exit wounds are bigger and show more damage is that **a bullet only expands after entry.** A bullet typically deforms or expands as it travels through the body, so **an exit wound is always more severe than the entry wound.**

There is uncertainty, however, as to what exactly WAS in the PC affidavit, because the court record differs from the prosecutor's own assertions. Specifically, the PC affidavit that Prosecutor Nic Lelecas provided me did not include the color photos above that would exonerate me and prove Philpott to be a liar. (See B&W photos, below), but it allegedly **did** include a couple of small, grainy, out of focus, black and white pictures that **do not show the detail**.

These black and white photos consist of one picture of Philpott laying in a hospital bed, looking sad, with wounds covered (no evidentiary value), and the other photo is a close-up of the large wound toward the rear of the leg which, by itself, shows nothing other than Philpott had been shot. **The photos that Wells withheld, however, are exculpatory evidence of the directional path of the bullet.** Those color photos show that Philpott was shot in the front of his thigh, and the bullet exited towards the rear, which corroborate the truth, consistent with the statement I made to Detective Frank Miller that night.

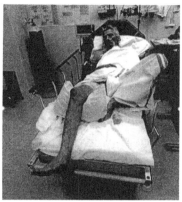

This photo, which tells nothing about the bullet wound was scanned in with the PC Affidavit documents by DCSO, making it appear as though it was part of the Affidavit. According to the prosecutor in my case, it was not part of the Affidavit. Original photo at RapeOfDelco.com/bw1.png Photo courtesy of DCSO

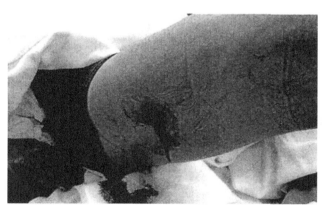

The second photo that Delaware County Sheriff's Office scanned into the PC Affidavit file. Like the first, it is black, white, grainy, and hard to see. This is obviously the exit wound, but Wells declared it the entry wound. By withholding the color photo of the MUCH smaller entry wound in the front, Deputy Wells manipulated the evidence. The withheld color photos clearly show the shot fired by me entered the front of Philpott's leg and exited from the back of it. photo at www.RapeOfDelco.com/bw2.png. Photo courtesy of DCSO

The "uncertainty" alluded to earlier is whether these black and white photos were actually in the PC affidavit. The court presented the black and white photos as part of a scanned "Adobe" format file titled, "PC Affadavit [*sic*] and Supporting Docs" given to me during the Discovery process, which led me to believe they were part of the PC Affidavit. However, Prosecutor Nic Lelecas claimed, in a letter to the Oklahoma bar Association, that the PC Affidavit was only "8 pages long".[22]The PC Affidavit is in the appendices of this book; note that the pages are numbered "1 of 17", "2 of 17", etc. The black and white photos are not even in the 17 pages of the PC Affidavit but were apparently scanned into the digital file at some point. This creates the appearance that the black and white photos *might* have been in the PC Affidavit. However, as is the case in so many of the details of the government handling of this case, the truth may be impossible to decipher.

There can be irregularities at the DCSO, however, according to Arawanah Buckett, who now dispatches for the Jay Police Department. Arawanah dispatched for six years as a radio dispatcher for DCSO, including three months under Sheriff Harland Moore, until she refused to perform an order from a supervisor that she felt was inappropriate. So, they fired her. Arawanah says the Radio Log is for the protecting the Sheriff, not the public, and can be altered at any time,

---

[22] Appendix H, Delaware County Prosecutor Nic Lelecas Response to Bar Complaint, page 1, para 3

making it worthless as defense evidence.[23]

Once I began to investigate Philpott, I discovered that Philpott's cousin, Joseph Bradley, worked in the Gravette, Arkansas emergency room. This is why Philpott and his accomplices drove to the Gravette ER (after changing clothes, and not calling the police). The people who work in an ER may believe the story that a patient tells them, and this may be reflected in the medical record, so it makes sense for Philpott to seek treatment where he can talk to a friend (or cousin). This would not be objective, of course, and that is why it is important to rely on the assessments of people who are specifically trained in specialty areas.

There just so happened to be a trained "wound nurse" on duty that evening, and his name is Renzil Reardon. A wound nurse can make an informed determination on the directional

---

[23] Arawanah is a patriot, and the descendent of Confederate Partisan Rangers. Her 4th great grandfather, James Buckett (Burkett) was an original member of Captain Stand Watie's company and rode with Watie through the duration of the war until he died in 1865. Arawanah > Charles Buckett & Jeanie Loux > Grover Buckett & Gladys Qualate > Samuel Buckett & Margarot Seabourn > David 'Di-Wi' Buckett & Aggie 'A-Ke' Ratler > James Buckett & T 'Di Ni' Colston. Arawanah's maternal grandfather, Bill Loux, was a Deputy in Delaware and Mayes Counties for almost 40 years. Arawanah and her sister Joey dispatch at Jay Police Department. Documentation at www.rapeofdelco.com/buckett.htm

path of the bullet, based on measuring and comparing wound sizes, fragment wounds, severity of the of the respective wounds, etc. Renzil Reardon, the Emergency Room wound nurse on duty, tended to Philpott's wounds. Reardon is **a Registered Nurse** who has the specialized wound training required to make an informed determination on the direction of the bullet. Mr. Reardon determined that the wound on the front of the leg was the entry wound, and the wound toward the rear was the exit wound, which corroborates my story, and contradicts Philpott.[24]   Shockingly, **Deputy Wells simply withheld this exculpatory evidence from the PC Affidavit and appears to have ignored it altogether.** See photo of gunshot wound (GSW) direction determination by Wound Nurse Renzil Reardon, R.N. (initials R.A.R.).

---

[24] Appendix I, Exculpatory Wound Nurse Medical Report Withheld by Deputy Wells from PC Affidavit

GSW R UPPER THIGH FROM ANTERIOR TO POST THROUGH
AND THROUGH BLEEDING CONTROLLED---DISTAL
SENSATION/CIRCULATION INTACT---NO DEFORMITY
OBSERVED-----------------------------------RAR
2040---XRAY AND LAB COMPLETE---------RAR
2120--TDAP EXP03/18/16--LT #JP44P----RAR
2310---REPORT CALLED TO P BURNETT RN-------RAR
2310---TRANSPORTED TO 350 VIA STRETCHER----RAR

Notes from ER nurse who attended to Darrell Philpott on 4/14/2014. Note they reveal that the GSW (gunshot wound) on the right upper thigh from anterior (front) to post (back). This is yet another piece of crucial evidence proving my claim that Philpott was coming toward me, not running away from me. However, Deputy Gayle Wells not only withheld it from the PC Affidavit, his police report stated the exact opposite. Complete GSW report at www.RapeofDelco.com/renzil.pdf

Then, in addition to withholding the clear, color photos which show Philpott was shot in the front (and prove Philpott was lying); and in addition to including (at most) the two grainy B&W photos that **only show the side wound, not the front**; Deputy Wells then goes so far as to assert that:

"THE WOUND APPEARED TO BE A THROUGH AND THROUGH SMALL CALIBER GUNSHOT TO THE RIGHT THIGH **FROM BACK TO FRONT**"[25]

---

[25] Appendix G, PC Affidavit, page 6/17, para. 6

In law, this is called a conclusory statement. A conclusory statement is an assertion that is made without supporting evidence. They are not allowed in a courtroom and competent and honest cops don't make them in their police reports. If Wells was conducting an unbiased investigation, this is where he would have measured both wounds in order to determine which was the entry and which was the exit, and he would have recorded these measurements in his report, like the Wound Nurse, Renzil Reardon, RN did in his report. Reardon, like any local juror would, came to the opposite conclusion as Wells. So, Wells just concealed Reardon's report from the Probable Cause Affidavit, just like he withheld the high resolution, color photographs of the wounds that actually told the viewer which wound the exit was, and which wound was the entry.

Deputy Wells withheld the medical records that would prove Philpott lied, and prove Philpott was advancing toward me.

No deputy concealed evidence to make me look good or fabricated evidence to make Philpott look bad.

WELLS DECLARES PHILPOTT THE VICTIM, NOW HE HAS TO BACK IT UP

The investigation had been decided before it started, then everything that followed was molded to fit that conclusion.

When investigators called Deputy Wells at his home at 8pm, **Wells declared Philpott "the VICTIM" before he even left his house to take over the investigation.**[26] This demonstrates a total lack of concern to even give the appearance of objectivity or fairness by the Sheriff, or his handpicked investigator, Gayle Wells.

Remember, at the time of the shooting, Darrell Philpott had been convicted for felony drug dealing, felony burglary, and felony theft, and he had two active warrants for his arrest for other dangerous crimes. Also remember that after his encounter with me, Philpott did not go to law enforcement, or even go to the hospital first. Instead, Philpott fled to his cousin Jack Thomas' house, where Philpott ditched the clothes he was wearing, changed into clean clothes, and then chose to seek treatment at a hospital in Arkansas, where Jack's brother, Joseph Bradley worked.

Why did Philpott ditch his clothes? I know he reeked of meth, and he admitted he drank a bottle of whiskey by that time. I believe he changed clothes so that the hospital staff, and possibly police officers, wouldn't smell the whiskey.

---

[26] Appendix G, PC Affidavit, page 3/17, paras. 8-9

*Philpott's clothes were recovered but they were never tested for methamphetamine residue or gunpowder residue. Comparing the amount of gunpowder residue on the front of the pants leg to the rear of the pants leg would have told investigators whether Philpott was shot in the front or the rear. Apparently, **this is something Deputy Wells didn't want to get into the record.** Darrell Philpott's clothes became another piece of manipulated or excluded evidence, and no further questions about them were asked by Deputy Wells.*

PROBLEMS WITH THE PC AFFIDAVIT

DID THE POLICE HAVE TO "LOCATE" ME?

The law enforcement records for the Turlington/Philpott case reflect poorly on Delaware County officials, generally. Some problems are omissions or half-truths, while others are simply dishonest. For example, the record reflects that I was "LOCATED AND DETAINED AT JAY...",[27] as if they had to go look for me. This misrepresentation omits the fact that I actually reported the incident by calling 911, told the DCSO that I was on my way to town to make a statement, and then was stopped *within sight of the Sheriff's Office.*[28] The record intentionally omits the facts that make me look like a responsible citizen.

---

[27] Appendix G, PC Affidavit, page 3/7, para. 5

[28] Ibid., Radio Log Record, lines 5, 11-12

The worst omissions, however, are in the PC Affidavit. Gayle Wells, the officer hand-selected by the Sheriff to handle the case, who began by declaring Philpott "the victim" before the investigation even began, had one more task to perform: shape the PC Affidavit to form a criminal case against me.[29]

WAS PHILPOT DRUNK, HIGH, OR SOBER?

While law enforcement officers can and do take statements from witnesses who are under the influence of drugs and or alcohol, the officer must of course note the fact that the witness made his statement while under the influence. If the witness is a convicted drug felon or has admitted to the officer that he was drinking prior to making his statement, or if the witness has admitted to medical personnel to being addicted to drugs or being an alcoholic, then the investigating officer orders a toxicology report. If the officer does not, he is derelict and in violation of standard police procedure.

---

[29] Ibid., PC Affidavit, p.3/17, paras. 5,8 and

E. H. Turlington, II, "Career Felon Philpott Police Interview," April 14, 2014, accessed July 28, 2019,
http://RapeOfDelco.com/philpott.mp3. (3:02)

Problem: *Philpott in fact testified that he was drinking a bottle of whiskey immediately* **before the shooting,**[30] *finished the bottle and then threw in the wood stove at his cousin's house after the shooting.*[31] *Philpott also testified that he drank a bottle of whiskey* **on the way to the E.R.,**[32] *after they left the house. Despite Philpott having three felony convictions (including one for intent to deal drugs) multiple drunk driving convictions, warrants for his arrest (including one for drunk driving) and admitting to drinking at least TWO bottles of whiskey that evening to Deputy Wells and admitting to the hospital staff he drank "... a 6 to 12-pack most days" and "...smokes a little weed", Wells protected his felon's credibility making it a point to go on the record saying, "Philpott appeared to be sober"*[33] *and failing to order a toxicology report on Philpott.*

---

[30] Appendix R, Preliminary Hearing Transcripts, page 51, *Philpott Drinks Hard Whiskey Prior to Shooting*

[31] Appendix M, Preliminary Hearing Transcripts, page 76, *More Perjury, Philpott Changes Clothes and Destroys Evidence,* and

E. H. Turlington, II, "Career Felon Philpott Police Interview," April 14, 2014, accessed July 28, 2019,

http://RapeOfDelco.com/philpott.mp3(4:44)

[32] Appendix K, Preliminary Hearing Transcripts, page 53, *Philpott Drinks Second Bottle of Whiskey Minutes Before Police Interview*

[33] Appendix G, PC Affidavit, page 4/17, para.10

AS I TALKED WITH MR. PHILPOTT. I ASKED HIM IF HE'D BEEN DRINKING EARLIER IN THE DAY. HE SAID, "YES. BUT ONLY A HALF PINT." I ASK HIM WHAT HE WAS DRINKING AND HE TOLD ME, "1/2 PINT OF WHISKEY." I COULD NOT SMELL ALCOHOLIC BEVERAGE ON OR ABOUT HIS BODY AT THE TIME OF CONTACT. PHILPOTT APPEARED TO BE SOBER.

SOCIAL HISTORY: He is a handy man, lives at home. He is self employed. He smokes one pack of cigarettes daily, occasionally smokes a little 'weed'. He drinks a 6 to 12-pack most days.

DISCHARGE DIAGNOSES:
1. Gunshot wound with cellulitis, right thigh.
2. Daily alcohol use.
3. Tobacco use.

THE HOSPITAL LATER PROVIDED ME WITH A COPY OF HIS MEDICAL RECORDS AND AN XRAY COMPACT DISC. THERE WERE LATER PLACED IN THE CASE FILE.

I TALKED WITH CNA GARRETT. I ASKED HIM IF HE WAS GOING TO RE-DRESS AND WRAP MR. PHILPOTT'S INJURY. HE TOLD ME HE WAS. AS I WATCHED, GARRETT REMOVED THE BANDAGE. I TOOK PHOTOS OF THE EXPOSED INJURY.

THE WOUND APPEARED TO BE A THROUGH AND THROUGH SMALL CALIBER GUNSHOT TO THE RIGHT THIGH FROM BACK TO FRONT.

Problem: *As proven earlier in this chapter, the Wound Nurse, Renzil Reardon, contradicts Deputy Wells' claim[34] on this, as the Wound Nurse determined the gunshot wound was front-to-back.[35]*

I ALSO TOLD MR. PHILPOTT I WAS GOING TO PERFORM A GUNSHOT RESIDUE KIT ON HIS HANDS AND FACE TO CHECK TO SEE IF HE'D FIRED A WEAPON RECENTLY. HE SAID, "NOT TODAY ANYWAY, " AND AGREED. I FOLLOWED THE DIRECTIONS ON THE GSR KIT; DOING BOTH HANDS IN ORDER AND THEN HIS FACE. I SECURED THE SAMPLES IN THE INDIVIDUAL VILES AND RETURNED THEM TO THE KIT ENVELOPE. THEY WERE SEALED WITH EVIDENCE TAPE.

---

[34] Appendix G PC Affidavit, page 6/17, para. 6

[35] Appendix I, Wound Nurse Medical Report Withheld by Deputy Wells

Problem: *No one claimed Philpott fired a weapon. Philpott admitted he had a glass bottle. The only reason to order this test was to prove Philpott didn't have a gun, which was never contested. However, the direction of the gunshot wound (front to back or vice versa) WAS disputed. Wells did NOT order a residue test of Philpott's pants or his leg wound, which WOULD have shown the directional path of the bullet, as there would be gunpowder residue at the entry wound.*

SOCIAL HISTORY: He is a handy man, lives at home. He is self employed. He smokes one pack of cigarettes daily, occasionally smokes a little 'weed'. He drinks a 6 to 12-pack most days.

REVIEW OF SYSTEMS:

Constitutional:	Negative for fevers or chills.
HEENT:	Negative.
Respiratory:	Negative for any shortness of breath.
CV:	Negative for chest pain.

Continued on page 2

HISTORY AND PHYSICAL
K. Marcus Poemoceah, MD
4/18/14 06:34

Problem : Gayle Wells claims he obtained Philpott's medical records from the staff. That means Gayle Wells knew **Philpott admitted to drug use and daily alcohol abuse, yet Wells omitted this information.** It is relevant as it affects both Philpott's credibility, and also calls into question his level of rational thought at the time of the incident, and his ability to clearly recall what had happened. Much more significantly, however, is the fact that if Gayle Wells had the medical records, then he also had the determination of the wound Nurse (Renzil Reardon, R.N.) that the bullet path was from front to back. This contradicts the concocted Wells/Philpott story about poor Philpott being shot in the back. By omitting the wound nurse determination, Wells proves that his misrepresentation of the facts was intentional. This was no good faith error.

PROBLEMS WITH WELLS' INTERVIEW[36]

After declaring Philpott to be the victim for the second time (before hearing either Philpott's or my version of events), Wells proceeded to conduct a 40 minute interview.[37] Throughout the interview Wells can be heard giggling, cooing, and otherwise fawning over the violent felon (who at the time had multiple warrants for his arrest). At one point Wells can be heard complimenting Philpott on his "working man's hands" and telling Philpott he was going to hold them.[38] Wells asks Philpott what his hobbies are, and what he "does for fun".[39] This is a very awkward moment in the interview as evidenced by Philpott's refusal to answer. It sounds like Wells is asking Philpott to fill out an online dating profile. Finally, Wells goes on to give Philpott his personal mobile phone number, telling him to call, "anytime, day or night".[40]

During the interview, Wells leads Philpott, alters Philpott's testimony, and fails to follow up on any self-contradictory, clearly false, incriminating or just plain insensible statements.

---

[36] Both Turlington's and Philpott's Police Interviews are available at www.RapeOfDelco.com

[37] E. H. Turlington, II, "Career Felon Philpott Police Interview," The Rape of Delaware County, April 14, 2014, accessed July 28, 2019, http://RapeOfDelco.com/philpott.mp3. (3:02)

[38] Ibid., 24:00, 24:20

[39] Ibid., 28:23

[40] Ibid., 39:13

Nobody from the Sheriff's office complimented my body parts (except for the "muscular" description in the PC Affidavit),[41] *or offered to hold my hand, or gave me their phone number (much less invited me to call them off the record). The detective who interviewed me didn't feed me optimal answers or finish my sentences for me.*

WELLS ALTERS WITNESS TESTIMONY MULTIPLE TIMES

In one instance of altering witness testimony, Wells changed the time of day Philpott told him he had been drinking whiskey. At 4:45 in the interview, Deputy Wells asks Philpott, "You've been drinking or using any kind of drugs *tonight?*". Philpott responds, "Yeah, I's drinkin". Wells changed both the wording and the meaning of Philpott's answer in the Probable Cause Affidavit[42] by stating Philpott admitted to drinking a half pint of whiskey *earlier in the day*, instead of that *night*. This is a significant change to Philpott's testimony, as the body processes alcohol at the approximate rate of an ounce per hour. Wells concealed Philpott's admittedly drunken state during the interview and ignored Philpott's drunken state at the time of the shooting. The investigator chose to not have toxicology work done that would have established Philpott's estimated blood alcohol content at the time of the confrontation. **This information would have been exculpatory.**

---

[41] Appendix G, PC Affidavit, page 1/17

[42] Appendix G, page 3, Line 5

In another example, Deputy Wells actually coaches Philpott to change his testimony from his initial (true) answer that Philpott was unemployed, to actually claiming he is employed.

After asking Philpott his occupation, and then having to explain to Philpott the meaning of "occupation", Wells asks Philpott "what is your job?" Philpott answers "none", but rather than documenting Philpott's unemployment, Wells suggests to Philpott he is a "laborer" to which Philpott answers "uh, yeah" (28:00, 4:39 and 4:42).[43] Of course, there are no questions about who he worked for, where he worked, or any specific jobs he had done. Once Wells coaxed Philpott to say "uh, yeah", Wells had what he wanted: Now, Wells can portray Darrell Philpott on the record as a productively employed citizen!

In a third example, when Philpott is asked whose land he was on, Philpott *gave two different answers.* Philpott first answered "Mike Raney", then changed the answer to "not really Michael Raney's but it's really Shorty Somebody's that's kin to Michael."[44] Philpott clearly had no idea whose land he was on. Sheriff Harlan Moore gave the Tulsa World a third version: that Jack Thomas (Philpott's cousin) sent

---

[43] E. H. Turlington, II, "Career Felon Philpott Police Interview, "The Rape of Delaware County, 14 April 2014, accessed July 28, 2019, http://RapeOfDelco.com/philpott.mp3.

[44] Ibid., 11:00 minutes

Philpott to *a foreclosed property*.[45] The property that is now my family farm, where Philpott trespassed, was in foreclosure prior to our acquiring it. At 13:07 Philpott admits I told him he was trespassing. Also, stealing firewood and burning someone else's land without permission are both illegal. Wells could have arrested Philpott, the triple felon with active warrants for his arrest, for stealing or burning on someone else's property, in addition to arresting him for trespassing. Wells wasn't going to do anything to harm Philpott; **Wells actually told Philpott "All I'm trying to do is help you",** [46] **and that's exactly what he did.**

None of the witnesses (neither Philpott, nor Philpott's accomplices, nor I) mentioned "Michael Raney's **buddy**". That was Wells' invention. This is a significant change to the testimony that was given, because everyone knew they weren't on Michael Raney's land. They needed a different story, so Wells provided them with one: They were on Raney's *buddy's* land. Of course, no one ever named Raney's buddy- that Wells invented- because he didn't exist.

---

[45] Dee Duren, "Fight Over Trespassing Ends In Delaware County Shooting, Arrest," News On 6, April 15, 2014, , accessed July 26, 2019, https://www.newson6.com/story/25254867/fight-over-tresspassing-ends-in-delaware-county-shooting and Appendix S, "News on 6 Article"

[46] E. H. Turlington, II, "Career Felon Philpott Police Interview," The Rape of Delaware County, April 14, 2014, accessed July 28, 2019, http://RapeOfDelco.com/philpott.mp3. (07:02)

The problem with admitting they thought they were on foreclosed property is that **they were admitting to a crime**, so Wells tried to change it. By claiming they were on "Michael Raney's **buddy's**" land, Wells and Philpott could make the argument that they thought they had permission to be there. This was just another attempt by Wells to distract from the admission that Philpott and his accomplices were engaged in criminal conduct.

In the fourth example of altering witness testimony, Joseph Bradley is falsely quoted in the PC Affidavit. The PC Affidavit claimed I asked Bradley whose land they were on. [47]

Another neighbor, Joseph Bradley DOB 05/12/1980 was driving westbound past James Barrett and Darrell Philpot. Joseph Bradley stated he was stopped by a white male later identified as Edwin Turlington driving a black Ford truck. Edwin Turlington asked if he was on his property and Joseph Bradley stated "no". Joseph Bradley stated he observed

If this were true, it would show that I wasn't sure whose land they were on. However, I knew exactly whose land they were on, and the affidavit misquotes Bradley anyway. According to both Bradley's and my sworn statements, the question I asked Bradley was, if he was *with the trespassers*.[48]

---

[47] Appendix G, PC Affidavit, page 2/7 para. 2

[48] Appendix Y, Joseph's Bradley's Sworn Statement

When it started to go on phone a newer black ford pickup was coming down the hill, he stopped me about 75 to 100 yards from where ste A Steve and Darrel were at. He asked me if they were with me, I said no and continue went on home.

At 4:15 into my interview with Deputy Miller, I said that I approached (who turned out to be Joseph Bradley) and asked him, "Are you with them? Do you know who they are?"[49]

My statement was consistent with Bradley's statement, and they were both consistent with the truth. But once again, another alteration of witness testimony makes me look bad; specifically, they tried to make it look like I didn't know whose land they were on. I knew exactly where they were.

Also, it is standard procedure for law enforcement officers to take witness' employment information when taking sworn statements. Joseph Bradley is Jack Thomas's brother. Joseph was employed at the Gravette, Arkansas Emergency Room when Darrell was taken there for his gunshot wound. It would have helped my case, but harmed Philpott's case for a

---

[49]E. H. Turlington, II, "Turlington Police Interview," The Rape of Delaware County, July 15, 2018, accessed July 28, 2019, http://RapeOfDelco.com/turlington.mp3.

jury (or DA) to know this considering that the Gravette ER is in another state. Either the investigating officer didn't ask Joseph about his employment status, or the investigator asked but didn't like the answer, or the investigating officer did his job and recorded Joseph's employment, but Deputy Gayle Wells tampered with the evidence like he did so much other evidence in my case.

Philpott's statements about when he was drinking, his employment status, and whose land he was on, were altered. Bradley's and my statements about what I said to Bradley were also altered. The one thing all of these changes have in common is the result always makes Philpott look better, and always makes me look worse.

WELLS FEEDS PHILPOTT OPTIMAL ANSWERS (OPTIMAL FOR PHILPOTT)

Wells' coaching can be heard throughout his interview with Philpott,[50] but some of his more harmful tampering follows:

As stated above in the third example of altering evidence, Wells claimed in his PC Affidavit that Philpott named "Michael Raney's buddy" as the owner of the land he was on. This was mentioned earlier but is another example of Wells

---

[50] E. H. Turlington, II, "Career Felon Philpott Police Interview," The Rape of Delaware County, April 14, 2014, accessed July 28, 2019, http://RapeOfDelco.com/philpott.mp3

putting words in Philpott's mouth. After Wells asks Philpott whose land he was on, and Philpott gives him his series of names, Wells pauses a couple seconds then encourages Philpott with, "Michael Raney's......buddy?"[51] Philpott did not pick up on Wells' suggestion this time, but Wells used it in the PC Affidavit anyway.

Another example of Wells feeding optimal answers to Philpott is after Philpott flatly stated "No" when asked if he was employed.[52] Wells asks Philpott if he is employed *again* twenty four minutes later.[53] This time, Wells suggests, "laborer?" to which Philpott agrees, as though his earlier denial never took place. Or, as if Wells and Philpott had an off the record discussion since the first denial.

A third example of Wells feeding Philpott optimal answers is when Philpott tells him I pulled my vehicle up to Philpott. Wells, asks, "Does he jump out of his vehicle?". (9:41) Philpott never claimed that I "jumped" out of my vehicle, or even exited my vehicle. The idea that I "jumped" out of my vehicle sounds aggressive and was initiated by Wells.

A fourth example was after Wells had ended the "working part" of Well's interview and was trying to go over the official narrative one more time before leaving Philpott. At 39:43 into the interview,[54] Wells tells Philpott, "I just want to double check with you before I leave." After Philpott

---

[51] Ibid., 11:00

[52] Ibid., 4:39

[53] Ibid., 28:02

[54] Ibid.

repeatedly admitted that he called me a motherfucker and challenged me to fight, Wells then instructed Philpott "He shot you without any provocation."[55] Curiously, Philpott answers, "That's the way I see it". Wells immediately corrects him, "You weren't, you weren't, you didn't threaten him." Obviously, Wells was upset that Philpott wasn't picking up on what he was being told. Emboldened by making it through the interview without getting arrested, Philpott continues, "I told him to put the gun down and we could get it on-" Wells interrupts, "Okay, alright". " -if you're gonna be a man-" Wells interrupts again, this time louder, "ALRIGHT." Philpott finally finishes "- be a man!", Wells exclaims, "Very good!" and changes the subject, "Anything else?"

Wells did not want Philpott to describe any further how he was challenging me to fight as he advanced toward me.

When Wells went over the narrative one last time with Philpott, he ignored what Philpott had already told him in the interview, what Philpott was trying to tell him right then, and is telling Philpott the official version that Wells is putting in his report – that poor innocent Philpott was shot in

---

[55] Had Wells asked instead, "He shot you without provocation, correct?", it would still be leading the witness, but didn't even try to hide drilling the official narrative into Philpott. Wells of course had no idea anyone would ever hear the interview, much less his coaching the witness afterward.

the back for absolutely no reason. Philpott was either too drunk or too stupid to know that Wells was giving him the narrative, so Wells had to interrupt Philpott repeatedly to get him back to that narrative.

When Philpott had no idea whose land he had been tres-passing, Well's suggested "Michael Raney's... buddy?", even though Philpott had said nothing of the sort. When Wells asked Philpott if he was employed, Philpott flatly answered, "No.", but by the end of the interview Philpott was a laborer and a handyman. Well's coaching Philpott to claim that I "jumped" out of my truck portrays me as acting aggressively. However, Philpott never claimed this happened. After Philpott boasting to Wells throughout the interview how he had cursed me and challenged me to fight, Wells literally took everything Philpott said, then reasserted the opposite to Philpott to get him back on track with the narrative that poor inno-cent Philpott got shot in the back for no reason.

WELLS IGNORES INCRIMINATING EVIDENCE AGAINST PHILPOTT

As stated above, Sheriff Harlan Moore told the Tulsa World that Philpott was cutting wood on *a foreclosed property.*[56]

---

[56] Appendix S, News on 6 Article

Dee Duren, "Fight Over Trespassing Ends In Delaware County Shooting, Arrest," News On 6, April 15, 2014, , accessed

Entering someone else's property without their permission is trespassing, regardless of if it's the Turlington land, or the Bank's foreclosed land, or anyone else's land. Wells ignored that.

Every landowner adjacent to my farm was available for questioning, but no investigator even tried to contact any of them. At no time in the *more than five years* that passed between my arrest and the charges being dropped, did the Prosecution *ever* find *anyone* to claim that Philpott was on *their land*, much less that Philpott was on their land with permission.

*Within months of the shooting, the county bulldozed the scene of the shooting, making it unrecognizable. When my brother informed the prosecutor of this, the prosecutor did not know this. So, who **did** know about the bulldozing? Did the Sheriff have it done? What county official had an interest in altering the scene?*

The first thing the prosecution should have done is determine whether or not Philpott was trespassing. The government was willing to prosecute Turlington for over five years without knowing that answer. They still don't.

July 26, 2019, https://www.newson6.com/story/25254867/fight-over-tresspassing-ends-in-delaware-county-shooting.

Wells ignored Philpott's admission that he set and abandoned a fire on someone else's property with no one to tend it (12:00). [57]

Wells ignored the fact that despite claiming they were cutting wood,[58] there was **no chainsaw, no firewood** in the truck, **no stumps**, and no explanation for the Coleman fuel-based pallet-lab. Despite multiple deputies responding to the scene, at no point in the investigation did *any* deputy note any evidence of cut wood (stumps, a pile of firewood, etc.). Over one hundred photos were taken of the area and NOT ONE showed any evidence of "cutting wood". Wells ignored that.

No one asked why Philpott and Barret would decide "burn trash" on someone else's property rather than take it to the public dumpsters less than a quarter mile from where they burned it (and half a mile from Jack Thomas house). Wells ignored that.

Five minutes into the interview, Philpott is asked the location of the (**first**) whiskey bottle he admitted to drinking earlier. He answers his customary "uh..." and paused. He eventually admitted he "... threw the bottle in the wood stove." And that's it. Wells fails to ask Philpott if throwing glass bottles in his wood stove is normal for Philpott, or why

---

[57] E. H. Turlington, II, "Career Felon Philpott Police Interview," The Rape of Delaware County, April 14, 2014, accessed July 28, 2019, http://RapeOfDelco.com/philpott.mp3 (12:00)

[58] Appendix G, PC Affidavit, page 2, first paragraph, last sentence and throughout Philpott's interview

he would do that. Was Philpott destroying evidence? Wells changed the subject.

Wells certainly did not want to ask what the men were doing out there with a wooden pallet set up with plastic sheeting and a can of Coleman camp fuel (which the DCSO photographed). He especially didn't want to enter into the record the photo that shows this scene directly under the Turlington "No Trespassing" sign. Nothing to see here; move on.

Regarding Philpott's memory, honesty, or ability to keep a story straight, or perhaps all three, **Philpott actually admitted to Wells that he will "never give the same answer twice,"[59] Wells accepts it with, "Okay", and changes the subject.**

---

[59] E. H. Turlington, II, "Career Felon Philpott Police Interview," The Rape of Delaware County, April 14, 2014, accessed July 28, 2019, http://RapeOfDelco.com/philpott.mp3 (30:25)

These photos weren't taken when Deputy Wells was in charge of the investigation. Detective Miller took them the following day, on his personal time.

OTHER PROBLEMS WITH THE INVESTIGATION

WHAT DID THE TRESPASSERS INTEND TO DO?

As mentioned previously, according to the Sheriff's news release, the trespassers intended to go to a place where they **"thought the property was in foreclosure"** to cut down trees and take firewood. The Sheriff made a mistake, however, in his early news media blasts: he actually let some truth slip into the story. This was before Deputy Wells came up with the *"Raney's buddy's land"* story.

In truth, they planned on going to foreclosed property to do *something*. The evidence contradicts the "cutting wood" story. I believe they were cooking meth. What we know for sure is this: the trespassers didn't know that the property was no longer in foreclosure, because it had been recently purchased by my family. Still, whether they went there to "cut wood" or to cook meth, **they went to the Turlington property with criminal intent**, because:

1) Cutting wood on foreclosed property is a crime. It is literally stealing from the bank, because the land and the timber is owned by the bank, and

2) The plat map below (obtained by DCSO during their investigation) shows that the only "foreclosed" property near the scene was the property purchased by the Turlingtons on March 28, 2014. The land *had been* in foreclosure

for several years but had been recently purchased by the Turlingtons.

This is what we know for a fact: the men went out to the Turlington property with criminal intent, and they had no right to be there. Turlington did have a right to be there, and he had a right to confront them, and to defend himself.

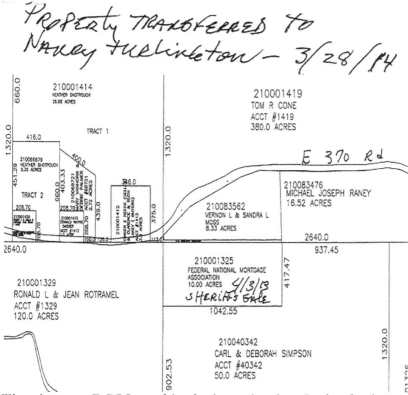

PROPERTY TRANSFERRED TO
NANCY Turlington – 3/28/14

210001414
HEATHER SHOTPOUCH
26.96 ACRES

210001419
TOM R CONE
ACCT #1419
380.0 ACRES

TRACT 1

E 370 Rd

210066679
HEATHER SHOTPOUCH
5.30 ACRES

210083476
MICHAEL JOSEPH RANEY
16.52 ACRES

TRACT 2

210083562
VERNON L & SANDRA L
MOSS
8.33 ACRES

210001329
RONALD L & JEAN ROTRAMEL
ACCT #1329
120.0 ACRES

210001325
FEDERAL NATIONAL MORTGAGE
ASSOCIATION
10.00 ACRES *4/3/13*
SHERIFFS SALE

210040342
CARL & DEBORAH SIMPSON
ACCT #40342
50.0 ACRES

The plat map DCSO used in the investigation. It clearly shows the 'foreclosed property' that Philpott went to was sold to Turlingtons by that time ("sold" note written by DCSO). Deputy Wells withheld it from the Probable Cause report to the District Attorney. Original plat map at www.RapeOfDelco.com/map.jpg. The Turlington farm is surrounded by descendants of Stand Watie's Cherokee Mounted Rifle regiment. Ron Rotramel, an 88 year old active farmer and Air Force retiree is the grandson of John Rotramel, Company L, of Stand Watie's Cherokee Mounted Rifle Regiment.[iii] Heather Shotpouch's 3rd great grandfather is "Shotpouch", Co. G, Col. Adair's 2nd Cherokee Mounted Volunteers, and later Co. O, Col Watie's 1st Cherokee Mounted Volunteers. He was the progenitor of the Delaware County Shotpouches. His son, Charley Shotpouch fought for the Union. Charley's son Bird fought in WWI and Bird's son Mike fought in WWII.[iv] Leroy Summerfield (opposite page) was the great grandson of Joseph Summerfield of Company A of Watie's Cherokee Braves. Leroy lost his leg in Vietnam[v]

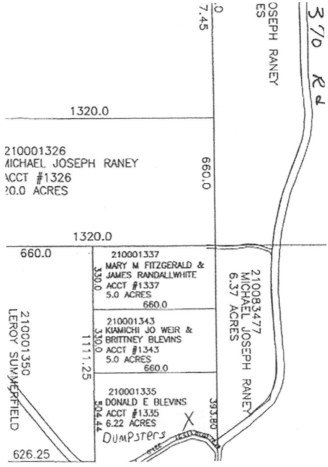

This map used in the DCSO investigation shows where 3, twenty three feet long, bright green, county trash dumpsters sat less than a mile from where Philpott and his accomplices chose to 'burn trash' on land they thought was foreclosed (according to Sheriff Moore). These dumpsters were in plain sight from the road. Deputy Wells knew this and knew there was no reason to start a fire in the wood line to burn trash.

The Information Operation

Deception (Misinformation)
And Concealing Evidence (Withholding Information)

While I sat in the Delaware County jail and Deputy Gayle Wells cobbled together (and concealed evidence from) the Probable Cause Affidavit, Sheriff Harlan Moore was busy misinforming journalists in order to shape public opinion (including that of the local DA and judges).

The Sheriff employed two deceptive methods to mislead the journalists: *deception* (lying) and *concealing* information (withholding evidence). *Sheriff Moore deceived the public* by saying things that weren't true about Philpott to portray him in a sympathetic light[60] and things about me that weren't true to portray me in a bad light. Moore made Philpott and his accomplices appear to be hard working, good old country boys by telling reporters they were driving home after a long day of "cutting wood" when I drove my pickup in front of theirs, forcing them to stop, then jumped out of my vehicle cursing and threatening them. Of course, none of that is true. Remember, the story that I jumped out of my truck, etc. came from Wells, not Philpott. Also, remember there was no cut wood or saw, etc. in the trespasser's truck nor at his house. Then Moore quoted Philpott as saying that Philpott and I

---

[60] This was necessary, because if anyone knew the truth about Philpott, they would have no sympathy at all for him.

"had an exchange of unfriendly conversation."[61] There was no "conversation", friendly or otherwise, just Philpott calling me a "punk motherfucker" and challenging me to "settle it like a man", according to his own testimony. Finally, the article quotes gentle, peace loving Philpott as saying I shot him in the back as he turned away from me avoiding a confrontation. Remember, the Sheriff told this lie *after* the wound nurse determined Philpott was shot in the front of his leg.

Moore continued to omit information about me that would exonerate me, or portray me in a favorable light, and omit information about Philpott that would portray him in an accurate light. If Sheriff Moore was honest, instead of giving fabricated information to reporters to make the arrest appear legitimate, he would have accurately depicted the situation by telling them the truth. The Sheriff *could* have told reporters that the wound expert who examined Philpott said he was shot from the front of his leg. Or Moore could have told the reporter that I was a veteran, or private investigator, or a family man, and he could have told reporters that Philpott was a violent triple felon with active warrants for his arrest and a nearly 40 year long RAP sheet. But, regrettably for both the Sheriff and me, the truth didn't corroborate his story.

---

[61] This quote is absurd. Philpott talks like an excited Earnest T. Bass. Preliminary Hearing Transcripts are online at www.RapeOfDelco.com/prelim.pdf. Philpott doesn't use a 4-syllable word in the entire 121 pages.

The Sheriff also lied about the investigation itself. Moore told reporters that "...investigators worked through the night trying to piece together details of the incident..." and that "investigators determined the bullet entered Philpott's leg from the back side", **as though this was a super complex case, and in the end they, collectively, concluded Philpott was the victim and shot in the back.** The truth is that only one law enforcement officer in the entire investigation (Deputy Wells) stated that Philpott was shot in the rear of the leg.

This is the scene Sheriff Moore painted for the public. In reality, the lead investigator Deputy Wells decided Philpott was the victim prior to starting the investigation.

Finally, most of the articles (like Duren's) conclude with my arrest. Duren continues, stating I called 911 to identify myself as the shooter and tell them Philpott and his accomplices were committing arson. The very next statement quotes Moore misquoting me, "I didn't want to do it, but I couldn't get them to stop", as if I shot Philpott over arson.

To be clear, I never told anyone that I shot Philpott because I couldn't get him to stop committing arson, or for trespassing, or for any reason other than self-defense. And there is no evidence that I ever have. He was threatening me and cursing me while coming at me with a glass bottle in his hand. It's also interesting the article doesn't give the reason I *did* call 911. I told 911 that I shot a trespasser in self-defense and was coming in to town to make a statement as the victim of a crime, not to "turn myself in". The fact that Moore intentionally misrepresented what I told the 911 dispatcher shows that his intent was to manipulate the official message to the public.

The last few lines of Duren's article state that "Deputies took Turlington into custody, impounding his truck and recovering his .380 pistol. They are requesting he be charged with felony assault with a firearm and shooting with intent to kill Philpott. Turlington is in the Delaware County Jail." As for deputies taking me into custody, this is technically true, but misleading. The only reason they were able to "take" me anywhere, was because I went to them *voluntarily*, after I called ahead to tell them I was coming, *as a victim of crime*. As for them impounding my truck, this is true, but what they didn't report is that the Judge ordered them to give it back to me because they had no justification to take it in the first place. As for deputies "recovering" my .380 pistol, the wording makes it sound like they found it during the investigation. When in truth, the *only* reason they were able to take it was that I unloaded and brought it to town to give to them *voluntarily*. I also gave them advance notice of this over the telephone. There were no surprises. As for my charges, the DA never charged me with either assaulting Barret or intending to kill Philpott.

> *The journalists covering my arrest did not lie themselves, but they were used by Sheriff Harlan Moore to push a false narrative. For example, every single line of Dee Duren's article contained a provable outright lie or misrepresentation.*

ON THE RECORD, OFF THE RECORD, AND "THE DEAL"

At different places in the record, **Deputy Wells refers to going "on the record"**, revealing that there are conversations that are on the record, and conversations that are **off the record**. This is significant, because there were no "off the record" conversations with *me*, only Philpott. Remember, Philpott admitted to Wells that he would **"never give the same answer twice"** (30:25). Philpott needed help keeping his story straight. This reinforces the feeling you get when you listen to the interview, that Deputy Wells and Philpott have had unrecorded conversations, because *Wells has to repeatedly remind Philpott what he was supposed to say.*

After going "**off the record**" but still briefly captured on the tape recording, **you can hear Philpott admit to Wells that he had been shot before.** This is profound, and any honest investigator would have asked when, where, and who shot you? Why did they shoot you? *What were you doing* the *last time you got shot?* Did Wells ask anything at all? No; **Wells immediately changed the subject**. Listen for yourself at minute 23:19 of the interview, posted online at www.RapeOf-Delco.com/philpott.mp3.

Furthermore, **while off the record,** you can hear Wells *laughing* about how Philpott drank a half pint of whiskey prior to the interview and how it stung his gums. (33:09)

However, the interview begins with Wells declaring, **on the record,** that Philpott was sober (with at least two bottles of whiskey in his gut).

Perhaps most importantly, in the recorded interview, at 36 minutes and 51 seconds, you can actually hear Wells refer to them wrapping up the working part of "**the deal**". Shortly thereafter, the audio is shut off, so only Wells and Philpott know what was said **off the record** beyond that point, and we will probably never know what "the deal" was that Wells had with Philpott.

All I know is that I didn't get a "deal", or any "off the record" practice runs at getting a story right. We do know, however, that the recording captures Deputy Wells giving Philpott his cell phone number, and inviting Philpott to call "anytime, day or night". I didn't get that offer, either. Of course, whether Philpott did call Wells to discuss their deal, or Philpott's story, or anything else, we will never know, because that was "**off the record**".

Philpott Finally Understands His Role As " Victim"

Well's admission that he was just trying to help Philpott was not just small talk. Wells had to reassure Philpott that he was not the one who was in trouble.

Remember that Philpott was so evasive, he wouldn't even say where he lived. (06:49). Philpott also claimed (at first) that *he had no idea who shot him.* (5:50). The only reason for someone like Philpott to claim he had *no idea* who shot him was his own belief that he in the wrong and he was in trouble. At that point in the interview, Philpott didn't want the police talking to me.

*It was only **after** Wells assured Philpott that the whole point of the investigation was to help **him** (07:02), that Philpott:*

1. *changed his answer from having "no idea" who shot him to "the man that moved in the house below" (07:30), "second place on the left, I think he just bought it... I think he just moved there." (09:22),*
2. *admitted to Wells that he didn't want to go to the hospital after I shot him (19:22)*
3. *admitted to Wells that he had been shot in the past (23:14)*
4. *and that the last time he was shot he didn't go to the hospital or call police (23:19)*

This evasiveness is consistent with his pattern of getting himself shot. He gets shot and doesn't notify the police. The only reason to avoid the police or hospitals after getting shot is if you know you were doing something wrong when you got yourself shot again.

Wells never questioned why Philpott changed his answer from *not knowing who I was* to *knowing where I lived and that I had just bought the house.* Instead of asking Philpott why he didn't want to go to the hospital after being shot, Wells giggled and reassured him, "Darrell, you have good friends." When Philpott admitted to Wells that he had been shot before, instead of asking about the details surrounding that incident, Wells abruptly changed the subject. Once again, Wells didn't want to draw attention to anything affecting Philpott's 'credibility'.

How many people do you know who have been shot on multiple occasions, but never called the police? More importantly, would an objective investigator, upon hearing this, dig further, or abruptly change the subject?

McDonald County Press | 9 Mar 2017

BOOKING

Pineville, probation violation
   Darrell Eugene Philpott,
55, no address given, DWI
- alcohol, possession of a
controlled substance except
35 grams or less of marijuana,
pursue/take/kill/possess or
dispose of wildlife illegally,
operated motor vehicle on
highway without a valid
license, operated motor
vehicle in a careless and
imprudent manner - involving
an accident, and driver failed
to secure child less than
sixteen years old in properly/
adjusted safety restraint

45th Infantry Brigade Dining Out, Norman, Oklahoma, 2017

As Ed "Hoss" Turlington retired from the military in May 2017, District Attorney Kenny Wright's star witness against him, violent career criminal Darrell Philpot, was sitting in an Arkansas jail on a litany of charges, including his fourth felony (of which he was later convicted).

[3]

ROOTS

"The Oklahoma and Indian Territory...a happy hunting ground
filled with bushwhackers, horse thieves, whiskey peddlers,
counterfeiters, hide peelers, marauders. They'll kill ya for a hat
band."

- Judge Fenton (actor Pat Hingle) describing early Oklahomans
to Jeb Cooper (Clint Eastwood) in Hang 'em High. Both
Eastwood and Hingle are military veterans. Eastwood is a
member of the Sons of Confederate Veterans

...look unto the rock whence ye are hewn
Isaiah 51:1

PIONEERS AND VETERANS

THE FIRST FAMILIES OF THE TWIN TERRITORIES (FFTT) is a lineage association sponsored by the Oklahoma Genealogical Society. It is composed of the direct descendants of Indians and Pioneers who settled in Indian Territory or Oklahoma Territory prior to statehood. Many of those Indians and Pioneers were former Confederates, especially those along the eastern border. My family belongs to the FFTT under 8 of my ancestors[62] who pioneered Indian Territory in what is now Delaware and Ottawa counties. My wife Julie's third great grandfather, Texas Partisan Ranger Henry Price, pioneered Oklahoma Territory. Many, if not most Ottawa and Delaware county citizens are descended from Missourians and Arkansawyers (who, in turn, descend from Kentuckians and Tennesseans). The majority of Delaware County Indians descend from Stand Watie's Confederates. Military historians regard Watie as a genius of guerilla warfare.

---

[62] Adam Harmon and Nancy Swango, Phineas Baugher and Jessie Ann Harmon, John Duke Kelly and Muta Angeline Davis, William Kelly and Emma Gertrude Baugher,
   see www.rapeofdelco.com/fftt.htm

The "Southern Culture of Honor", [63] *which includes in-tolerance of improper conduct by others, is deeply entrenched in both the White and Indian populations in the area (see Oklahoma Citizen Arrest Statutes, page 3, footnote 9, above)*

South Carolina seceded from the Union on 20 December 1860. Six days later, US Army Major Robert Anderson, a former slave owner, moved his forces to Fort Sumter, an island fortress that guarded the entrance to Charleston Bay. This marine invasion and military occupation of a seceded, independent state was received exactly the same way as British military incursions were received by our independent colonies in 1776.[64]

---

[63] Cohen, Dov, Richard E. Nisbett, Brian F. Bowdle, and Norbert Schwarz. "Insult, Aggression, and the Southern Culture of Honor: An 'Experimental Ethnography."." *Journal of Personality and Social Psychology* 70, no. 5 (1996): 945–60. https://doi.org/10.1037/0022-3514.70.5.945.

[64] "Any people anywhere being inclined and having the power have the right to rise up and shake off the existing government and form a new one that suits them better. This is a most valuable, a most sacred right – a right which we hope and believe is to liberate the world. Nor is the right confined to cases in which the whole people of an existing government may choose to exercise it. Any portion of such people that can, may revolutionize and make their own of so much of the territory as they inhabit. More than this, a majority of any such portion may revolutionize, putting

The Confederate States of America was formed in February 1860, and on 12 April, began an artillery attack on the foreign occupation of Fort Sumter. Major Anderson surrendered in less than 48 hours. On 15 April, newly elected President Lincoln issued a request for a 75,000 man militia to the Governors of the United States. His request resulted in 4 more States seceding to the Confederacy and included the following Governors' responses:

Missouri Governor Claiborne Fox Jackson: 'Your requisition is illegal, unconstitutional, revolutionary, inhuman, diabolical, and cannot and will not be complied with.'"

Arkansas Governor Henry Rector: "The people of this Commonwealth are freemen, not slaves, and will defend to the last extremity their honor, lives, and property, against Northern mendacity and usurpation."

---

down a minority, intermingled with or near about them, who may oppose this movement. Such minority was precisely the case of the Tories of our own Revolution. It is a quality of revolutions not to go by old lines or old laws; but to break up both and make new ones." – Abraham Lincoln, January 12, 1848

Kentucky Governor Beriah Magoffin: "I will send not a man nor a dollar for the wicked purpose of subduing my sister Southern States."

Tennessee Governor Isham Harris stated in a telegram to Lincoln, "Tennessee will furnish not a single man for the purpose of coercion, but fifty thousand if necessary for the defense of our rights and those of our Southern brothers."

People are generally aware that the Cherokees, along with the Chickasaw, Choctaw, Creek, and Seminole ("The 5 Civilised Tribes") allied with the Confederacy in the "War Between the States". The federals had already forcibly removed the Indians out of their homes in the southeastern states and had quit making payments to them required by treaty. The Confederates promised to make those payments and did so throughout the war. Former New York Governor and Anti-Mason William Seward,[65] while campaigning for

---

[65] Seward was actually the leading Republican candidate for the 1860 presidential election but because of his (at the time) radical anti-slavery and pro-immigrant views lost to the more (in those time) moderate, **racist, anti-war** candidate Lincoln. In the years leading up to the election, Lincoln repeatedly assured voters of not only the right of **States to secede**, but of the legitimacy of slavery, (see **footnote 62 and 65**). In his first inaugural speech, Lincoln promised to protect slavery where it already existed, and that he believed this right was already protected in the United States

Lincoln in 1860, promoted kicking the Indians out of both Kansas and the Indian Territory (Kansas had not become a state yet). He said, "Kansas comes and asks or demands to be admitted into the Union. The Indian Territory, also, south of Kansas, must be vacated by the Indians..."[66] Upon being elected President, the vociferously racial segregationist Lincoln[67] appointed Seward as Secretary of State. Joining

---

Constitution, and that the Corwin Amendment (which protected slavery from federal power and at the time had already been passed by both houses of congress) merely reiterated what the US Constitution already recognized.

[66] Chicago, 3 October 1860 www.rapeofdelco.com/seward.pdf

[67] *I have no purpose to introduce political and social equality between the white and the black races.*

I will say then that I am not, nor ever have been, in favor of bringing about in any way the social and political equality of the white and black races; *I am not nor ever have been in favor of making voters or jurors of negroes, nor of qualifying them to hold office, nor to intermarry with white people.*

I will say in addition to this that there is a physical difference between the white and black races which I believe will forever forbid the two races living together on terms of social and political equality. And inasmuch as they cannot so live, while they do remain together there must be the position of superior and inferior, and *I, as much as any other man, am in favor of having the superior position assigned to the white race.* -Abraham Lincoln, first debate with Stephen Douglas, August 1858

the Confederacy was not a difficult decision for the Indians to make.

With 27 battles and countless skirmishes fought across Indian Territory, into eastern Missouri,[68] eastern Arkansas, southern Kansas and northern Texas, Confederate Brigadier General Stand Waite's "Cherokee Braves" fought in more engagements than any other unit west of the Mississippi.

Termed "The Most Complete Battle" by President Jefferson Davis and considered by military historians as "one of the most brilliant and daring raids of the Civil War", the Second Battle of Cabin Creek is known to Union sympathizers as "The Cabin Creek Disaster". Fought in today's Mayes County, Oklahoma, the battle was a raid on a 2nd Kansas Cavalry supply wagon train. Watie planned the attack. Texan Brigadier General Richard M. Gano[69] led a brigade composed of 1200 Cavalry and Artillery while Waite led the Indians, composed of two Cherokee regiments, two Creek regiments, and a Seminole battalion. The raid netted the Confederacy **740 mules and 130 wagons full of supplies worth over 75 million dollars** in modern currency. Waite led

---

[68] Both Watie and John Duke Kelly fought at the battle of Oak Hills (known as Wilson's Creek to Yankees and known as the 'Bull Run of the West' to historians). It was the first major battle fought west of the Mississippi River.

[69] Julie Turlington's 3rd great grandfather, Henry Price was assigned to Gano's Brigade as part of the 1st Texas Partisan Rangers and fought alongside Watie's regiment at the Battles of Cabin Creek, Indian Territory, among others.

his multi-tribal cavalry brigade throughout the War in the Cherokee nation and into Arkansas for the Battle (known by Yankees as the Battle of Pea Ridge). Watie was the last Confederate General to surrender.

Confederate Brigadier General Stand Watie, Cherokee Chief, Guerilla Warfare Genius, Freemason, Attorney, wealthiest man west of the Mississippi, and Turlington's country neighbor

Hardee, 10 years old, cleaning Stand Watie's tombstone
Polson[vi] Cemetery, Jay, Oklahoma, 2019

Jay, the Delaware County seat, is named after Confederate Jay Washbourne, nephew of Stand Waite and grandson of Confederate Captain J. W. Washbourne. Watie is buried in the country two miles from my house with Washbourne. My son Hardee maintains his head stone and those of the other Confederate families, including the Boudinots, Adairs, and Ridges. Lake Eucha is just outside of Jay. It was named after Oochelata (David Thompson). Oochelata was a Confederate in the 1st Cherokee Mounted Rifles and later, the Principal Cherokee Chief. It is understood in our area that the "o'" in "Grand Lake o' the Cherokees" is an abbreviation of "over": alluding to the countless Cherokee graves the man-made lake covers.

My wife Julie, and my mother Nancy Turlington, belong to the Cowskin Prairie chapter of the United Daughters of the Confederacy (UDC) under Partisan Rangers who fought in the Indian Territory, Missouri, and Arkansas region then pioneered the Twin Territories after the war.

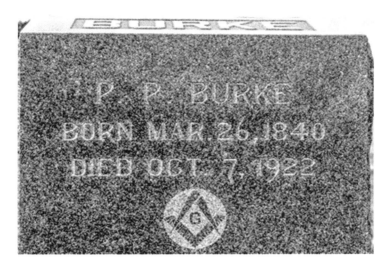

Julie's third great grandfather, native Arkansawyer Peter Pressler Burke,[vii] and both of his brothers were Confederates.[viii] Peter was one of the first to enlist in Waul's Legion when it was formed in the spring of 1862. He was assigned to Company C, Cavalry battalion and remained until the end of the war, when he was taken prisoner on May 4, 1865 almost a month after Lee's surrender at Appomattox. Peter's father James fought in the 1st Regiment Mississippi Volunteers in the War of 1812. Peter's father in law, Julie's 4th great grandfather, Jacob Butler Smith, served the Confederacy as a Tennessee infantryman. Peter Burke was a Master Mason.

Burke. Peter. P.

Co. *E*, Waul's Texas Legion.

(Infantry, Cavalry and Artillery.)

After the fall of Vicksburg the Cavalry Batt'n was also known as Willis' Batt n Texas Cav., serving later in Steel's Command Texas Cav. In 1864 part of the Art'y Batt'n became the 1st Texas Field Batt'y and the remainder was transferred to the 2d Texas Field Batt'y. The Infantry Batt'ns were consolidated in 1864 to form Timmons' Reg't Texas Infantry.

(Confederate.)

Burke, James

1 Regiment U. S. Volunteers.

(1 Reg't Miss. Territorial Vols.)

Julie's 3rd Great Grandfather Alabama born Henry Price. Price moved to Texas as a young man. He belonged to the 1st Texas Partisan Rangers and fought alongside Stand Watie's Cherokee Braves in Indian Territory under Brigadier General Richard Montgomery Gano. After the war, Price pioneered Oklahoma Territory. General Gano was the great grandfather of aerospace engineer, aviator, inventor, investor, philanthropist Howard Hughes through Hughes' mother, Allene Stone Gano.

Henry Price of Company D, Thirtieth Texas Cavalry, (Gurley's 1st Partisan Rangers) is Julie's 3rd great grandfather.[ix] He fought in the Battles of Poison Spring and Camden in Arkansas and the Roseville skirmishes near Fort Smith as well as Indian Territory battles, including the Cabin Creek battles. The Cabin Creek Battles took place in what is now Mayes county, which is adjacent to Delaware County.[70] Mayes County is named after former Confederate and Cherokee Principal Chief, Samuel Houston Mayes.

After the war, Price pioneered Lexington, Oklahoma Territory. He outlived both his wives and died in Big Horn County, Wyoming in 1912. Henry was a Master Mason.[x]

---

[70] Two of Turlington's 3rd great grandparents, Kentuckians Adam Harmon and Nancy Swango, pioneered Big Cabin and Vinita (now Mayes County), Indian Territory. Adam's grandfather was longhunter Dan Harmon of Harman's Station, Kentucky. Nancy Swango's grandfather tended Washington's farm after the first Revolutionary war.

http://www.rapeofdelco.com/fftt.htm

Henry Price on the 1900 Oklahoma Territory Census. Price was born, orphaned, adopted and raised in Benton County,[71] Alabama. His father was a Virginian and his mother from Alabama. Thomas was born in Texas to Henry and Martha. Martha was born in Missouri.

---

[71] Benton County, Alabama and Benton County Arkansas (which borders Delaware County on the east) were named for Missouri Senator Thomas Hart Benton, a War of 1812 veteran.

John Duke Kelly (on left) with David Kennedy,
photo courtesy www.rulen.com

My 2nd great grandfather, John Duke Kelly,[xi] was born to Missouri Territory pioneers Thomas Kelly and Nancy Zumwalt. He was an officer in Co A, 7th Missouri Volunteer

Cavalry, Missouri State Guard (the Vernon County Partisan Rangers),[xii] prior to riding with William Quantrill. Vernon County was known as the "Bushwhacker Capitol" of the West. Kelly fought in the battles of Carthage, Oak Hills,[72] and Dry Wood Creek under General Sterling Price. Later in the war, he rode with Quantrill,[xiii] and could personally take new recruits to both Price and Quantrill.

---

[72] The Battle of Carthage the first major battle after Lincoln invoked "the war power" in lieu of a Declaration of War in his Message to Congress on July 4, 1861, The Battle of Carthage was historically, strategically, and tactically significant.

The battle marks the only time a sitting U.S. State governor has led troops in the field. It is also the only time a sitting U.S. State Governor has led soldiers against the Union to which his state belonged.

Captain Jo Shelby, a Missouri farmer. spearheaded Governor Jackson's army, with a band of 150 independent Partisan Rangers . Pro Confederate Missouri earned their first victory in the war largely due to Shelby's battlefield maneuvers under fire by Sigel's artillery, followed by Shelby's Rangers chasing Sigel's troops from Carthage to Sarcoxie. By war's end, Shelby as known to both sides as one of the greatest, if not greatest, cavalry officers to have ever lived.

The Battle of Oak Hills (known as Wilson's Creek to Federals) was a Confederate victory fought near Springfield, Missouri. It was the second major battle in the War Between the States and the first west of the Mississippi. It is often referred to as the "Bull Run of the West".

1862 letter by James Long, to the Provost Marshal after his capture. Long wrote that he was poor, both his parents were dead, he had no home and couldn't afford bond. He closed by stating he had never taken any oath before but would rather fight for the Confederates than the Federals, as he couldn't "fight against all his people".

Letter at www.rapeofdelco.com/jameslong.jpg

The Partisan Rangers were sometimes referred to as "Bushwhackers", which means "one who beats the bush, or an outdoorsman". Their history is recorded in numerous publications, books, and artifacts, most notably in the Bushwhacker Museum in Nevada, Missouri. Nevada is in Vernon County, Missouri, and was known as the "Bushwhacker capitol" during the war. John Duke Kelly lived in Nevada when John Brown, who was already an indicted murderer at this point, led two dozen Kansans on a murder spree in Vernon County during Christmas, 1958. An excellent collection of Partisan Ranger history is also available at Rulen.com.

SCHEDULE 1.—Free Inhabitants in _Center Township_ in the County of _Vernon_ of _Missouri_ enumerated by me, on the _3_ day of _July_ 1860. _Nelson M Blanco_ Post Office _Nevada City Mo_ .

Dwelling-houses numbered in the order of visitation.	Families numbered in the order of visitation.	The name of every person whose usual place of abode on the first day of June, 1860, was in this family.	Age.	Sex	Color	Profession, Occupation, or Trade of each person, male and female, over 15 years of age.	Value of Real Estate.	Value of Personal Estate.	Place of Birth, Naming the State, Territory, or Country.	Married within the year.	Attended School within the year.
1	2	3	4	5	6	7	8	9	10	11	12
162	158	J Duke Kelly	30	M		Merchant	5520	8521	Missouri		
		M A Kelly	26	F					Missouri		
		Theodore Kelly	4	M					Missouri		

J Duke Kelly was a 30 years old merchant with $5,520 in real estate and $8,521 in personal estate in 1860. Although a wealthy Southerner, he did not own slaves. His wife M.A. (Muta Angeline) was 26, and their firstborn Theodore was 4 months old. All three were born in Missouri. 1860 Federal Census for Center Township, Vernon County, Missouri

After the war, the Kellys were forced to retreat to Indian Territory. The regular Confederate Soldiers were mostly pardoned after the war, but the "bushwhackers" were not considered lawful combatants entitled to due process. In fact, most were executed when captured, and Kansas "Redlegs" hunted down the southern guerillas after the war and killed them without trial. So, men like John Duke Kelly frequently retreated to the Indian Territory for two reasons: 1) they could escape federal jurisdiction, and 2) they were in the company of like-minded Cherokees and Choctaws, many of whom they served with in the war, and shared a rightful distrust of the federal government.

John Duke Kelly moved to Afton, Oklahoma. There, he raised and raced horses into his sixties, was a city councilmember, and owned a livery and a saloon on main street. Main street later became part of Route 66. He had three wives over the years, including one Cherokee, so the Kelly descendants include both whites and Cherokees.

> One mile dash, 3-year-olds, free to all for $35, three entries: Water Leap, owned by E. J. Waud; Kirby, owned by J. M. Williams; Little Buckton, owned by J. D. Kelly; won by Little Buckton.

Former Confederate Cavalryman John Duke Kelly
wins mile dash on "Little Buckton" at 1886 **Vinita** *Fair.*
The Weekly Chieftain, Vinita, Indian Territory, October 21,
1886

Little Buckton, J. D. Kelly.

Trotting, mile heats:

Jno. B. Sprague, E. C. Scammon.
Bay Diamond, R. L. Blair.
Uncle Joe, W. H. Miller.

Frank Bruce, trombone player with the Richards comedy company will make the balloon ascension to-day.

Yesterday's Races.

Mile dash:

Buckton 1st, $100.
Broadhead 2nd, $30.

61 year old John Duke Kelly takes 1st again on same horse. The Weekly Chieftain, Vinita, Indian Territory, September 24, 1891

THE AWARDS.

From the data at hand and to be obtained it was impossible to give a complete statement of the awards in detail and we therefore give the names of the parties who took premiums:

CLASS A—HORSES.

J. D. Kelley, G. W. Dixon, Dr. Littleton, D. S. Warren, M. L. Harlan, Mrs. Ironside, A. Westfork, Ralph Green, D. Hughs, M. Casto.

John Duke Kelly 1st Place in horse show, 1891 Vinita fair The Weekly Chieftain, Vinita, Indian Territory, September 24, 1891

AFTON IN ASHES!

Nothing Remains of the Business Section of the Town.

BEFORE THE HIGH WIND OF LAST EVENING THE BUILDINGS MELT LIKE WAX.

Detailed Account of the Devastation Prepared by a "Chieftain" Office Man a Few Moments After the Fire was Under Control and Presented Smoking Hot from the Ruins for the Information of its Readers.

Afton suffered a fire Friday afternoon which made a clean sweep of its business houses, not the one next to it belonged to Jno. "Keg" Landrum.

J. D. Kelly, saloon; loss $600.

John Duke Kelly's saloon burns in City Fire
The Weekly Chieftain, Vinita, Indian Territory,
30 September 1897

Vinita city election: Mayor, L. B. Bell; council, B. S. Landrum, T. R. Knight, A. B. Nichols, T. F. Thompson, F. L. Chouteau. Afton city election: Mayor, James Lamar; council, W. H. Donaldson, Tom Ballard, J. D. Kelley, Wiley Melton, Dr. James R. Dawson. G. W. Wells was elected marshal and George W. Taylor clerk.

John Duke Kelly, Afton City Council, 1895
The Weekly Chieftain, Vinita, Indian Territory,
September 5, 1895

William Kelly, son of J.D. Kelly and Muta Angeline neè Davis, was proprietor of the Fairland City snooker hall during prohibition.[73] He married Emma Gertrude Baugher, daughter of Delaware District, Indian Territory Marshal Phineas Albion Baugher.

NAMES.	OCCUPATION.	RACE OR NATIONALITY.	AGE	SEX	BY WHOM EMPLOYED.	Number in Family	DATE OF ARRIVAL IN THE NATION.	REMARKS.
1	2	3	4	5	6	7	8	9
...arles E. Shields	Farming	White	28	Male	Silas Bluejacket	4	1882	5 horses 7 Cattle 8 hogs
...gherly David	"	"	24	"	"	1	April 1890	

The 1890 Cherokee Nation Census included a segregated list of Whites living in the district under permit, "either by the Nation or U.S."

Phineas Baugher married Jessian Harmon, daughter of Adam Harmon and Nancy neè Swango in Kentucky. Phineas is listed in the 1890 "Whites with Permits" Indian Territory census as a 44 year-old farmer, arriving in Indian Territory in November 1887, having 9 family members, (Jessian died earlier that year) and employed by James Harmon, Jessian's brother. Phineas served as constable for Afton and later, city Marshal. Phineas' father, John Jacob Moyer Baugher, served in the Virginia militia during the War of 1812.

---

[73] "William Kelly" (1930) U.S. Census for Fairland City, Ottawa County, (1030), Enumeration District 58-12, Sheet A

> A novel case come up before Mayor Moore of this place last Monday morning. The town of Afton vs George W Eden charged with an assault on the editor of this paper on account of his advocacy for free schools. Complaint was sworn out by Marshal Baugher. The defendant plead not

George Eden assaults the newspaper editor for promoting socialism; Marshal Baugher files a complaint on behalf of the city of Afton. *"Afton Advance", 2 September 1892, as cited by Fredrea Gregath, "Afton (Indian Territory- Oklahoma) Some Early History", 198.*

Jessian Harmon's parent's Adam Harmon and Nancy nee' Swango, moved to Indian Territory from Kentucky about the same time as Phineas and Jessian.

Adam's grandfather Daniel, and Daniel's brother Mathias, defended the frontier as scouts for the Montgomery County, Virginia militia during the Revolutionary War.[74] Their father, famed Indian fighter cavalry Captain Heinrich Adam Harman (Herrmann), founded Harman's Station in Kentucky.[xiv]

---

[74] Militia of Montgomery County, Virginia, 1777-1790. (1990). United States: Kegley Books (pp 27 ,60) and Connelley, W. E. (1910). Eastern Kentucky Papers: The Founding of Harman's Station, with an Account of the Indian Captivity of Mrs. Jennie Wiley and the Exploration and Settlement of the Big Sandy Valley in the Virginias and Kentucky. United States: Torch Press.

*Harmans battle Indians at Hunting Camp,
Big Sandy Valley, Kentucky, 1788.
-Connelley, William, "The Founding of Harman's Station
and the Wiley Captivity" p. 29. 1910.*

Nancy's father, uncles, grandfather and grand uncles were Kentucky Confederates, Nancy's grandfather, "Little Abe" Swango served in the War of 1812, and his grandfather, Abraham Swango tended future President George Washington's apple orchards.[xv]

Robert Kelly, WW II Army Sergeant, Philippines, 1940
(back row, right end), and in front of Fairland home, 1940

John Duke Kelly's grandson, Robert Leroy Kelly gave his life in the Philippines during World War II. Robert's body was lost in the Pacific along with the rest of his B-25 Mitchell Bomber crew. Robert was raised in Fairland where his father William Kelly was proprietor of the town pool hall (see sign on bench opposite page). Robert's name is on the Ottawa County Veteran's Memorial at the Courthouse in Miami, and on the Fairland WW2 Veteran's Memorial in the city park. Robert married Myrle Maxine Simmons of Afton. Their son Ronnie served in the Army in Korea, and Robert's grandson's Edwin "Hoss" Turlington and Lance Turlington, are both Army veterans as well (Ed has retired from service in 2017, and Lance is still on active duty). The first row of names in front of the Delaware County Courthouse on the Veterans' Walk of Fame lists John Duke Kelly, Robert Leroy Kelly, Edwin Turlington Sr., Edwin Turlington Jr., Lance Turlington, REB Turlington, and family friend and local Pastor, Dean Bridges.

The Delaware County Courthouse WWII memorial lists 5 Kelly men.[75] Paul Duke Kelly's grandfather, John Duke Kelly, was named after Missouri Cavalryman John Duke Kelly sr (above and pages 61-66). When my family lived in Zena in the 70s, Paul Duke Kelly owned

---

[75] Earnest, brother of Clyde and Paul Duke, served in the war but isn't listed on the memorial.

one of the two general stores and John Hampton owned the other. John and his wife Lizzie neé Kelly[76] were Kelly Hampton's parents. Paul Duke Kelly had three sons, Roy, *John Duke*, and Tommy. John Duke was a sailor, Tommy was a marine, Roy was a soldier. Roy, and two of Roy's children graduated from West Point.

All four of Kelly Hampton's great grandparents were Indian Territory pioneers. His great grandfather JF Hampton brought the Kellys to Delaware District in 1903. Kelly's 2nd great grandfather, Turley Hampton rode in North Carolina's Company B, 3rd Mounted Infantry during the War Between the States. Hampton's 6th great grandfather, Colonel Andrew Hampton, commanded the Rutherford County Regiment of North Carolina militia during the Revolutionary War.

Kelly retired after 44 years as a Delaware County educator and his wife, Lonna taught for 48. All three of their children (David, Robert, and Kristi) grew up to be Delaware County educators. Kelly played football at OSU, his grandson Ben played football at OU and Ben's brother Casey, played at NEO.

---

[76] Clyde and Paul Duke Kelly's sister

Hampton's General Store, Zena, Oklahoma

The last thing any of the people involved in Turlington's prosecution see before entering the Courthouse, and the first thing they see upon leaving, is a reminder of what Turlington and his family have contributed to Delaware County. Turlington's false felony charges were active at the time his markers were placed at the entrance to the courthouse, and the local Veterans association responsible for their placement knew this. The markers' placement was a message to the District Attorney.

Parents

Ed and Nancy Turlington,
Miami, Oklahoma 1963

Nancy Lynn Kelly, 1964

Ed's mother, Nancy, was raised as a "Gold Star" daughter, having lost her father in WWII. Her mother, Myrle, was presented with a 48 star American flag at Robert Leroy Kelly's memorial service, and Myrle flew that same flag on her porch on Mulberry Street in Afton every Memorial Day, Veteran's Day, and Independence Day. Both of Myrle's sons, Ronnie, and Johnny, served in the Army.

Nancy attended college at NEO A&M at Miami on an Ottawa County Junior Miss Scholarship. She received her Bachelor of Education at Oklahoma State University and her

Master of Education at NSU in Tahlequah. She taught elementary school in Afton, and later served as a principal at Fort Gibson. Sapulpa hired her to be the first principal of Freedom Elementary. She emphasized citizenship, civic duty, and patriotism as a defining trait of Freedom Elementary, and every Memorial Day and Veterans' Day was observed with formal programs.

From The Tulsa World:

Principal works to keep Freedom ringing

NORA FROESCHLE World Staff Writer Jul 4, 2007

PATRIOTIC PRINCIPAL Nancy Turlington: "I have spent a lifetime teaching kids about appreciating the freedoms that we have. Everything in here is the stars and stripes — red, white and blue."   Kelly Kerr / Tulsa World

Nancy was invited to join the WWII Veterans' Association as a Gold Star Daughter, and she formed lifelong friendships with the association's founding members, Al Price and Paul Andert,[77] [xvi]along with many others. The WWII veterans

---

[77] Andert is one of the most highly decorated combat veterans alive. The movie "Fury", starring Brad Pitt, was loosely based on Paul's World War II service. Brad, the son of an Oklahoma trucker, got his first 12 gauge shotgun "in kindergarten or 1st grade", and has made it clear that he owns a handgun for defensive, not sport purposes. Brad told reporters at the 2019 Venice Film Festival that he grew up being "... taught to be strong, not show weakness, don't be disrespected, and so on...". According to Gwyneth Paltrow, Brad told Harvey Weinstein, the most powerful man in Hollywood at the time, that he would "kill him if he ever made (Gwyneth) feel uncomfortable again." Brad explained the confrontation to CNN, "I was a boy from the Ozarks... and that's how we confronted things". After spending time with Brad, Paul referred to Pitt as a "true patriot". (Appendix CC, Tulsan WWII hero advises Brad Pitt, movie team making 'Fury") Brad is Turlington's cousin through the Fullertons (http://www.rapeof-delco.com/samfullerton.htm). Brad is the 3rd great grandson of Confederate William Pitt of the 16th Texas Cavalry (known as the Bloody 16th). Brad > William Alvin Pitt & Jane Etta Hillhouse > Alvin Monroe Pitt & Elizabeth Jean Brown > Oliver Pitt & Rosa Lee Dorris > Thomas Monroe Pitt & Mary Isabelle Armer > William Pitt & Cynthia Parker

Turlington is currently putting together a Sons of American Revolution application for Brad under their common ancestor John Alexander Fullerton. Brad > William Alvin Pitt & Jane Etta

became regular visitors at Freedom Elementary and were incorporated not only into the national holiday observances, but the history and social studies classes as well.

The veterans didn't just talk about battle experiences, however. They also told the students about serving something greater than themselves, and what our national values are supposed to be. They talked about respect, faith and family in ways that would not be tolerated in public schools on the east and west coast. In small town Oklahoma, however, they were well received and appreciated.

Lance Turlington with Paul Andert, Tulsa, 2010

Hillhouse > Hal Knox Hillhouse & Clara Mae Cell > Emory A Hillhouse & Etta Coleman Williams > Henry Thomas Williams & Ida Mae Isbell > Francis C Williams & Sarah Green Fullerton > John McCune Fullerton & Ann Rawls Fort > Thomas Elder Fullerton & Isabella McCune > Alexander Fullerton & Mary Jane Sharp

Hardee, Paul Andert, and Nancy, Tulsa, 2018

ED TURLINGTON
fullback

Ed Turlington, Miami, Oklahoma, 1963

Edwin "Ed" Turlington, Sr. is descended from 7 Confederate Veterans and at least as many Revolutionary War

Veterans. [xvii] He came to Oklahoma from Sebastian, Florida on a football and track scholarship. At NEO A&M, he played fullback and anchored several relay teams, running the 100 yard sprint in 10 seconds flat.[78] After meeting Nancy at NEO in Miami, they were married and went to Oklahoma State. Ed was commissioned into the Air Force upon graduation and served from 1968-1972. After serving as an assistant headmaster and football coach at Palmer Preparatory High School for a year, Ed moved to Oklahoma where he served as an administrator in several Ottawa and Delaware county schools from the 70s to the 00s. When Ed was High School Principal at Grove, his sons' elementary school principal was their cousin, Earl Kelly. Their cousin Kelly Hampton was the High School counselor. Later, when Hampton was Superintendent at Colcord, Ed was his High School principal. Ed was Superintendent at Afton and at Oaks Indian Mission.

Ed was an Infantry officer in Oklahoma's 45th Infantry Brigade in the 80s.

---

[78] See Appendix T, "Turlington Busiest Player" and "10 Seconds Flat" articles, Miami News Record.

Ed Turlington with students, Grove High School, 1978

During Ed's career as an educator, more than a few wayward boys were given the choice of expulsion from school and legal consequences or enlisting in the military. Ed Sr. always believed that a young man would be forced to grow up in a hurry in the military.

It isn't a coincidence that all three of Ed's sons served in the military, as he raised them to believe it was their obligation as able bodied male citizens. Although his sons would serve in various capacities, including active duty Army, Army Reserves and National Guard, one military experience they all shared with their father was serving in Oklahoma's 45th Infantry Brigade.

1LT John Cooper and PFC Lance Turlington at the French Commando Course in Martinique, 1991. Coop was Lance's Detachment Commander in Steven's Raiders (Det. 1, C. Co., 1/279th Infantry Battalion), and remains a family friend. In 2017 Coop ("Deep C") and Gordon Carlin [xxiii] ("Safecracker") sponsored Ed into the Bedouin Shrine in Muskogee. Lance joined in the Shrine in the 90s. Both Deep C and Safecracker are descended from Louisiana Confederates. Coop is descended from Indians and Pioneers of Indian Territory and Louisiana Confederates. [xviii]

CSM Dean Bridges and SGT REB Turlington. Dean was Ed's platoon sergeant in D Company, 1/279th Infantry at Tulsa and C Company, 1/279th Infantry in Claremore. Dean was Lance's squad leader in Steven's Raiders.

REB and Dean served together in the Joint Area Support Group for the International Zone (Green Zone) in Baghdad. REB was a squad leader for the Commanding General's Protective Services Detachment in Iraq and Dean was Command Sergeant Major of the 45th Infantry Brigade Combat Team. As senior enlisted advisor to the Commanding General, Dean got to visit with REB on a daily basis during the war.

Dean is descended from Confederate Veterans on both his Father's and Mother's sides. His 2nd great grandfather, James Marion Bridges fought for the Confederacy in Company E, 4th Infantry Regiment, 1st Missouri State Guard. Dean's 2nd Great Grandfather [xix] Solomon K. Huffman fought for the Confederacy in Company H, 58th Virginia Volunteer Infantry Regiment and Company H, 7th Virginia Cavalry Regiment. Solomon's grandfather, Christian Hoffman, fought in Pennsylvania's 3rd Regiment during the Revolutionary War.

Bringing the 7th Generation Home

Ed "Fabric of Our Nation" Turlington, his wife Julie and their firstborn Edwin "Hardee" Turlington III. The photo was taken at the National Archives in Washington, D.C. during a weeklong ceremony marking the Army Reserves 103rd birthday. Turlington was chosen to represent the state of Kansas, where he was stationed at the time. The Commanding General of the Army Reserves reenlisted Turlington in front of the actual Declaration of Independence and Constitution.

Shooting violent felon Darrell Philpott is just the most recent contribution Turlington has made to the War on Drugs. Turlington fought his first battle in that war in "Operation Flete", a US Customs interdiction operation in Miami, Florida in 1988.

JUNGLE OPERATIONS TRAINING CENTER

Certificate

This is to certify that

having

successfully completed

the

Jungle Warfare Training Course

PVE Edwin Turlington

is hereby designated a

Jungle Expert

AWARDED THIS ___6th___ DAY
OF ___DECEMBER___ 19 _40_
AT FORT SHERMAN, PANAMA

LTC, INFANTRY
COMMANDER

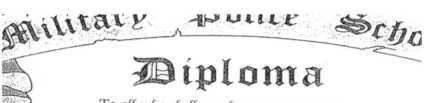

Military Police School

Diploma

To all who shall see these presents greeting.
Be it known that
EDWIN. H. TURLINGTON Jr.

having successfully fulfilled the requirements
of the course of instruction in the
TERRORIST SURVEILLANCE DETECTION COURSE
10 – 14 SEPTEMBER 1990 (40 HOURS)

and having achieved the prescribed grade, has been declared a
Graduate
In testimony whereof, and by the authority vested in us

This is to certify that

SPC EDWIN H. TURLINGTON

has successfully completed

VIP TACTICAL POLICE RESCUE COURSE

17 – 21 SEP 90   (40 HOURS)

PATCH BARRACKS, STUTTGART, FRG

THOMAS G. TAYLOR
GS-11, USAMPS
SPECIAL OPERATIONS

I was teaching in Tulsa during the blizzard of 07-08 that took out that city's power for more than a week. While applying for a loan at the bank next to my school, I met my soul mate, Julie. We married 7 months later on July 4th.

Just like her future husband, Julie liked guns (obviously), was a certified scuba diver, was formally schooled in Latin and had studied museum artifacts in Paris and London, was a martial artist, and was descended from a Confederate Partisan Ranger who pioneered Indian Territory after the war. Julie is a master parachutist, having over 300 skydives.

Ed "Hoss" Turlington's home, Sand Springs, Oklahoma
Spring 2008. Turlington was 39 years old.

Ed and Julie, 4 July 2008, Tulsa, Oklahoma

In 2008, Julie was teaching Spanish in southwest Oklahoma and I was her school resource officer.[79] Our firstborn, Hardee, was born in Paris, Texas, the following year, and I reminded Julie of something I told her on our very first date; that when I became a father, I would raise my family where I was raised, in the Ozarks of Northeast Oklahoma. It would still be another three years.

---

[79] A resource officer is a sworn law enforcement officer responsible for safety and crime prevention in schools. Future DCSO Deputy Chris Hardison lived on the other side of town.

Ed and Julie, pregnant with Hardee, Tulsa, 2009

Julie, Hardee, and Coach Turlington,
Hardesty, Oklahoma, 2009

Ed's 41st birthday, October 2009, Big D's Café, Hardesty,
Oklahoma . Hardee was six months old.

In the summer of 2010, Shodai Gary Dill certified Lance, Julie, and me as Jeet Kune Do instructors. I first became Shodai Dill's student after Dean Bridges introduced me to Shodai in 1992 after my Army discharge. Shodai Dill had conferred a black belt in Bushido Kempo to Dean two years earlier.

Mark Roach, Lance and Eddie Turlington, Dean Bridges with Tai Koshi Do Grandmaster Wayne Davis.

Dean is now the Grandmaster of Tai Koshi Do.

Shodai Gary Dill conferring a Black Belts
in Bushido Kempo and Akai Jitsu to Dean

Dill holds an 8th degree Black Sash from mainland China in Kung Fu and is the founder and Grandmaster of Bushido Kempo, which is often referred to as the Japanese version of Jeet Kune Do. He is internationally recognized as a first generation Jeet Kune Do student of Bruce Lee's Oakland school. Dill is a Vietnam Veteran, having served in both the Marine Corps and the Navy.

Dill was a Special Agent with the Naval Investigative Service, Office of Naval Intelligence and Oklahoma Bureau of Investigation. A former Chief of Police of two Oklahoma cities, he is known as "Chief" to his close students.

Dill with James Lee at the Oakland JKD School (James' garage). Bruce Lee lived at James' house when he developed JKD. James is the only person to receive the title "Co-Instructor" from Bruce.

One of Dill's many published articles on Jeet Kune Do

Shodai Gary Dill advertisement for JKD seminar
at the Roman Colosseum

Second Indictment

Escorted by OSBI agent Gary Dill, Undersheriff Bill Holderby reads charges levied against him by a grand jury as he leaves arraignment Wednesday afternoon. Holderby was indicted for soliciting a bribe and he and Sheriff Delbert Hamby were suspended from duty. Holderby's indictment follows that of Paul Center charged with perjury for denying making a phone call to warn an area club of an impending raid.

Photo by Bob Hewgley

Dill escorts dirty cops to court. Many years ago, Chief told
me his favorite part of being a Special Agent
was busting corrupt cops.

Grandmaster Gary Dill, Jun Fan Jeet Kune Do Nucleus,
3rd Annual JFJKD Seminar, Seattle Washington, 1999

Julie, Associate Instructor, Sokedai Jill Hernandez, 9th
Degree Black Belt, and Shihan Jenny Benn, 4th Dan,
Tahlequah Oklahoma, 2011

Lance and Ed, Bushido Kempo Camp, Tahlequah, 2011

Shodai Dill, Dragon Lady, Mongo and Major Pain in front of Asian Winds Dojo, Tahlequah Oklahoma, 2010. Shodai christened the Turlington brothers and Julie with new names upon certifying them as Jeet Kune Do Instructors. Lance was an Army Major at the time.

Shodai Dill with 13 month old Hardee

Ed and Hardee, Motorcycle Rally, Liberal, Kansas, 2011

In 2011, my wife taught science in the Oklahoma panhandle while I worked as a dual status civil servant across the border in Kansas when Julie, our son Hardee, and I were chosen to represent the State of Kansas at a weeklong ceremony in Washington DC to celebrate the Army Reserves 103rd birthday. The Reserves put us up at the Ritz Carlton at Pentagon Square, and treated us to tours of Arlington Cemetery, the National Archives, the Smithsonian and of course Army briefings. Day meals were buffet and evening meals were banquet. The Army Drum and Fife band played for us one evening after supper.[80] The Commanding General of the US Army Reserves reenlisted me under the Declaration of Independence and Constitution. On our last day, Army journalists interviewed us.[81]

According to the Miami News Record:

"Sgt. Edwin H. Turlington, Jr. was one of 57 U.S.
Army Reserve Soldiers who were honored ... in
Washington, D.C. Turlington attended Afton and
Miami Public Schools, Northeastern State University, John Brown University, Oklahoma State, and
Regent's College. The ceremony ...provided an opportunity to recognize the 57 hand-selected Soldiers
and their families for their accomplishment and

---

[80] www.rapeofdelco.com/drum.mp4

[81] Stay Army Reserve magazine, May 2011, and online at https://web.archive.org/web/20120302164645/https://stayarmyreserve.wordpress.com/events/2011_qolfr_ncrc/turlington/

dedication... Lt. General Jack C. Stultz, commanding general of the U.S. Army Reserve said, "*This ceremony celebrates the fabric of our nation: the citizen-soldier.*" [82]

Julie, Ed and Hardee at the National Museum of Natural History, Smithsonian Institution, Washington, DC 2011

[82] "Turlington Honored", The Miami News Record, June 5, 2011,

https://www.miamiok.com/news/article_c8a69398-a42f-569e-9874-120a95033cbb.html

Sgt. Edwin H. Turlington

Sgt. Edwin H. Turlington, and my brothers, Staff Sgt. Reb Turlington and Maj. Lance Turlington

Why I Stay Army Reserve

"I like being in the military. I started out in the Florida National Guard and after a break in service I went Active Duty for 4 years and then I got an opportunity to go to Germany. I had a second break in service and I came back again, this time with the Army Reserve. An and after serving for 18 years, I'm ready to Reenlist for three more years. Both of my brothers, my father and myself have all served in the 45th Infantry Division."

Sgt. Edwin H. Turlington

So far SGT Turlington has been with the 45th Infantry Division, 82nd Airborne, Military Police, as a Watercraft Operator (88K), in Civil Affairs and currently in the Army Firefighter Unit, as a Detachment NCOIC in Garden City, Kansas. He had most fun as a Watercraft operator which he really enjoyed.

He is married to Julie, when asked about her experience as a military wife, the first things she replied was: "You need something to wear for formal occasions and he looks great in uniform." Which she said with a big smile and made her husband burst into a laugh. After that she added:"The military has enriched our lives in many ways and has also helped us professionally". They have a two-year old son and are currently expecting a baby boy, as his father assured.

Ed, Julie, and Hardee Turlington, pregnant with Hoss,
Pike's Peak, Denver, Colorado, 2011

Hoss Britton Turlington, Chesapeake Bay,
Virginia, February 2017

Hoss and Aunt Christiane, Camp Lejeune, North Carolina, March 2015. You can't tell it now, but Hoss didn't talk until he was 4. Christiane was instrumental in his speech development and taught him to read. He still reads several years above his grade level.

Hoss loses a tooth for the first time. March 2019

Cherokee Restaurant prid

Photo by Denton Thomason

Little Hoss Turlington chows down on a plate of Mickey Mouse pancakes at Cherokee Restaurant. The classic diner is famous for their affordable and filling breakfasts, which are served 24/7.

Hoss Britton Turlington, Big Cabin Truck Plaza, Big Cabin, Oklahoma. Hoss's maternal 4th Great Grandfather, Texas Partisan Ranger Henry Price, fought in the Battles of Cabin Creek at Big Cabin. Hoss belongs to the First Families of the Twin Territories under his paternal 4th Great Grandparents Adam Harmon and Nancy Swango,[83] who pioneered Big Cabin, Indian Territory. xx

---

[83] Page 463, Hoss' FFTT certificate for Adam Harmon and Nancy Swango

Lance challenges his big brother at Fall Jeet Kune Do Camp, Tahlequah, Oklahoma, 2012...

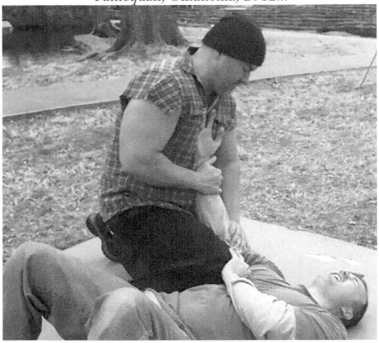

...and immediately regrets it!

Descendants of Manns and Moodys of Lawrence County, Missouri: Anna, Hardee, Jacob, Nathan and Hoss Turlington, September 2013

Sons of the American Revolution Induction with Viet Nam veteran Fred Morris, Ottawa County Veterans Memorial, 26 October 2013

During the spring of 2013, my wife Julie and I were certified as Private Investigators. Julie graduated top in our class,[84] I was second. The retired Delaware County Deputy who took our class did not pass. He seemed like an honest man and from our discussions I know he was not stupid. His failing the class goes to show how rigorous the class was, but also, that I understood the law better than a career DCSO deputy.

That fall, my brother Lance brought his family to visit for Thanksgiving and we went out to look at a foreclosed property in the country where the borders of Oklahoma, Arkansas, and Missouri meet. It was a long drive from where Julie was teaching in Miami, but when we pulled up though the driveway, out of the shade of the trees and into the clearing with the house, big barn, and chicken coop, I knew this was it.[85]

Lance bought the adjacent parcel of land as a quick means to settle an easement issue, and the real estate closing on the farm was 7 April 2014. Julie was 4 months pregnant with our daughter, Audrey Maxine Turlington. Exactly one week after closing, I caught convicted drug dealer / felon burglar / felon thief career criminal Darrell Philpott with two accomplices trespassing and engaging in what appeared to be drug

---

[84] Julie has a degree from Baylor, and graduated from St Thomas Episcopal, a private school in Houston. She is a smart woman.

[85] Video of first time driving into farm, www.hossturlingtons.com/firsttime.mp4

related activities while standing around a fire they had set on my farm. At the time, Philpott had two active *2009* Missouri warrants for his arrests. (see the rest of the book for how that turned out).Lance's daughter, Anna shot her first buck on top of our holler that fall. Lance said it was the best deer hunt he had ever been on and that the buck wandered around their tree stand for a half hour before Anna could get a clear shot.

10 year-old Nathan Turlington with his first deer,
November 2014

12 year-old Anna Turlington with her first buck, 2014.
Bullet hole in heart. Turlingtons are proficient marksmen.
Turlington farm, Jay, Oklahoma.

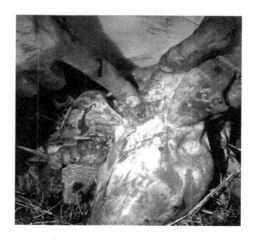

Julie pregnant with Audrey Maxine, Summer 2014.
Hoss Turlingtons Bee and Goat Farm Jay Oklahoma

Audrey Maxine Turlington 2014 and 2016. Audrey is
named after Julie's maternal grandmother, Marilyn Audrey
née Hawthorne and Ed's maternal grandmother,
Myrle Maxine née Simmons.

Audrey, 2018, Memorial Day, with her Great Grandfather
Kelly, who died in the Philippines in WW II

Audrey, 2019

Audrey and Dad, April 2018

John Duke Kelly Turlington, 2018

Duke, Audrey, Hoss and Hardee, Grandma's House, Miami, 2018

Audrey, 5 years old, and her little brother, Duke, 3 years old, Grandma's House, Miami, September 2019

Farm boys. 2019

Hoss catches a trout, Ft. Knox, Kentucky, March, 2020

Hardee with his first revolver, Cecilia, Kentucky, January 2020

Disabled Veterans Dean Bridges, John Cooper, and Ed
Turlington Delaware County Courthouse, 2014.
Dean was Ed's platoon sergeant in the 90s and Cooper was
Lance Turlington's platoon leader when Lance in the 90s.
Cooper ("Deep C") and Gordon ("Safecracker") Carlin,[xxiii] both
aware of his charges, sponsored Ed into the Bedouin Shrine in
Muskogee in 2017. Gordon was Lance's team leader when Coop
was his Platoon Leader.

Grove, 2014

Miller & Bayou Roots; Below: Teen Fiddlers; Fiddle Champ Instructor Jake Duncan; Instructor Susan Duncan with Young Fiddlers; Adult Fiddlers; Young Fiddler Hardee Turlington

Hardee attends Jana Jae Fiddle Camp,
Grove, Oklahoma, 2016

Photo by Joe Capolino

The Jana Jae Fiddle Camp and Fiddle Fest not only handled string instrument instruction but percussion as well. Drummers Ed Turlington, left, David Karnes (instructor), Alicia Jaycobson and Zach Carroll practiced drumming in the back of the Grove Civic Center, near the bathrooms, on Saturday, September 3. The camp/festival lasted Labor Day weekend, from Friday, September 2, to Sunday, September 4.

Ed drums while Hardee attends classes, Joe Capolino,
"Fiddle Camp", The American, September 18, 2016

Hardee with Country Western Megastar Jana Jae

11 years old Hardee knocks teenager down sparring,
May 2020

Xxiii

Hardee learns Jeet Kune Do from his father, May 2021

Hardee and his instructor, former national sparring champion
and Senior Olympic Coach for Team USA,

Cody Springsguth

Hardee learns Krav Maga from Grandmaster Dean Bridges, December 2020

David "Robocop" Sergeant,[xxi] Arkansas and Missouri State sparring champion, teaches Hardee Hwa Rang Do, July 2020

Ed "Hoss" and Julie Turlington, Bedouin Shrine Ball, Tulsa, 2017. Ed sr, Ed, and Ed's brothers Lance and REB are 32d degree Freemasons and Shriners. Ed sr was made a Mason at Grove, Oklahoma Lodge #187 in the 70s when he was Grove High School Principal. Ed sr's friends, former Grove School Superintendent Jim Bradford and Grove native and former GHS Football coach Charlie Hampton also belong to the Grove lodge. Ed jr got to attend lodge with Charlie the last year of Charlie's life (2017).

Grove, Oklahoma Ancient Free and Accepted Masons:
Paul Paquin, Cassidy Kuningas, Ed Turlington, Ron Coppedge
Back row: Bill Miller , Todd Deakins

32nd Degree Masons, Scottish Rite Induction, Tulsa 2016
Ed Turlington, Paul Paquin, Kyle Arnall, Jarrod McKibben

Bedouin Shriners Ring Race Spring 2017, Muskogee Oklahoma.
"Polo" Hendrix, "Pinball" Smith, "Hoss" Turlington,
"Backwoods" Howe, Gordon "Safecracker" Carlin,xxii "Boss
Hogg" Turner, "Bowtie" Holman, "Fast Eddy" Smith, "Juicy"
Green, "Smiley" Blackwood.

Gold Star Family meets
Oklahoma Medal of Honor recipient

Edwin Hardee Turlington III, his sister, Audrey, and Grandmother, Nancy Turlington were honored to meet Melvin Morris, Oklahoma Medal of Honor recipient, at a ceremony in Tulsa last week. During the ceremony, Hardee, Audrey, and Nancy were recognized as a Gold Star Family as Nancy's father Sgt. Robert LeRoy Kelly, died overseas during WWII. Nancy Kelly Turlington grew up in Afton and currently lives in Miami, Robert LeRoy Kelly grew up in Fairland, Hardee and Audrey live between Jay and Grove.

Nancy, Hardee, and Audrey Turlington with Medal of Honor recipient Melvin Morris. Morris, Gold Star Family ceremony, Tulsa. Morris served with 5th Special Forces in Vietnam. He was born and raised in Okmulgee. "Gold Star Family meets Oklahoma Medal of Honor recipient", The American, May 9, 2019, page 1

Friend in need: First responder seeks t helpless

By Kaylea M. Hutson-Miller news@joplinglobe.com   Sep 13, 2020   2 min to read

Afton City Hall

FTON, Okla. — As a kindergarten-er, Lane Carroll made a decision that set the course of his life. The young man told everyone at his kindergarten graduation he planned to have a career in law enforcement.

Now, decades later, the 24-year-old Afton man has made good on his decision. He works as a first responder as a member of the Delaware County Sheriff's Office and the Afton Volunteer Fire Department.

"I always wanted to be a cop, and when I got out of (high school), I still wanted to be a cop," Carroll said, explaining he went to the reserve academy at the age of 21 and later completed the bridge academy to be-

At first, Carroll said, the chance to take part in "car chases and gun fights" is what drew him to the job. But now, he said, the job is more about helping people — especially those most in need of help.

"Some people can't help themselves," Carroll said. "Those are the people who need the most help, and they can't or don't know how to help themselves."

This past week, Carroll earned kudos on social media after he came to the assistance of Nancy Turlington and her grandchildren after Duke Turlington hurt himself while playing at a park in Afton.

Audrey Maxine and Duke make the Joplin Globe, 13 September 2020. Afton Fireman and Delaware County Reserve Deputy Lane Carroll administers aid to Duke after a playground accident. Duke's father grew up with Lane's aunt, Michelle Carroll.   The author of the article, former Delaware County Journal managing editor Kaylea Miller, is married to former Delaware County Detective Frank Miller (pp. iii, 3-6, 21, 39, 47). Kaylea now teaches at Miami High School with Julie Turlington. "Friend in Need: First responder seeks to help the helpless", The Joplin Globe, Sep 13, 2020, pages 1C-2C

Turlington and native, undisclosed location

"Hoss" Turlington", firstborn "Hardee" and Lance
Turlington farm, Delaware County, Oklahoma, 2017

Eddie and Lance Turlington go hunting,
Delaware County, Oklahoma, 1977

[4]

THE PRELIMINARY HEARING

preliminary hearing. A criminal hearing (usu. conducted by a magistrate) to determine whether there is sufficient evidence to prosecute an accused person.

Due Process Clause. The constitutional provision that prohibits the government from unfairly or arbitrarily depriving a person of life, liberty, or property.

–BLACK'S LAW DICTIONARY, 7TH EDITION

"THE PURPOSE OF THE PRELIMINARY HEARING is to establish probable cause that a crime was committed and probable cause that the defendant committed the crime".[86] A preliminary hearing is a proceeding that takes place before a criminal trial. The presiding judge uses the "probable

---

[86] 22 OK Stat § 22-258 Preliminary Examinations and Proceedings Thereon

cause" standard[87] to decide. The preliminary hearing was my attorney Winston Connor's opportunity to introduce the exculpatory evidence that Chief of Criminal Investigations Gayle Wells withheld, to show that Well's altered witness testimony, and to impeach the State's only witness to the crime that testified that day. Connor failed to do any of the above as shown in this chapter and Chapter 6.

When the preliminary hearing finally took place, it turned out to be a circus, where the State's only witness to the alleged crime could barely complete a sentence. That same witness failed three times to identify me as the shooter (I was the only man in the court room who was not an officer of the court), and committed perjury multiple times, and admitted to using firearms as a felon (which is a felony in itself).[88]

The State apparently called their only other "witness", "Jack (Bradley) Thomas" with no previous prosecutorial inquiry at all, as he could answer none of their questions about the alleged crime.

Finally, during the Preliminary Hearing, Prosecutor Nic Lelecas entered a falsehood he knew to be false into the record at least three times and allowed the above mentioned perjury.

---

[87] See "probable cause", pages 10-11

[88] A. ... it shall be unlawful for any person convicted of any felony in any court of this state or of another state or of the United States to have in his or her possession or under his or her immediate control, ...any ... firearm.

THE RIGHT TO A SPEEDY TRIAL

In case you're thinking five years is an extremely long time for a District Attorney to drop charges on a case, it is. According to Oklahoma's Trial "time limits act", "If any person charged with a felony crime who is held to answer on an appearance bond is not brought to trial within eighteen (18) months after arrest, the court shall set the case for immediate review..." .[89] District Attorney Kenny Wright wasn't even able to bring me to a preliminary hearing in 18 months (it was a week shy of 20 months).

THE PROSECUTOR ALLOWS HIS WITNESS TO TESTIFY WITH ACTIVE WARRANTS FOR HIS ARREST

When I shot Darrell Philpott in self-defense in 2014, he had two active warrants for his arrest from *2009*. These warrants were still active when Nic Lelecas allowed Philpott to testify against me 20 months later in the Preliminary Hearing. I found these warrants during my initial investigation, the week of my arrest, and showed them to Connor. Connor never mentioned these warrants during the hearing.

THE STATE'S SOLE WITNESS CAN'T IDENTIFY THE SHOOTER, THE PROSECUTOR FALSIFIES THE RECORD

Nic Lelecas, the prosecutor in my case, entered evidence he knew to be false at least three times. An irrefutable example is recorded verbatim on the preliminary hearing

[87] 22 OK Stat § 22-812.1 (b)

transcript.[90] The prosecutor asked Philpott, the **only** government witness, to identify the shooter. Keep in mind the only men present were the officers of the court and me. This was not a hard question to answer. When asked to identify the shooter, Philpott pointed toward the defense attorney, Winston, stating, "I believe that's him". The prosecutor was unable to conceal his shock that the witness was unable to identify the man who had shot him from arm's length away the previous year. Philpott couldn't figure out the defendant was not the one making objections and addressing the court, but the man sitting silently next to him. The prosecutor asked, "You *believe* that's him?" to which his witness answered, "Yeah". The prosecutor then asked Philpott to, "...describe the clothing of the individual that you identified as the person who pulled the gun out?", to which Philpott answered a "gray jacket" with a "white shirt" that "might have kind of a greenish tint" and a tie. As you will see below, I was wearing a tan sports coat, not gray, and a white shirt, not a "greenish" white shirt. However, my attorney, Winston, was wearing a gray jacket with a greenish white shirt. Despite Philpott identifying Winston Connor as the shooter, the prosecutor asked, "that the record reflect he's identified

---

[90] Appendix Q Preliminary Hearing Transcripts, pages 13-15, "Philpott is Unable to Identify the Shooter, The Prosecutor Attempts to Knowingly Enter a Falsehood into the Record THREE TIMES"

the person that pulled the gun, for purposes of the preliminary hearing."[91]

Testimony is a form of evidence. The prosecutor offering evidence he knew to be false was the first instance of prosecutorial misconduct in the preliminary hearing, but the worst was yet to come.

After the State's sole witness failed to identify me as the defendant **three times,** and the Prosecutor entered evidence into the record that he knew to be false **three times**, Winston stated the obvious, that, "based on the description", the State's witness had not identified me. The prosecutor verified to his witness, "Mr. Philpott, you pointed to an individual ...as the person... with the gun, correct?" Philpott replied he had, then the prosecutor continued, "Can you tell me, from the head down, what he's wearing today?" Philpott answered, a "gray" jacket and a "plaid" tie. **For the third time** , the State's witness failed to identify me as the shooter, and instead identified the defense attorney. **For the second time**, Philpott described *in detail* what my attorney was wearing, not me.

For the third time, Prosecutor Lelecas entered into the record that his witness had identified me, when he had actually identified my attorney. Winston informed the court that he was the only one with a gray jacket and a plaid tie and assured the court that he had not shot Philpott. On his fourth

---

[91] Ibid.

attempt, *and only with help from Winston Connor*, Philpott finally changed his story to identify me as the shooter. [xxiii]

It should be emphasized that no one is claiming that Winston Connor is actually the shooter (no one except Philpott, anyway). The point is that Philpott has such a ruined mind from decades of hard drug use, that he actually thought that the defense attorney was the shooter, which proves that Philpott has no recollection whatsoever. If Philpott can't even identify me as the shooter, then he has no credibility to describe what actually happened on the day of the shooting.

To fully appreciate how far gone Philpott's mind is, you have to understand what he saw in that courtroom when he identified Connor as the shooter. There were only five men in the courtroom other than Philpott: the judge, the court recorder, the bailiff, the prosecutor, and me. This was not a situation where Philpott had to pick me out of a lineup. All he had to do was pick the only man in the room who was not an officer of the court, and he was unable to do that. Any normal person off the street, with no knowledge of my case, would have been able to figure out I was the defendant (the shooter).

If there were ANY integrity in this process, the prosecution would have gone on the record to state that Philpott could not even identify the shooter. A reasonable prosecutor at that point would have to stop and at least *consider* dropping the charges on the spot. However, the prosecution continued as if nothing had happened.

The astonishing part is after Darrell Philpott went on the stand in the Delaware County Courtroom, under oath, on the record, and identified Winston Connor as the shooter THREE TIMES, going so far as to describe Connor's shirt, jacket and tie pattern so there could be no confusion, **the prosecutor then AGAIN knowingly entered false evidence into the record to reflect that the witness had identified the shooter,** *implying that Philpott had identified Turlington for the sake of the record.* **That is a falsehood before the court, spoken by Philpott, then misrepresented on the record, by the prosecutor.** *If the prosecutor had been successful in his multiple attempts to manipulate the record, a jury would have no idea the State's sole witness lacked the ability to recall the most basic facts of the incident. Philpott identified the defense attorney as "the shooter",* **three times,** *and Prosecutor Nic Lelecas tried* **three times** *to have the record reflect that Philpott had identified Turlington.*

THE PROSECUTOR ALLOWS HIS WITNESS TO COMMIT PERJURY IN COURT; THE DEFENSE ATTORNEY FAILS TO IMPEACH

Impeach, *vb.* **2.** To discredit the veracity of (a witness)

THERE ARE SEVERAL WAYS TO IMPEACH A WITNESS IN OKLAHOMA, and Darrell Philpott must be among the most impeachable witnesses to ever testify in a courtroom. According to 12 OK Stat § 12-2404,[92] witness impeachment is the process of calling into question the credibility of an individual testifying in court. Several of the methods to impeach are by prior conviction (if the conviction were for a felony or a crime of moral turpitude), inconsistent and contra-indicatory statements, bad character for truthfulness, prior bad acts, and mental disability. As I would learn from my personal investigation of Philpott, government documents prove that he is impeachable by all these methods. As you read the following pages, remember, this was District Attorney Kenny Wright's star witness against

---

[92] 12 OK Stat § 12-2404, Character Evidence Not Admissible to Prove Conduct - Exceptions - Other Crimes A. Evidence of a person's character or a trait of his character is not admissible for the purpose of proving action in conformity therewith on a particular occasion, except: 1. Evidence of a pertinent trait of character offered by an accused or by the prosecution to rebut the same; 2. Evidence of a pertinent trait of character of the victim of the crime offered by an accused, or by the prosecution to rebut the same, or evidence of a character trait of peacefulness of the victim offered by the prosecution in a homicide case to rebut evidence that the victim was the first aggressor; or 3. Evidence of the character of a witness, as provided in Sections 2607, 2608 and 2609 of this Code. B. Evidence of other crimes, wrongs, or acts is not admissible to prove the character of a person in order to show action in conformity therewith. It may, however, be admissible for other purposes, such as proof of motive, opportunity, intent, preparation, plan, knowledge, identity or absence of mistake or accident.

me for over five years. What follows are examples of the various ways in which Philpott is thoroughly impeached (his credibility is proven to be deficient):

1.IMPEACHMENT BY CONVICTION OF CRIME (FELONIES)

DEPUTY CRANE FINDS PHILPOTT DRUNK AND PASSED OUT IN THE MIDDLE OF THE ROAD; PHILPOTT EARNS HIS 4TH FELONY CONVICTION

According to Oklahoma Title 12-2609, a witness may be impeached if he has been convicted of a felony in the previous 10 years.[93]

In 2016, Benton County, Arkansas Deputy Justin Crane found Philpott drunk and passed out in the middle of a highway with his foot on the brake pedal and his car engine running.[94] That arrest resulted in Philpott's most recent drug felony conviction, as well as his most recent drunk driving conviction and Class VI drug conviction because they found Philpott's stash of meth while he was being booked.[95]

---

[93] 12 OK Stat § 12-2609 Impeachment by Evidence of Conviction of Crime

A. For the purpose of attacking the credibility of a witness: 1. Evidence that a witness other than an accused has been convicted of a crime shall be admitted, subject to Section 2403 of this title, if the crime was punishable by death or imprisonment in excess of one (1) year...

[94] Appendix Z, 2016 Philpott PC Affidavit for Felony Meth, DWI and Class VI Drugs

[95] Appendix C, 2017 Philpott Drug Felony Conviction and Appendix FF Philpott's 2017 DWI Conviction

At this moment if you were to assume that Philpott would probably just jump bail again, you would be right; he did.[96]

Darrell Philpott's credibility is impeachable by his 2017 felony methamphetamine conviction.

PHILPOTT'S CREDIBILITY IS IMPEACHABLE BY HIS THREE 1981 FELONY CONVICTIONS FOR ROBBERY, THEFT, AND DRUG DEALING

Subsection (B.) of the above impeachment statute continues with the following exception, "Evidence of a conviction under this section is not admissible if a period of more than *ten (10) years has elapsed since the date of the conviction* or of the release of the witness from the confinement imposed for that conviction, whichever is later, to the date of the witness's testimony... **unless**, *during the ten-year period,* **the witness has been convicted of a subsequent crime** *which is a misdemeanor involving moral turpitude* **or** *a felony.*"

The State decided that if a felon can just go ten years without committing another felony or crime of moral turpitude, then his credibility can't be impeached for conviction. But Darrell Philpott is the kind of person who doesn't take advantage of second chances. Philpott takes advantage of those that would give him a second chance. Oklahoma is not the only state to give Philpott a second chance. Arkansas tried as well.

---

[96] Appendix AA, Philpott's 2017 Arrest Warrant for 2016 Felony Meth, DWI, etc.

Like most career criminals, Philpott's public record began when he was still a teenager.[97] Philpott earned his first felony convictions at age 20 for robbery and theft.[98] But Philpott got the chance of a lifetime under Arkansas Act 378. Arkansas Act 378 was an expungement program that totally erased a criminal history as though it never happened, and restored all civil liberties, to include firearm possession. It was a once in a lifetime opportunity for a young man to avoid prison time, start life as a productive member of society and have his crimes forgiven and forgotten. All Philpott had to do to keep his crimes sealed was stop committing crimes *for three years from his felony sentencing date of June 8, 1981.*[99]

However, Philpott, being true to form, was able to last exactly *one week* before getting arrested again from the time of his convictions for felony robbery and felony theft. On the eighth day, he was arrested[100] (and later convicted)[101] **for felony drug dealing**. *As a convicted felon, Philpott cannot possess firearms. Remember that.*

---

[97] 1979 Minor in Possession conviction, see Appendix EE

[98] Appendix A, "Philpott's 1981 Robbery Felony and Theft Felony"

[99] AR Code § 5-4-303, "Conditions of suspension or probation": (b) The court shall provide as an express condition of every suspension or probation that the defendant not commit an offense punishable by imprisonment during the period of suspension or probation.

[100] Appendix BB 1981 Pre-Sentencing Report, page 1, para. 4

[101] Appendix B Philpott's 1981 Drug Dealing Felony

When given the chance of a lifetime to redeem himself, violent felon Darrell Philpott was unable to last eight days without getting caught committing another felony.

2. IMPEACHMENT BY CONVICTION OF CRIMES OF MORAL TURPITUDE

"[M]oral turpitude is `anything done contrary to justice, honesty, modesty, or good morals.' [In re Williams, 64 Okl. 316, 167 P. 1149 (1917)]

In Oklahoma, "A witness may be asked, for the purpose of affecting his credibility, if he has been convicted of a crime which involves want of moral character. Drunk driving would be such an offense... This opinion is predicated upon the fact that such an activity is inherently dangerous to the public in general and such a crime shows a lack of personal integrity and a lack of concern for and respect of the person of others and their property."[102]

PHILPOTT'S MULTITUDE OF DRUNK DRIVING CONVICTIONS

Philpott's criminal career spans five decades and includes repeated incidents of drunk driving charges and convictions

---

[102] BUNN v. STATE,1977 OK CR 52, 561 P.2d 969 quoting Starns v. State, Okl.[561 P.2d 972] Cr., 297 P.2d 421 (1956)

from 1979[103] to his 2017 Arkansas convictions.[104,105]Remember, when I arrested him, he had multiple active warrants for his arrest for failing to appear on Missouri criminal charges, including a 2009 drunk driving charge.[106] However, Sheriff Moore and Deputy Wells chose to protect the multiple felon with multiple active warrants for his arrest (Philpott), rather than listen to the disabled veteran and family man (me). So, those warrants weren't discharged for another two years, when Philpott plead guilty[107] after being arrested in Arkansas committing a felony and other dangerous crimes .[108]

---

[103] See Chronology, p. for 1979 DWI

[104] See Appendix FF "Philpott's 2017 DWI Conviction"

[105] Far too many to include in this book. For a partial accounting, see Chronology, p.

[106] Appendix D, "Philpott's 2009 Arrest Warrants that were Active in 2014 when Sheriff Moore Protected Him"

[107] Appendix 2017 conviction on 2009 Drunk Driving

[108] See Philpott's 2017 Arkansas DWI conviction (Appendix FF "Philpott's 2017 DWI Conviction") and his 2017 Missouri Conviction on his 2009 DWI charge (Appendix E, Philpott's 2017 Conviction on his 2009 Missouri DWI Arrest)

*Remember at the time I shot Philpott in self-defense, he had this 5 year old warrant for his arrest for failing to appear in court on that 2009 arrest, and Delaware County Prosecutor Nic Lelecas 18 months later allowed Philpott to walk into the Delaware County Courthouse with that arrest warrant still active, and commit provable perjury against me multiple times, and leave the courthouse a free man). It wasn't until Philpott was arrested by Arkansas authorities on an unrelated felony that the **then** 7 year old arrest warrant was discharged.*

It only takes one DWI conviction to impeach a witness for moral turpitude in Oklahoma. For a partial list of Philpott's other convictions and charges for driving drunk or high, see Chronology, page 350 (the charges are hyperlinked to online documentation in the digital version of this book).

3. IMPEACHMENT FOR PRIOR INCONSISTENT STATEMENT[109]

The most obvious contraindicatory statement Philpott made was in the courtroom when he identified my attorney, Winston Connor, *three times,* as the man who shot him (instead of me). After the third time, Winston finally announced to the court he was not the shooter, leaving me as the only other

---

[109] 12 OK Stat § 12-2613 Prior Statements of Witnesses

person the shooter could be. Only then did Philpott identify me as the shooter.[110]

4. IMPEACHMENT FOR BAD CHARACTER FOR TRUTHFULNESS

In Oklahoma, a witness may be impeached for bad character by showing criminal convictions, inquiring about bad acts (as long as they have to do with truthfulness or untruthfulness), or by showing a bad reputation or opinion of another witness.

The easiest method to impeach Philpott for bad character would be to show his felony perjury from the preliminary hearing, but prosecutor Nic Lelecas refused to acknowledge Philpott committed perjury. To recap, Philpott lied under oath by specifically denying he had been convicted for a drug dealing charge, when he had been.[111] Philpott also lied under oath when he denied that he had other felony convictions which he had, for theft and robbery.[112]

---

[110] Appendix Q Preliminary Hearing Transcripts, pages 13-15, Philpott is Unable to Identify the Shooter, The Prosecutor Attempts to Knowingly Enter a Falsehood into the Record THREE TIMES

[111] Appendix L, "Philpott Commits Perjury by Omitting Theft and Burglary Felonies and Denying Possession with Intent", Appendix A, "Philpott's 1981 Theft and Robbery Felonies", and Appendix B, "Philpott's 1981 Drug Dealing Felony"

[112] Ibid.

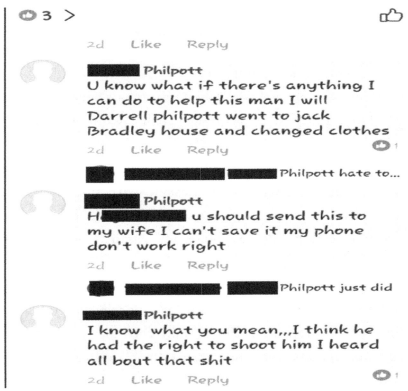

Philpott has a reputation for bad character with his own family. Even though Deputy Wells demonstrates a decades long relationship of covering for Philpott, Philpott's own kin don't believe he deserves protection. Here, they offer to help me in this case against their own relative.

5. IMPEACHMENT FOR PRIOR BAD ACTS

In Oklahoma, a witness may be impeached for prior bad acts, but this is where the types of impeachments overlap for Philpott, because his bad acts included perjury, which is also a type of bad character for truthfulness, mentioned above, but I will provide some detail:

During the Preliminary Hearing, Philpott committed felony perjury multiple times as my attorney went through the motions of cross examination.

When Connor asked Philpott if he had been convicted of a felony, Philpott answered, "Yeah". Connor asked, "On what"? Philpott answered, "half a bag" of controlled substances (when pressed, Philpott clarified it was a "half a *trash* bag"). **Connor clarified, "Possession with Intent"?** (Possession with Intent to Distribute, in other words, to deal drugs). **Philpott, stated, "Possession. Yeah" Again, Connor clarified, "Trafficking"? to which Philpott answers, "No; Possession."** [113] (see Appendix A for Philpott's Possession with Intent Felony Conviction). Philpott didn't mention his felony robbery conviction,[114] or felony theft conviction, or his multitude of arrests and convictions for drunk driving,[115] his convictions for assaulting a woman,[116] fleeing an officer[117] or any of the other dozens of violent and dangerous charges he had racked up over the previous thirty-six years.

Before Connor released Philpott, Connor asked me if I wanted him to ask Philpott anything else. I told Connor to get on the record Philpott's poaching charge. Remember,

---

[113] Ibid.

[114] Appendix A, Philpott's 1981 Theft and Robbery Felonies

[115] See partial RAP sheet in Chronology, p. 350. Philpott has too many drunk driving charges to list individually.

[116] Appendix JJ, Felon Philpott Grabs Gun, Assaults Woman, Daughter, and Destroys Their Home

[117] Appendix LL, Philpott Flees from Arrest

when Philpott testified against me, he had the same active bench warrants for his arrest that he had when I had arrested him over a year and a half earlier. Those warrants were for failing to appear on poaching and drunk driving charges in neighboring McDonald county, Missouri.

When Connor asked Philpott specifically about the poaching charges, Philpott flagrantly denied it, under oath. This perjury is documented in Appendix D of this book. Once again, if there were any integrity in this process, the prosecution would not go forward based on the testimony of Darrell Philpott. He is an impeached witness who lied on the stand about his criminal record and couldn't even identify me as the shooter. And yet, *Darrell Philpott, the perjurer with convictions for felony drug dealing, felony burglary, and felony theft and multiple active warrants out for his arrest, walked out of the Delaware County Courtroom as a free man, and I was still going to be prosecuted.*

Because I paid to have the PC hearing recorded, there is a record of Philpott's perjury.[118] When I showed proof of this (the court record) to the prosecutor, he simply denied it was perjury and made it clear he wouldn't do anything about it (see chapters 5 and 6, on Connor and the Prosecutor).

---

[118] Transcripts for the Probable Cause, or Preliminary, Hearing are online at RapeOfDelco.com/prelim.pdf .

14   CROSS EXAMINATION

15   BY MR. CONNOR:

16   Q   Mr. Philpott, let's start out with, have you ever been

17   convicted of a felony?

18   A   Yeah.

19   Q   Of what?

20   A   Half a bag full of weed.

21   Q   Possession with intent?

22   A   Possession; yeah.

23   Q   Trafficking?

24   A   No; possession.

25   Q   Where was that at?

                                                  30

1   A   Arkansas.

6. IMPEACHMENT FOR MENTAL DISABILITY

PHILPOTT HAS A HABIT OF VIOLENT ATTACK WHEN HE'S CAUGHT COMMITTING CRIMES

According to McCormick on Evidence,[xxiv] page 340, "A habit ...is the person's regular practice of meeting a particular kind of situation with a specific type of conduct... ."

Section 2406 of Oklahoma Title 12[119] provides for the admissibility of a person's habit to prove that the conduct of the person on a particular occasion was in conformity with the habit. In other words, if you act a certain way in similar circumstances, it can be considered a habit. One very consistent habit Philpott has demonstrated is that when an armed man tries to stop him from committing a crime, Philpott attacks the armed man. In just the time since he assaulted me, he has assaulted Arkansas Deputies Crane and Lampkin (on different occasions), and the responding medics who tried to subdue him, all during or immediately after he was placed under arrest.[xxv]

Winston Connor chose not to impeach the convicted drug dealer Darrell Philpott, possibly the most impeachable man to ever set foot in a Delaware County Court.

PHILPOTT ADMITS TO USING FIREARMS AS A FELON

It is a felony in Arkansas, Missouri, and Oklahoma for a felon to have a firearm in his possession. [120] Philpott casually

---

[119] 12 OK Stat § 12-2406 Habit – Routine practice: Evidence of a person's habit or of an organization's routine practice, whether corroborated or not and regardless of the presence of eyewitnesses, is relevant to prove that the conduct of the person or organization on a particular occasion was in conformity with the habit or routine practice.

[120] 12 OK Stat § 12-1283, **A.C.A. § 5-73-103, and** Section 571.070.1(1) RSMo.

admitted to being around guns all his life (he has been a felon since he was 20 years old)[121] and he admitted to using a .308 Savage rifle while being a felon (a .308 is the same caliber as used in an M60 machine gun). Philpott actually had been convicted on three felonies at the time of his admission but perjured himself on the most recent two felonies.[122] At this point, Winston should have stopped the procedure and gotten to the bottom of Philpott using firearms as a felon. And if Winston failed to do so (for whatever reason), then the Prosecutor in my case should have. Instead, Philpott explained that he was allowed to possess a firearm in spite of being a felon because of an expungement law. Both Prosecutor Lelecas and my defense attorney, Winston Connor, accepted Philpott's *legal opinion* at face value, and nothing more was asked about it. Chapter 7 tells how I showed Nic Lelecas the documentation for the three felonies (that were not expunged) that Philpott had at the time he perjured himself (as well as the Meth felony, and Drunk Driving convictions Philpott earned since the time of my arrest.)

At one point in the hearing, Philpott testified to hunting deer on the morning of 14 April 2014 (the day I caught him

---

[121] Appendix II, Preliminary Transcripts, page 68. Considering Philpott earned three felonies at the age of 22, and was 53 at the time of the hearing, that was just another admission that Philpott committed felonies his almost his entire adult life.

[122] Appendix A, Philpott's 1981 Felony Theft and Felony Burglary Convictions

trespassing).[123] Poaching is consistent with Philpott's trend of illegal hunting.[124]

Violent Career Criminal Philpott, with felonies stretching from the age of 20 to the age of 56, admitted to being around guns all his life (which is a felony) and specifically on the morning he attacked me (another felony). Both the Prosecutor, Nic Lelecas, and my defense attorney, Winston Connor, accepted this police informant's legal opinion that he was allowed to have firearms.

State's "Witness" Jack (Bradley) Thomas and What the Prosecutor Did Not Do and Never Did

The final "witness" to testify was Jack Thomas.[xxvi] Jack testified that he believed a road leading to the place I caught Philpott trespassing belonged to his nephew, Mike Raney. Jack admitted he never saw property lines and didn't know.

It is interesting that Mike Raney didn't testify to it being his land, much less that Philpott had permission to be on it. Not once during the five years I was charged did the Delaware County DA subpoena Mike Raney (or anyone else) to claim the shooting site belonged to him, much less that

---

[123] Appendix II, Preliminary Transcripts, Page 31

[124] Appendix D Philpott's Active Arrest Warrants When the Sheriff Protected Him

Philpott had permission to be on it. Apparently, that's what the DA thought that Jack would establish. The DA's office couldn't even come up with a sworn statement from anyone (except Philpott) that Philpott was on anyone's land but mine.

The Sheriff and DA had five years to come up with a single witness that the shooting took place anywhere but my farm, but they could not do it.

DEFENSE ATTORNEY WINSTON "BACK DOOR" [125] CONNOR FAILS (INTENTIONALLY?)

In addition to Connor failing to Impeach Philpott on the myriad of issues listed above, Connor failed to mention the exculpatory medical records or photographs that Wells withheld from the PC Affidavit. Connor failed to mention Wells' altering Philpott's testimony multiple times, or the altering of Joseph Bradley's sworn statement. Connor did nothing when Philpott lied about the nature of his drug dealing conviction. Connor failed to point out that Philpott lied by omission regarding his felony theft conviction and felony robbery conviction. Connor failed to bring up Philpott's arrest warrants that were not only active the night I shot him in self-defense but were still active as he testified against me.

---

[125] See page 164

When Philpott denied being in trouble other than the one felony he admitted and traffic tickets, Connor failed to even begin to list Philpott's 8 page RAP sheet.

Connor failed to ask Wells why he didn't order a toxicology report on Philpott, a convicted drug dealer with a known substance abuse problem who admitted to drinking that evening. Connor failed to ask Wells why he didn't take a gunpowder residue test of Philpott's jeans or legs. Connor failed to ask Wells why he withheld the medical report from the PC Affidavit, or the photos of both sides of the bullet wound.

Remember, Philpott admitted to Deputy Wells he had been shot in the past, before I ever met him. Connor didn't even ask what Philpott was doing the first time he was shot, or why he didn't go to the hospital the first time he was shot, or why Philpott didn't call the police either of the two separate times he has gotten himself shot. When Philpott answered, "No" to Connor's asking him if he called law enforcement after I shot him, Connor failed to ask him why he hadn't.

Finally, both Connor and Lelecas failed to act when Philpott admitted to felonies when he confessed to the felony of possessing guns as a felon and poaching deer. Both Connor and Lelecas failed to act when Philpott omitted his felony theft and felony burglary conviction and misrepresented his drug dealing felony conviction as a mere "possession" conviction. I informed Winston about Philpott's charges prior to the hearing.[126] As a prosecutor, Lelecas had access to all of Philpott's criminal records. According to my brother Lance, who supervises prosecutors, the government has a duty to assess the credibility of their witnesses. This should include a criminal background check, but even this wouldn't be necessary with Darrell Philpott, because Nic Lelecas had prosecuted Philpott in the past.

> *Prosecutor Nic Lelecas made a mockery of the Delaware County Court by allowing a violent felon with active warrants for his arrest to walk into the courthouse, perjure himself multiple times testifying against Turlington, and leave a free man. Lelecas never offered any proof that his felon star witness had permission to be on the land he was on, much less proof of whose land it was. Turlington's defense attorney, Winston Connor, had multiple opportunities to impeach Philpott but he chose not to.*

---

[126] See Appendix A, *Philpott's June 1981 Theft and Robbery Felonies* and Appendix B, *Philpott's 1981 Drug Dealing Felony*

Ed and Julie Turlington, pregnant with Duke Turlington Preliminary Hearing, Delaware County Courthouse, Jay, Oklahoma, 8 December 2015

Ed is wearing a tan jacket, white shirt and disc patterned tie, not the grey jacket, "greenish" shirt and plaid tie Philpott ascribed to the shooter in the Preliminary Hearing. It was Winston Connor who was wearing the grey jacket, greenish shirt, and plaid tie.

[5]

THE PROTECTED CAREER CRIMINAL

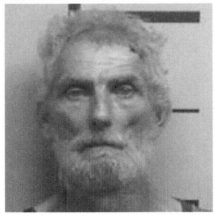

October 4, 2016. Drug dealing burglar Darrell Philpott the day after his 4th felony arrest (for which he was later convicted). His 2009 Arkansas arrest warrants were still active because Delaware County Sherriff Harlan Moore had Gayle Wells covered for Philpott when I arrested him in 2014.

Despite Philpott being the only State's Witness against me, it took District Attorney Kenny Wright more than three years to drop charges against me.

FOR OVER TWO HUNDRED YEARS, Wanted Men have crossed the border into what is now Oklahoma from Missouri and Arkansas to avoid the authorities. Prior to statehood, there were no counties, therefore no Sheriffs, and very little law enforcement. This has been the subject of both books and movies, True Grit, the Outlaw Josey Wales, and Hang 'Em High are a few well known westerns on this theme.

In the present day, criminals still migrate across the border from Missouri and Arkansas into Oklahoma, but for a vastly different reason. Whereas their criminal predecessors took advantage of the lack of law enforcement, today's criminals seek refuge in Oklahoma because of the law enforcement industry that has developed. Criminals who are not under police protection are arrested, make deals with the District Attorney to inform on other criminals, and are set free or receive greatly reduced sentences, depending on their alleged crime.

Rural law enforcement agencies, which often don't have the funding necessary to properly investigate crimes, have increasingly relied on the testimony of informants over the last several decades.

So much so that an informal system has developed of law enforcement agencies taking it easy, or even protecting informants. In return, informants tell the law enforcement agencies what they need to secure convictions. Bestselling author and attorney John Grisham[xxvii] wrote a nonfiction book titled "The Innocent Man" about rural Oklahoma cops doing exactly this, and it resulted in one man on Death Row before DNA evidence cleared him. In 2018, Netflix made a documentary series based on "The Innocent Man". I suggest you watch it.

In my case, the prosecutor based his position on a violent drug dealer informant's testimony, and (at best) on a fundamental misunderstanding of the photographs of the wounds that *show the exact opposite of what the prosecutor says they show.* More importantly, it's obvious that the drug dealer/snitch that I shot was being protected by law enforcement throughout the investigation.

If one didn't know Melvin Gayle Wells, they might be surprised listening to his interview with lifelong violent criminal Darrell Philpott. There was no pretext of an investigation, much less professionalism, but the silly, feminine manner at which Wells conducts his interview. The interview begins with Wells securing permission from Philpott to "*slip off*" his own jacket (in the ER), followed with 40 minutes of Wells giggling and cooing, showing an excessive familiarity with Philpott nearly nonstop. It is as though they don't just know each other, but as if they have some kind of relationship unknown to the listener.

My investigation into the Wells – Philpott relationship revealed its origins at least as early as 1991, in a legal violation written by Wells. The interesting thing about that citation was that it was dismissed for reasons not annotated. Even more interesting is those charges were dismissed at cost to the state. The government order has been redacted so the public cannot see which government official requested the dismissal or why.[127]

In 1991, Darrell Philpott was able to offer something to the government for them to drop the six year old arrest warrant and related charges (at cost to the state). We don't know what Philpott offered, but we do know Gayle Wells was the officer responsible for the charges. At the time of Turlington's arrest, the catch-and-release relationship between Philpott and Wells was at least 17 years old. Perhaps this is why, when Philpott assaulted a woman, her daughter, and their dog in a drunken rage, he exclaimed, "I can do anything I want!"

On 14 April 2001,[128] Philpott was fleeing Benton County Arkansas drunk driving yet again. Bentonville County Deputies requested assistance from DCSO in their pursuit. Once Philpott crossed into Delaware County, he parked his car and quit running because he thought he was in his safe space. By the time DCSO had caught Philpott, he was no longer in his vehicle. Unfortunately for Philpott, the responding Delaware County Deputy was not Gayle Wells, so Philpott was actually arrested for his crime.[129]

---

[127] Appendix KK, *Philpott's 28 year Witness Protection program begins.*

[128] Exactly 13 years before I arrested him

[129] Appendix II, Philpot flees (while driving drunk) from Benton County Deputies to Delaware County, Oklahoma

> —————, ———————, ———————— and physical abuse.
>
> *I had an order of protection on him before for threatening me & threatening to burn my house down. Put his fist through the gun case to get a gun, when we were having a drink.*
>
> *drunk, when asked by visitor not to hold her baby when drunk, he left & came back 30 minutes later in a rage, cussing kicking animals + telling us he could do anything he wants too. He told me not to come close to him cause he didn't know what he would do to me, then started laughing (a ver demented laugh) He kicked the bedroom + broke it, kicked the post on the couch cau...*

This is a 1997 sworn statement to police by a woman who was physically assaulted by Philpott. If you want to hear the "demented laugh", listen to the 2018 police video of Philpott's attack on Arkansas Deputy, Cedric Lampkin at *Rape.ofDelco.com/arrestvideos.mp4*

Philpott has not changed (for the better) over the years.

THE REAL PROBLEM

Beyond being a career criminal, whose credibility is impeached in every possible way that courts recognize impeachment, **Darrell Philpott is a danger to society, and he has been from at least 1979 until the present**. He has convictions in neighboring McDonald County, Missouri and Benton County, Arkansas for felony drug dealing, felony theft, felony robbery and felony meth, multiple possession charges and convictions, more drunk driving convictions than I can list, convictions for assaulting women, and dangerous misdemeanor charges such as poaching and fleeing from authorities. Philpott's most recent felony conviction and most recent *two* drunk driving convictions took place *after* I arrested him (while he was still Delaware County's sole witness against me. That's right –Delaware County District Attorney Kenny Wright had Philpott listed as his main witness against me *for years* prior to Philpott's most recent felony conviction and drunk driving convictions – and *for years* after those convictions.)

Almost without exception – except for those times Philpott was already detained during his arraignment- Philpott failed to appear in court to answer for his crimes, the courts issued warrants for his arrest, and Philpott would spend years hiding from the law until he was caught. In Philpott's dismissed Delaware County case from 1991, he jumped bail and it was almost six years before a Delaware County prosecutor (Winston Connor?) canceled the arrest warrant and dropped his charges. When Philpott committed aggravated assault against me, his active warrants were almost five years old. Because Gayle Wells covered for him instead of enforcing the law, those 2009 warrants were active another two years until real cops in Bentonville, Arkansas found him drunk driving again. In fact, Philpott has spent just 305 of the 3907 days since I shot him not in jail or wanted by police. He is wanted now for skipping bail on two 2018 charges from when another Arkansas deputy found him drunk and passed out in the middle of a road, this time laying on the pavement instead of passed out in his car.

Darrell Philpott is able to commit crimes in neighboring Arkansas and Missouri then return to Oklahoma, protected in his safe space by snitch immunity.

WANTED AGAIN

I have provided the documentation to show that Darrell Philpott is a violent man with felony convictions for drugs, theft and robbery spanning exactly *thirty-eight* years (8 June 1981 to 7 June 2017). He has dozens of additional dangerous and/or violent criminal convictions (including for the assault of a woman), and various charges and arrest warrants spanning his adult life. He has also admitted to government officials to at least 7 other felonies for which he was not convicted.[130] Darryl Philpott's current status is that he is a fugitive from the law, in hiding, and wanted by the police on Arkansas Arrest Warrant 51052018, issued 8 October 2018. This is the Delaware County snitch, whose spoon-fed testimony was shaped to create a probable cause affidavit, for the purpose of prosecuting me for defending my family farm.

---

[130] See Appendix BB Philpott's 1981 Pre- Sentencing Report, page 3, paragraph 5

"I can do *anything* I want!"
- Delaware County DA's Star Witness , Career Criminal and long term Police Informant, Darrell Philpott to a woman and her daughter after assaulting them

[6]

THE CRIMINAL LAWYER

Make crime pay. Be a lawyer.
— William Penn Adair[131] ("Will") Rogers,
Indian Territory pioneer, Cowboy Pundit, Freemason, and
son of Confederate Cherokee Braves Captain Clement
Vann[132] Rogers

---

[131] Colonel William Penn Adair commanded the 2nd Cherokee Mounted Volunteers while Colonel Stand Waite commanded the 1st Cherokee Mounted Volunteers

[132] Colonel Clement Vann commanded the 2nd Cherokee Regiment. Clement Vann Rogers was a Captain in the Cherokee Mounted Rifles.

Former Assistant DA Winston "Crime Pays Me"[133] Connor II was the premier defense attorney in the 13th Judicial District. He offered to "take care" of Turlington's charges but didn't. Winston made international headlines when he was arrested on ten felony charges in a murder-for-hire plot with convicted cop killer and local drug ring leader Slint Tate.[134]

Wiretap Audio of Winston and Tate is at www.RapeOfDelco.mp3

After notifying the Delaware County Sheriff's Office (DCSO) of the trespass and self-defense shooting, then coming into town to make a statement and being arrested **with a gun to my head**, I sat in the Delaware County jail. Even though my cellmates informed me that Darrell Philpott was a "snitch", I had no idea how deep the drug business infected the local legal system.

All I knew was that I had been charged with felony assault for defending myself against a well-known local criminal and police informant, I was facing serious prison time. On the recommendations of lawyers and inmates alike, I retained the services of Winston Connor. Interestingly, Connor was also a former **13th Judicial District Assistant District**

---

[133] See page 160

[134] Tate isn't from here. He moved to Oklahoma with his family when he was ten.

Attorney. As I later learned, Winston played both sides of the law.

After learning the case was a simple matter of a justifiable shooting of a violent, trespassing felon, Connor said he could "take care" of the charges for $10,000, assuring my family and me it would not go to court and that ten thousand would "take care of everything". Apparently, Winston meant that $10,000 would take care of Winston. Remember, this is Winston "Crime pays me" Connor.

> *Considering my defense attorney, Winston Connor, used to be the Assistant District Attorney for Delaware county, it is easy to understand how he would have contacts and relationships with criminal elements. But since those relationships appear to involve getting charges dismissed for the criminal who assaulted me, Winston **should have** told me about any potential conflict of interest, if he had a relationship for almost two decades that involved dropping charges and canceling arrest warrants for Philpott in exchange for... (?).*

> *I had no idea how connected they were, and Winston didn't tell me. Maybe a Winston-Philpott relationship explains why Winston made so many major decisions about my case without my permission.*

Major decisions affecting the client's case, *such as allowing the case dismissed* by the judge, are decided by the client. The Oklahoma Rules of Professional Conduct specifically notes, "**A lawyer shall abide by a client's decision whether to settle a matter.**"[135]

Because of the importance of a client's ability to make choices in his best interest, this lawyer's obligation is repeated in Rule 1.4, "Communication". To wit:

> (a) A lawyer shall: ... (2) reasonably consult with the client about the means by which the client's objectives are to be accomplished; (3) keep the client reasonably informed about the status of the matter; ... (b) *A lawyer shall explain a matter to the extent reasonably necessary to permit the client to make informed decisions regarding the representation.*

The above rule is explained immediately after in "Comment (1)": "Reasonable communication between the lawyer and the client is necessary for the client effectively to participate in the representation."

After 18 months had passed, Special District Court Judge Alicia Littlefield announced from the bench she was going to dismiss the charges. Winston told her not to, without asking me what I wanted, or even acknowledging my *presence.*

Afterward, I demanded to know why he didn't let her dismiss my charges. He explained that had she dismissed them, the Sheriff would just refile the charges, and that I would be

---

[135] See Rule 1.2, "Scope of Representation and Allocation of Authority Between Client and Lawyer", Title 5, Chapter 1, Appendix 3-A

arrested again, have to post bail again, and the whole process would begin again.

While all those things are technically possible, other attorneys have advised me that it is very unlikely the Sheriff would have refiled charges. I have no way of knowing if Winston actually knew the Sheriff's plans, if he was working with the Sheriff, or working with the drug ring. I just know that Winston was getting paid regardless of what happened to me.

Regardless, it was my decision to make. If Winston had followed the Rules of Professional Conduct and asked my permission, I would have definitely chosen to have them dropped and all of this over.

> *My case could have ended right there. The Judge offered to dismiss the case.* **Winston asked the Judge to not dismiss the case.** *This was my decision to make, but Winston made it for me, without my permission.* **The question is, why? Was he working the case for more money, or was he working with the other side?**

WINSTON HAS ME WAIVE RIGHT TO SPEEDY TRIAL

On 6 January 2016, the month after the preliminary hearing, and almost three months after the speedy trial review should have begun, Winston had me waive my right to a speedy trial for the first time, stating he had to visit his father who was in another state. My case should have been dropped for lack of timeliness, but instead, the speedy trial clock was reset because that's what Winston wanted. More than 18 months after that, the case still hadn't gone to trial.

Again, on 25 July 2015, Winston had me waive my right to a speedy trial for (his) personal reasons. Then on 15 December 2015 Winston had me waive my right to a speedy trial again. Then, **for the fourth time**, on 8 January 2018 (exactly three years and one month after the preliminary hearing) Winston had me waive my right to a speedy trial, again.

The Delaware County prosecutors needed justification to deny my Speedy Trial and Winston Connor, the former 13th Judicial District Assistant District Attorney, provided that justification.

WINSTON VIOLATES ATTORNEY ETHICS (BIG SURPRISE)

The Oklahoma Bar Association website lists the types of complaints that the Bar investigates. The first example is "- a lawyer holding money on your behalf will not return the money or provide you with a written accounting of how it was spent".[136] On 3 January 2018 I sent Connor a certified letter requesting an accounting of his $10,000 retainer. In response, Winston called me and explained he wanted another $20,000 to $30,000 to take my case to court. He said he would need half of that for himself and half for an expert witness ($10,00 to $15,000 to explain to a Delaware County,

---

[136] "Lawyer Complaint Process," Oklahoma Bar Association, August 5, 2019, https://www.okbar.org/gc/complaint/.

Oklahoma jury what bullet holes look like). I explained I could not afford more than what we agreed on for his trial retainer. In a letter to me dated 14 February 2018, Winston claimed that I was "clearly advised that the fee got (me) through the preliminary hearing". That is obviously a lie, as Winston continued to make appearances and file motions in my case to keep my trial going (including the above five waivers of my right to a speedy trial) *exactly three years and two months after the preliminary hearing* until his withdrawal in February 2018.

> *Due to Connor's failing to file any of the withheld exculpatory evidence with the court, or mention Philpott's impeachable crimes, or mention the fact Philpott had active warrants for his arrest at the time of his testifying, and because of the Connor's lack of familiarity with my case, and most of all for Winston's failure to act on my right to a speedy trial, I felt I was not being properly represented. After Connor demanded another $15000-$20,000 to continue representing me, I fired him, waived my right to an attorney so I could represent myself, and expanded the previous cursory investigation I had begun on Philpott.*

On 14 February 2018, the Court allowed Winston to withdraw as my attorney. A month later, I waived my right to counsel so I could approach the District Attorney's office in person with the evidence I had of criminal conduct of both the DCSO, the prosecutor, and the violent felon I shot in self-defense.

Winston withdrawing turned out to be the best thing that happened to my case.

BAR COMPLAINT, CONNOR LIES TO THE BAR AND ATTEMPTS TO VIOLATE THE ATTORNEY-CLIENT PRIVILEGE

Rule 1.4 (4), "Communication", of the Rules for Professional Conduct, states that lawyers are to "...promptly comply with reasonable requests for information".

After 5 months of Winston refusing to account for what he did for, or with, the retainer, I wrote a one-page letter to the Oklahoma Bar Association. I complained that Winston (1) was holding $10,000, and would not return the money or provide me with an accounting of how it was spent, (2) lied about the terms of the ten thousand dollar retainer, (3) failed to provide me with any written scope of representation documentation, (4) demanded $20,000-$30,000 in addition to the $10,000 he was paid, and (5) discharged me after I told him I could not afford to pay him more than what we had agreed to. I also informed the bar that Winston has done this to other clients (taken their money, dropped them without explanation, and kept their money).[137] Finally, I reported that Winston lied to me about the nature of my charges: he

---

[137] Instructions on filing Bar Complaints, as well as the complaints I filed against Winston Connor, prosecutor Nic Lelecas, their responses, and my counter response are available at www.RapeOfDelco.com/barcomplaints.htm

told me I was being charged with attempted murder, and that DA Eddie Wyant was offering me a plea bargain that was the same prison time and fines as if I were found guilty. I told the bar that of course I turned down the offer, figuring that Winston had paid off Eddie Wyant for the "attempted murder charge". This is a tactic that locals suspect the DA's office has been complicit with in the past: overcharge a crime that would be unprovable in court, and thus a guarantee a win for Winston. I mentioned my suspicions to Winston. He didn't deny that a payoff had taken place, but he was visibly agitated that I mentioned it.

I closed the letter noting Winston's email username ("crimepaysme"), his reveling in the "Godfather" image, and asking for a zealous investigation. I also included a newspaper article about Winston titled, "Wiretapped prison phone call links Jay attorney to alleged leader of drug ring".[138]

WINSTON ATTEMPTS TO VIOLATE CLIENT CONFIDENTIALITY, AND LIES TO THE BAR ASSOCIATION

The right of a client to be able to trust his attorney to not discuss his case is one of the most sacrosanct maxims in the law. It is also one of the oldest.

---

[138] Curtis Kilman, "Wiretapped Prison Phone Call Links Jay Attorney to Alleged Leader of Drug Ring," Tulsa World, September 1, 2017, https://www.tulsaworld.com/news/local/crime-and-courts/wiretapped-prison-phone-call-links-jay-attorney-to-alleged-leader/article_2f7a1df7-1512-53b1-adc3-4b9f2fdaae8e.html.

"The attorney–client privilege is the oldest of the privileges for confidential communications known to the common law. (It's purpose) is to encourage full and frank communication between attorneys and their clients and thereby promote broader public interests in the observance of law and administration of justice." – US Supreme Court Justice William Rehnquist[139]

Oklahomans feel it is so important that a client should be able to trust their lawyers that they codified that right no less than three times in their statutes.

According to 5 OK Stat § 5-3, the fourth duty of an attorney is, "(t)to maintain inviolate the confidence, and, *at any peril to himself,* to preserve the secrets of his client."[140] Section (4) of the preamble to the Oklahoma Rules of Professional Conduct[141] states, "A lawyer should keep in confidence information relating to representation of a client...". Section (a) of Rule 1.6, "Confidentiality of Information", *again* asserts the importance of lawyers to not betray their clients, "A lawyer shall not reveal information relating to the representation of a client...".[142]

---

[139] *Upjohn v. United States,* 449 U.S. 383 (1981)

[140]http://www.oscn.net/applications/oscn/DeliverDocument.asp?CiteID=64830

[141] Oklahoma Title 5, Chapter 1, Appendix 3-A, Preamble

[142]http://www.oscn.net/applications/oscn/DeliverDocument.asp?CiteID=479339

Section (b) (5) gives the following exception to confidentiality: "to establish a claim or defense on behalf of the lawyer in a controversy between the lawyer and the client...". Nowhere in my letter did I address the facts of my case. The facts of my case had nothing to do with my Bar complaint, so they were not relevant to any legitimate response Winston could have offered.

However, in his response, Winston stated he thought it was necessary for the bar to understand the facts of this case as they were explained to him by me, as well as facts reported to law enforcement, and the facts reported by medical professionals. Winston took almost two pages to repeat the Deputy Wells narrative about me, **which would have** violated his oath of confidentiality, if he was actually betraying me by repeating things I told him. The only reason I say he "attempted" to violate the attorney-client privilege, is that he just flat out lied about what I said. So, he didn't betray my secrets; he invented them.

Winston began his list of discrepancies by stating that in my "version of the facts", I encountered four (4) different [*sic*] male subjects standing around the fire... ." Then Winston told the Bar it was a "known fact" the trespassed land was neither my land, nor my family's land. Winston just asserted that what the drug dealer said was true, and what I said was not, providing no evidence for any of his claims.

Of course, none of this is true; on the night of the shooting, I stated there were three trespassers standing around the fire, not four. I have always maintained that number was three. More importantly, it is not a "known fact" the trespassed property does not belong to my family. No one has ever come forward to verify the Wells/Philpott assertion about where it happened. If Winston's best defense against being unethical is to convince the Bar that his client's testimony was different than someone else's testimony, then Winston's defense is to distract and deflect the charges about his unethical behavior. His response was not a denial; it was merely his attempt to say that I am, maybe, as bad as *he* is.

But even if these things were true, they had nothing to do with my Bar complaint, so *if I had* I told Winston any of it, he would be in violation of the Rules of Professional Conduct as well as violating 5 OK Stat § 5-3.

These weren't the only lies in Winston's letter, but for the sake of space and time, I will only address one more, because this one is demonstrably false according to Winston's own words.

Winston states on page 6, "I had been representing Mr. Turlington for a period of almost four (4) years when I had to withdraw from his representation for an amount consistent with the work to be performed." Although the statement as a whole is nonsensical, it does contain the admission he represented me for two and a half years after the preliminary hearing.

Here's the inconsistency: If I had paid Winston an "amount consistent with the work to be performed", then he is admitting here that we agreed for him to represent me long after the preliminary hearing in exchange for the $10,000.

He also claimed in his response that the $10,000 was only for the preliminary hearing, so there is a discrepancy of 30 months in Winston's own assertions.

> *Not only did Winston attempt to violate the Attorney-Client privilege, he lied multiple times to the OBA. His only defense to violating the privilege, is to admit that he lied about the conversations in his response to the OBA.*

After Winston demanded $15,000 to $20,000 in addition to the $10,000, I gave him to continue representing me, a close friend told me that Winston did the same thing to his wife. Then he told me about several others who had spent their savings on Winston, only to have Winston abruptly dump them or demand an exorbitant amount of money to continue representing them.

I did not pay a retainer of that amount the retainer was 4000 then he needed more $ more $ he went 2 court with me a couple times and did my preliminary hearing after that he needed another 8000 & I told him I was tapped after that had no more $ then when we went 2 the next court date John weedn filled n 4 him after court mr weedn sd to take this to jury trial it is going to cost 15000 or he can work in a plea Winston got started I asked where he was he sd he wasnt sure tried calling Conner never got a call back went 2 hisboffice and they would just tell me he was not in my wife sit there all day 1 day waiting to talk 2 him they sd he wasnt there all day

But never had a contract

> In a few days I will write a sim|
> told me. You can edit the amo|
> with the bar. if you want. it ma|
> getting him disbarred. he nee|

MON 2:39 PM

I will gladly help in total he fucked me on 21000 total so anything to get at him I am in on!!!!

In short, Winston took $21,000 from his client to tell him to make a plea deal. I have many communications from Winston's former clients like the one above.

Thankfully, I was able to recover from Winston cheating me and make my bar complaint as a free man. At least one of Connor's victims had to make his complaint while incarcerated.

In 2008, one of Winston's former clients wrote the Bar Association   from   the   Florence   ADMAX   prison   in

Colorado.[143] That former client complained that he also re-tained Winston for $10,000 but never saw nor heard from Winston again. In 2013 a former client, Delvin Melcher, sued Winston for malpractice. Melcher claimed failure to dis-charge fiduciary duties owed after payment, violation of at-torney-client relationship after payment, legal malpractice, and fraud, among others.

After speaking to other former clients, I learned two things that are common practice for Winston. The first is to claim to be able to "take care" of problems for ten thousand dollars, without going into detail how. The other is that he does not follow the best practice taught at Oklahoma law schools, which is to have a "scope of representation" or doc-ument that explains exactly what he will do for a set amount of money, so the client understands what they are paying for.

Apparently, $10,000 has been the usual fee since at least 2008. A naïve reader might think it odd Winston accepts cli-ents without benefit of a contract, but not having a contract allows Winston to drop clients at will. If a client doesn't have a contract, it is difficult for the client to argue a breach of contract, because the client has to argue there was a verbal contract with no documentation. Then, Winston, merely

---

[143] ADMAX stands for Administrative Maximum Facility. It is known as the "Alcatraz" of the Rockies and is a higher level of custody than a regular maximum security prison. For instance, prisoners are only allowed out of their cells for one hour a day. By comparison, *I was only let out of my cell a half hour each day the three days I spent at the Delaware County Jail.*

tells the Bar Association his former client lacks credibility because they are pending criminal charges. So, Winston has a business practice of ripping off people who are pending trial, i.e., his clients.

WINSTON THREATENS TO KILL HIS ADVERSARY'S BOYFRIEND

Most people Winston cheats don't have the resources to fight back, and even if they did, they are afraid of Winston's criminal connections, and for good reason. One local man who *was* willing to testify against Winston is local attorney and former Marine, David Anderson.[xxviii]

According to a Grove Sun article,[xxix] Connor contacted Anderson in 2017 in an attempt to get Anderson's female client to drop criminal charges. Anderson also testified that Connor threatened to "take out" the boyfriend[144] of Anderson's client. Anderson also testified that "Connor made a direct threat that he was going to ruin" the boyfriend's business.

The article continues,

> During the case, Connor allegedly offered (her) $100,000 if the criminal charges against his client went away, according to the affidavit.

---

[144] I am friends with the man that Winston threatened. He is a well-respected Doctor whose family pioneered Miami, Indian Territory.

Anderson also testified that Connor allegedly contacted (her) directly, in an attempt to get her to reconsider his offer of $100,000. Connor again threatened to destroy the business of the person close to CM.

In another instance, Connor allegedly contacted (her) and threatened her family if she did not drop Anderson as her attorney.

For the second time in a period of two years a member of the Oklahoma Bar has alleged that Winston Connor has ordered or threatened to murder someone. Talking to someone else's client is an ethics violation but threatening them is a crime. Winston's routine habit of violating the Oklahoma Lawyer's Code of Ethics pales in comparison to the ten felonies for which he currently awaits trial. However, Winston did violate the lawyer's Code of Ethics once again by contacting another Lawyer's client. He is awaiting trial for the above threats to a woman. At the heart of the issue was a criminal matter, making Winston's intimidating a witness threats an "obstruction of justice".

*Winston Connor has an established business practice of "taking care" of legal matters **outside of the courtroom**. He does this by threatening murder, threatening to " ruin" people's businesses, offering bribes, whatever it takes.*

I had my reservations about Winston Connor from the beginning, and as it turns out, I was right. The email address he gave me to contact him is CrimePaysMe@sbcglobal.net.

Apparently, crime paid Winston pretty well for a lot of years. According to a Daily Mail article titled, "The holiday's over!"[145] Connor was arrested on 12 January 2019 for 10 felonies including soliciting first-degree murder, racketeering, witness tampering, assault, and prostitution related offenses. The man Connor was wiretapped conspiring with was Slint Tate, a convicted cop killer and drug ring leader from Delaware county.

---

[145] Appendix P, "Winston Connor is Arrested on Ten Felony Charges" and Maxine Shen For Dailymail.com,

"Oklahoma Attorney Arrested for Soliciting a Murderer to Kill Another Convicted Killer While," Daily Mail Online, January 15, 2019, accessed July 26, 2019,

https://www.dailymail.co.uk/news/article-6590947/Oklahoma-attorney-arrested-soliciting-murderer-kill-convicted-killer.html.

Before you think it is just too crazy to believe that Delaware County officials could be conspiring with the drug ring, remember where Winston Connor got his start in Delaware County: *as the local prosecutor.*

Winston "Crime Pays Me" Connor, with his extravagant lifestyle, flashy clothes, and gangster persona, epitomized by his tagline **crime pays me,** *was practically bragging that he was the kingpin of the drug rings in Delaware County. It is debatable whether the true kingpin was Winston or Slint Tate, but there can be no doubt that Winston was the lynchpin between law enforcement and the drug dealers. These relationships did not begin when he was defense attorney. The record shows the ménage trois of criminal immunity between the DA's office, Philpott and Wells began at least as far back as 1999 (see preceding chapter). Of course, if Winston were honest with me, he would have told me about this history with Philpott and Wells, but he hid it from me. I had no idea they were as deeply connected as they were.*

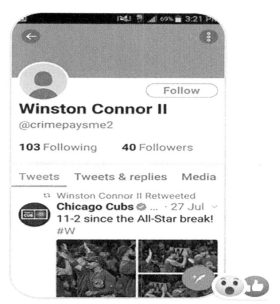

Winston Connor II @crimepaysme2.
Connor is a gangsta when it comes to tweeting.

Connor allegedly traded legal services for sex with prostitutes

Delaware County attorney Winston Connor allegedly traded legal services for sex in business owned or operated by (from the top) Loren Kristyn Sells and Chelsea Nance. Sells and Nance, along with Andrea "Cissy" Johnson, were charged with multiple felonies connected to the case in indictments filed by the 17th Multicounty Grand Jury on Nov. 16, 2018, and officials from the Oklahoma Attorney General's office.

Kaylea M. Hutson-Miller, "Connor Allegedly Traded Legal Services for Sex with Prostitutes," Grand Lake News (Grand Lake News, January 18, 2019), https://www.grandlakenews.com/news/20190118/connor-allegedly-traded-legal-services-for-sex-with-prostitutes

Happier Days: Winston and his beautiful (former) wife celebrating her 50th birthday in the Caribbean. Little did they know Winston would be arrested on 10 felony charges (including solicitation of a prostitute and pandering (pimping) when they stepped off the plane on their return home.

The object of Winston "Backdoor" Connor's unlawful desires?
Andrea Johnson*: Accused Backdoor of trading sex in exchange for legal services*

204 | *The Most Dangerous Man and The Rape of Delaware County*

According to a January 18, 2019 Tulsa World Article, titled "Attorney accused of solicitation advised Tulsa sex workers and prostitution ring leaders, search warrant reveals",[146]

> ... Connor, on numerous occasions, allegedly engaged in acts of prostitution with employees of Sells and Cousino, according to court documents. ...On one occasion, Connor sent Cousino a message indicating he was able to get "deferred deals" for women charged with prostitution-related offenses. Among those was a case against **Andrea Johnson** who Connor said had her case dismissed. *Johnson* is a defendant for racketeering and pandering. ...Connor is charged in a separate indictment with pandering[xxx] and solicitation.[xxxi]
>
> ... (A)n employee of Sells for nearly a decade, testified ... that Connor was treated differently than other clients by being allowed to get into the businesses through *back entrances*. She said that ensured he was not seen by anyone not directly

---

[146] Kendrick Marshall and Samantha Vicent, "Attorney Accused of Solicitation Advised Tulsa Sex Workers and Prostitution Ring Leaders, Search Warrant Reveals," Tulsa World, January 18, 2019, https://www.tulsaworld.com/news/local/crime-and-courts/attorney-accused-of-solicitation-advised-tulsa-sex-workers-and-prostitution/article_06ab318f-8594-5def-b4bd-b3b1556520da.html.

involved in his appointment (and that in) lieu of
meetings at his law office, Connor met with the
woman at the Swedish Relaxation Center for sex
services on a weekly basis...

Winston "back door" Connor had it all: a beautiful wife, a
big boat on the lake, the most successful law practice in the
judicial district, even a firstborn son who self identifies as a
weed fairy. Winston gambled it all on trying to be a gangster
with his "crimepaysme" moniker on email and twitter, and
(according to the State Attorney General) trading legal services for sexual favors and trying to trade legal services in
exchange for murder, and God knows what else. We'll see
how much of a gangster this soft, chubby lawyer is when he's
in a maximum security prison.

Winston Connor III
June 17 ·

Love is all there is ......and a weed fairy ....there's definitely a weed fairy

In fairness to the Connor family, just because they don't serve in the military doesn't mean they don't fight for their beliefs. Here "weed fairy" Winston Connor III stands up for his beliefs.
The Connors aren't from around here.

[7]

THE *CRIMINAL* PROSECUTOR

So, the prosecution can lie and mislead, and the defense still has "the burden" to show misconduct by the government?
-Supreme Court Justice Anthony Kennedy, Banks v. Dretke[147]

When police or prosecutors conceal significant exculpatory or impeaching material, we hold, it is ordinarily incumbent on the state to set the record straight.
-Supreme Court Justice Ruth Bader Ginsburg, Banks v. Dretke

The prosecutor has more control over life, liberty, and reputation than any other person in America.
His discretion is tremendous.
- Attorney General and Future U.S. Supreme Court Justice, Robert Jackson

---

[147] *Banks* is a 2003 Supreme Court case in which a man who had been convicted on snitch-based testimony spent over 20 years in prison. Just as in my case, the Prosecution withheld evidence that would have allowed the defendant to discredit their witness. Also, the Prosecution in Banks withheld that the State had previously made a deal with their witness. Banks was *ten minutes* from receiving lethal injection when Justices halted his execution.

(The prosecutor's role) ... is not that it shall win a case, but that justice shall be done.... **It is as much his duty to refrain from improper methods calculated to produce a wrongful conviction as it is to use every legitimate means to bring about a just one."**
-Berger v. United States, 295 US 78, 88-89 (1935)

THE PROSECUTOR'S PRIMARY RESPONSIBILITY is not to convict, as most believe, but to seek justice.[148] In other words, it is just as much his duty to protect the rights of the accused as it is his duty to prosecute the accused. Justice is not served when the State punishes an innocent man.

> The prosecutor speaks not solely for the victim, or the police, or those who support them, but for all the People. That body of "The People" includes the defendant and his family and those who care about him. It also includes the vast majority of citizens who know nothing about a particular case, but who give over to the prosecutor the authority to seek a just result in their name.
>
> — Lindsey v. State, 725 P.2d 649 (WY 1986)

---

[148] National District Attorneys Association Prosecution Standards, 1.1 Primary Responsibility: The primary responsibility of prosecution is to see that justice is accomplished. Also, the American Bar Association Standards for Criminal Justice, 3-1.2(c): The Function of the Prosecutor: The duty of the prosecutor is to seek justice, not merely to convict.

Prosecutorial misconduct is the act of breaking the law, or a code of ethics, while working as a prosecutor. Offering false, or inadmissible, evidence in court is one example, and allowing a witness to commit felony perjury is another.

In both *Mooney v. Holohan*, 294 U.S. 103 (1935), and *Napue v. Illinois*, 360 U.S. 264 (1959), the Supreme Court held that *prosecutors may not present false testimony or allow false testimony to go uncorrected.* The idea that prosecutors may not present false testimony or allow false testimony to go uncorrected is engrained in multiple Oklahoma statutes. The prosecutor in my case did both.

Every attorney licensed to practice in Oklahoma swears an oath[149] that they **will do no falsehood or consent that any be done in court**, and if they know of any, they will give knowledge thereof to the judges... that it may be reformed..."

In addition to the Oklahoma Attorney's Oath, the third duty listed in Oklahoma Title 5, section 3, "Duties of attorney and counselor" forbids attorneys "to seek to mislead the judges by any artifice or false statements of facts...".

Rule 3.3, "Candor toward the Tribunal", from the Attorney's "Code of Professional Responsibility" (Oklahoma Title 5, Section 1.5), states "(a) A lawyer shall not knowingly:(1)

---

[149] 5 OK Stat § 5-2, Upon being permitted to practice as attorneys and counselors at law, they shall, in open court, take the following oath: ...that you **will do no falsehood or consent that any be done in court, and if you know of any you will give knowledge thereof to the judges of the court, or some one of them, that it may be reformed**; ... so help you God.

make a false statement of fact or law to a tribunal or fail to correct a false statement of material fact... (3) offer evidence that the lawyer knows to be false.

Angela J. Davis, a Professor of Criminal Law and Criminal Procedure, quotes[150] the findings of an Innocence Project study on Prosecutorial Misconduct . Of the first 70 court rulings in the study that were overturned based on post- conviction evidence:

- Over 30 of them involved prosecutorial misconduct.
- Over 30 of them involved police misconduct which led to wrongful convictions.
- Approximately 15 of them involved false witness testimony.
- 34% of the police misconduct cases involved suppression of exculpatory evidence. 11% involved evidence fabrication.
- 37% of the prosecutorial misconduct cases involved suppression of exculpatory evidence. 25% involved knowing use of false testimony.

Every one of these elements has been demonstrated in my case.

---

[150]Angela Davis, "Prosecutors Who Intentionally Break the Law," Digital Commons @ American University Washington College of Law, accessed October 23, 2019

https://digitalcommons.wcl.american.edu/clb/vol1/iss1/2/

Nic Lelecas committed prosecutorial misconduct when he allowed Philpott to identify the defense attorney as "the shooter" three separate times, and even describe the defense attorney by the clothes he was wearing, so there could be no confusion that he was pointing at the defense attorney. Rather than stop the circus, Lelecas said "let the record reflect that the witness identified the shooter", as if Philpott had identified me. This is beyond Lelecas refusing to remedy a falsehood; he intentionally deceived the court record (See appendix Q).

Deputy Wells committed police misconduct repeatedly, but most obviously when he altered witness testimony on the record, and when he withheld exculpatory evidence from the PC affidavit (see chapter 2). He also helped Philpott craft a false narrative, which means Wells was involved with all three varieties of police misconduct identified in the study: suppression of exculpatory evidence, evidence fabrication, and knowingly using false testimony.

ABUSE OF PROSECUTORIAL AND POLICE DISCRETION

discretion (di-skresh-an). **1.** A public official's power or right to act in certain circumstances according to personal judgment and conscience. - Also termed *discretionary power.*

- Black's Law Dictionary

Malicious prosecution is when a prosecutor uses a civil proceeding against the plaintiff, despite the prosecutor knowing he doesn't have a case.

The very first responsibility of a prosecutor according to the Oklahoma Rules of Professional Conduct is to "refrain from prosecuting a charge that the prosecutor knows is not supported by probable cause".[151] As you read the following chapter about Delaware County Prosecutor Nic Lelecas, ask yourself if he knew my charges weren't supported by Probable Cause.

FAILURE TO ADDRESS PERJURY

At the preliminary hearing Winston Connor cross examined Philpott in a manner that demonstrated a general lack of preparation or familiarity with the case. However, before he concluded his cross examination, I reminded him to ask about Philpott's criminal record. I had previously found the court records of Philpott's arrest warrant for poaching charges in Missouri, as well as his three felony convictions for robbery, theft, and drug dealing.

Keep in mind, that while Philpott was on the stand, perjuring himself and identifying the defense attorney as the

---

[151] "Special Responsibilities of a Prosecutor," OSCN (Oklahoma Bar Association), accessed October 23, 2019,

http://www.oscn.net/applications/oscn/DeliverDocument.asp?CiteID=481037.

shooter, he had two active warrants out for his arrest.[152] However, he was not going to be arrested by Delaware County officials. Neither would he be arrested for perjury. Philpott had a blank check to do what he wanted in Delaware County. This is consistent with the "testify and walk" scheme of snitch-based prosecution. He was immune from any accountability, as long as he delivered his lines.

Thankfully, before the preliminary hearing, I requested and paid for the hearing to be recorded. Had I not done that, I would not have the proof of Philpott's perjury and the prosecution's malfeasance. I still thought that maybe, *just maybe*, the prosecution was against me because the Sheriff's Department had so thoroughly skewed the PC Affidavit, and the DA's office thought I was *actually* guilty.

On March 16th, 2018, I filed my waiver of right to an attorney with the Court Clerk; so, the judge could sign to subpoena Philpott's medical records. Attorneys can subpoena evidence themselves, but litigants acting without an attorney [*pro se*] must get a judge to authorize subpoenas. The court clerk, who apparently had not dealt with a *pro se* litigant before, sent me to presiding Judge Denney. Judge Denney told me I needed an attorney.

So, I went to the prosecutor myself.

---

[152] Appendix D, "Philpott's 2009 Arrest Warrants that were Active in 2014 when Sheriff Moore Protected Him"

FOUR MEETINGS WITH THE PROSECUTOR

In all, I had four face-to-face meetings with the prosecutor in my case, Nic Lelecas. They were April 3rd, May 3rd, June 14th, and July 19th, all 2018. [153]

At the first meeting I provided Nic a 3 ring binder containing my entire defense in good faith, believing that the DA would not pursue a case against someone who was not guilty, or at the very least, would not pursue charges against someone he could not beat in court. I soon learned that neither prosecuting the guilty, nor winning in court were the goals of the DA's office, but to teach a lesson to anyone audacious enough to exercise his statutory right[154] to make a citizen's arrest.

The binder contained:

1. a concise narrative of what happened at the scene
2. witness statements
3. interview recordings on CD
4. police photographs
5. dozens of Philpott's criminal records and prosecutions and arrest warrants over a 39 year period, including the three 1981 felonies he perjured himself over during the preliminary hearing
6. the warrants for poaching and DWI that were active when he assaulted me, when he testified against me 18 months later, and were active when

---

[153] Appendix H, Nic Lelecas Response to Bar Complaint
[154] See page 2, footnote 9, above

Philpott committed perjury about them in the Delaware County Courtroom

7. Philpott's five year old arrest warrants that were active when I shot him, and when he testified against me 18 months later, and 10 months later when Arkansas Deputy Justin Crane found him passed out behind the wheel of a car "just off Hwy 72"

8. The police report from Philpott's 4 October 2016 Arkansas drug related felony arrest and DWI arrest.

9. Philpott's 10 January 2017 arrest warrant for jumping bail on the 4 October 2016 arrests.

10. Philpott's 22 March 2017 Missouri DWI conviction[155]

The report also showed Deputy Wells' altering of witness testimony, including Philpott's interview answers concerning whose land he trespassed, the time he was drinking, as well as his being unemployed.

Everything in the book was cited to either page and paragraph number in the PC Affidavit, to exact times in Philpott's Police Interview, to Preliminary Hearing Transcript pages, or to written witness statements from the investigation. I even included an audio CD of both Philpott and my

---

[155] Appendix E, "Philpott's 2017 Missouri Conviction for 2009 DWI"

interviews, the PC Affidavit, and the referenced transcripts pages and witness statements.

Perhaps most importantly, the binder report included the exculpatory evidence that Deputy Gayle Wells withheld from the PC Affidavit. Examples of this excluded evidence included:

1) the Wound Nurse's determination that Philpott had been shot from front to back,

2) the high resolution color photographs of those wounds that showed how the Wound Nurse came to that determination, and DCSO photos of :

3) photos of my family's "No Trespassing" sign, that Detective Miller took

4) photos of Philpott's makeshift meth lab that Detective Miller took

5) photos of the empty truck bed that was supposedly held a half rick of wood[156] (and presumably chain saws, etc.) that Deputy Hardison[xxxii] took

6) photos of the same truck missing a license plate that Deputy Houston took and noted in his police report[157]

The evidence was presented in a simple format that anyone could understand. However, I also cited everything I said from government sources, so that it was undeniable. This was not merely a defendant claiming, "I didn't do it!", this binder was full of hard evidence from government sources.

---

[156] Preliminary Transcripts, page 3, line 19 at www.RapeOf-Delco.com/prelim.pdf

[157] Appendix G, PC Affidavit, p.9/17, paragraph 16

On my second meeting, Nic provided me with Discovery evidence. Since it had been exactly a month since our first meeting (more than enough time for Nic to consider the evidence in my report), I asked Nic what he thought about the proof of Philpott's perjury and Well's withholding and altering evidence. He told me he was still looking at it.

My third meeting with Nic was the following month for the sole purpose of updating me with the Prosecution's position on the case. I asked Nic again about Wells' withholding of exculpatory evidence, this time specifying the medical report, the photos of the wounds, and the photographs of the "No Trespassing" sign, the photos of the truck with missing license plates (as well as the police report noting they were missing), the empty truck bed, and the remains from Philpott's meth processing. Although Nic could not or would not discuss the investigatory report I gave him, he did perk up when I told him my brother Lance was a member of the Oklahoma bar. Nic asked if there was any way he could meet Lance. I responded in the affirmative and put Nic on the phone with Lance. Lance explained to Nic that he had given me legal advice on my way to town after I shot Philpott, thus becoming my counsel. Lance explained to Nic that the first time he called the Sheriff's office they didn't tell him I had been apprehended in the street enroute to make a statement. The Sheriff's office told Lance I would call after I was finished making my statement. Lance waited a while and when I hadn't called back, he called a second time and was told again that I was making a statement and I would call him back when I finished. Lance explained he was an attorney and my counsel again and gave them his Bar Association number. He told them again he wanted to speak to me as my counsel. They assured him again I would call him after making my statement. By the fourth time Lance called, he realized he was being deceived and the Sheriff's office never had any intention of letting him speak to me. By this time, I was already in the jail cell being told about Philpott's snitch immunity by my cell mates.

When Lance was finished telling Nic how the Sheriff's office lied to him by telling him I would be allowed to call him after making my statement, and how I was denied my right to counsel as they continued to press me for as much information as they could get, Nic asked if Lance could meet us in person next time.

> *Keep in mind that the entire time the Sheriff's office was denying me counsel and lying to Lance, that Lance repeatedly told the Sheriff's office he was my counsel and wanted to speak to me.*

Before our meeting closed, I told Nic that if this case weren't closed soon, I was going to make it public. He chuckled (not facetiously) and replied, "It's already public knowledge, Mr. Turlington. It's been in the papers many times." I answered, "No, Nic. Your side of the story has been in the paper several times. I am going to make it public by telling my side of what happened, including all of Gayle Wells' crimes and also that your star witness is a multiple felon and has even been convicted of another felony since he assaulted me, and his perjuries, and that you've been informed of them." Then I produced a hardbacked copy of *"Afton (Indian Territory – Oklahoma) Some Early History"*,[158] I explained the authoress went to High School with my mother and belonged to the same UDC chapter as my mother and my wife, and that she owned a printing press, and I would be writing a book on my arrest if my charges weren't dropped soon.

According to Nic, **my fourth and final meeting** with him was on July 19th. Lance took leave from Ft Knox, Kentucky. It had been over three months since I gave Nic the binder full of exculpatory evidence. I asked Nic again if he had checked Philpott's testimony against his lengthy criminal record to see his perjury. Nic replied, in front of Lance, that he had checked the transcripts and there was no perjury. [159] I wondered if Nic had actually seen the transcripts, and for a moment wondered if Nic was even familiar with the Oklahoma perjury statutes.

I asked Nic about the other exculpatory evidence I had shared with him in good faith. He provided excuses: As for the truck bed, it was possible the trespassers emptied the cut

---

[158] Fredrea Gregath Cook, *Afton (Indian Territory - Oklahoma) Some Early History* (Wyandotte, Oklahoma: Gregath Company, Inc., 2016), www.aftonhistory.com.

[159] According to court records, Nic didn't check out the Preliminary Hearing transcripts until 9 January 2019, over six months later.

wood and the deputies failed to ask about it or take pictures. As for the missing license plate- it wasn't a concern, and neither was my family's "No Trespassing" sign that Wells withheld from the PC Affidavit.

When I asked about the photo of the camp fuel can (see page 47), Nic replied that he had spoken to *Deputy Wells* about it. According to Wells, Philpott and his accomplices could not have been making meth because Meth manufacturing was a complicated, involved process that required a complete laboratory.[160] I asked Nic what he thought a convicted drug dealer and meth addict was doing with camp fuel, and a pallet, and glass bottles, and plastic sheeting. Nic just shrugged.

Finally, I asked Nic what he thought about the photos that clearly showed Philpott was shot in the front of the leg that Wells withheld. Nic maintained that Philpott was shot in the back of his leg and launched into a discourse on ballistics. For the first time in our meeting, Lance interrupted Nic and flatly told him, "You're wrong. That is factually incorrect. Bullets do not normally do that." Then Lance gave Nic a lesson on ballistics and wounds.

Keep in mind that between us, Lance and I had close to 50 years military service. We both have been recognized by the

---

[160] Meth manufacturing is simple enough that teenagers can make it in their bedrooms without their parents knowing. However, Philpott was living with his cousin, who would not allow it in his home. To see how simple the meth making process is, do an internet search for "Shake and Bake Method for Making Meth".

Army as expert marksmen and we are both gun enthusiasts. Lance in particular has been hunting since he was ten years old and has shot more deer than he can count. Before he was an Army lawyer, Lance was an infantryman and an expert field medic. He has five trophies for marksmanship competitions on Army posts competing with other professional Soldiers.

He has over 41 months of deployments, including Mosul, Baghdad, and other Middle Eastern combat zones. He has literally carried wounded soldiers into the medical station after an attack on his base. It is no exaggeration to say that Lance has probably had more blood on his hands (both human and animal) than any other Oklahoma lawyer. So, when a liberal New England lawyer tries to teach Lance and me how bullets work, it is a ridiculous thing to behold.

Left: 9mm Pistol Champion, Ft. Sill, Oklahoma Right: Trophies from Various Military Shooting Competitions

Lance with 10 point White Tail Deer, November 2019

A PRAGMATIC APPEAL TO THE PROSECUTOR

At every meeting (including this one) I showed Nic my utmost respect. On every visit I was professional and spoke to him as a detective might speak to a prosecutor, and never strayed from the facts of the case. Now Lance, an attorney, was present. Even though Lance was there as my brother and not representing me, he did most of the talking about law after the initial questions I asked Nic.

One should understand that when Lance discusses the law with Prosecutor Nic Lelecas (or any other Attorney from the DA's office), it is not a meeting of equal legal minds. Lance has *fifty* attorneys and paralegals who work for him. The prosecutors who work for Lance have supervisors *who have supervisors* who report to Lance.

However, the legal points Lance made to Nic that day made no more difference to Nic than the exculpatory evidence, or the impeachment evidence I had shown Nic earlier.

Because Lance, an attorney, was present on my behalf, I felt I could speak frankly to Nic on a more pragmatic, if not personal level, and leave the particulars of the case to Lance and Nic to discuss. This obscene prosecution had gone on for more than 4 years at this point and, out of exasperation, I tried to level with Nic politically, since the law and evidence clearly did not concern him. The following line of questions (which must have made mild mannered Nic uncomfortable to say the least) was spontaneous. I certainly hadn't discussed them with Lance prior.

I asked Nic what he believed the District Attorney was trying to accomplish by prosecuting me and told Nic that he would never be District Attorney in the 13th (Judicial District) by prosecuting a local farmer for arresting a violent felon like Darrell Philpott. I asked him if he even realized that he was already at a disadvantage as a New England liberal - he responded by stating he didn't know what being pro-abortion had to do with being a District Attorney. I asked him if the District Attorney understood the voting community was firmly on my side of this case and asked if he realized my family had pioneered the 13th Judicial District when it was still Indian Territory, and that the first presiding judge of the 13th was my cousin. Before Lance could step in and try to get the conversation back on track, I asked Nic, " Nic I realize you haven't served and don't understand veterans, but have you ever paid much attention to the thousand veterans' names in front of the courthouse you pass by every day when you come to work?" I actually waited for a response. When I didn't get one, I asked, "Have you ever stopped to read *any* of them?" He answered he had. I asked him if he ever noticed the very first name when he left the front doors of the court house every day. Of course, he had not. I told him "It's *my* name. And his", nodding to my brother. And our brother's and our father's, and grandfather's, and his grandfather's. You should take a look today when you go home." Nic was speechless. I appeared to really have his attention for the first time in the 8 or so hours I had spent face to face with him. "Nic, those names, *including mine*, were put there after Wells framed me. The old sailor who had them put them there knew about my charges when he did it. He was born and raised in Jay and knows Gayle Wells, and what outsiders like you and him and the Sheriff have done to our county. The people here are patriots, and they don't like what's happening to their county and they don't like what is happening to me. Tell Kenny to drop these charges for his own job security if he won't drop them in the interests of justice."

My impromptu monologue over, our meeting ended. The next time Nic asked to meet Lance, he requested I not attend.

On 6 January 2019, Lance gave a briefing[161] at the Grove Mazzio's to concerned citizens about Gayle Wells and Harlan Moore's corruption. Afterward, Lance gave the same briefing to Nic Lelecas. Although the briefing contained no new information, Lance constructed poster boards with photographs, court records, police and witness statements, and the property map of where the shooting took place and gave the same briefing he would to a jury. Although these things were in the binder, I gave to Nic, I had no way of knowing that Nic actually looked at them. From the lack of concern he showed, it appeared as though he had not. After Lance's briefing, Lance and I knew with certainty that Nic had all the facts.

---

[161] Audio of the briefing is at RapeOfDelco.com/briefing.mp3 a reconstructed video at RapeOfDelco.com/briefingvideo.mp4

OKLAHOMA BAR ASSOCIATION COMPLAINT AND RESPONSE

Several months passed with no word from Nic. Now that I knew Nic had seen the evidence of Gayle Wells' crimes and Sheriff Harlan Moore's lies, as well as Philpott's perjuries and 2017 felony conviction and drunk driving convictions, it was time to send a warning shot to Nic. Remember, up until now I had no proof that I showed Nic any of the above. But by complaining to the Bar Association, Nic would be forced to do *something* with the information I had shown him. He could lie to the Bar (which he did) and tell them he didn't know about Philpott's perjuries and recent felony conviction and drunk driving convictions, but once they forwarded my complaint to Nic, he could no longer pretend like he didn't know. At the very least Nic would be forced to report to the Judge that Philpott had committed perjury in court (a felony in Oklahoma). Not only would Philpott be impeached from his perjury, but also from his most recent felony (if not the other three), and drunk driving convictions, etc. Also, considering my experience with Nic thus far, there would be a good chance he would mislead, if not outright lie, to the Bar Association in his response and I would be able to prove it. And he did, and I can.

On 30 November 2018, I complained to the Oklahoma Bar Association about Nic's many ethics violations. His response is in Appendix H.[162] I made the tactical decision to

---

[162] I have not included my Bar Complaint on Winston Connor in the appendix in the event that Winston will further violate the

not tell the Bar about the worst thing Nic did when he entered a falsehood into the record (three times).

My goal was not to get Nic disbarred, or even in trouble, but to get him and Kenny to stop playing their obscene games with my freedom and drop charges. Besides, I wanted to keep at least one card up my sleeve in case they didn't drop charges.

To see how Nic knowingly entered a falsehood into the court record, see pages 119-121 and Appendix Q, "The State's Sole Witness Can't Identify the Shooter, The Prosecutor Attempts to Falsify the Record Three Times".

If the 30 November Bar complaint about Nic didn't result in my charges being dropped, I would write a second complaint outlining Nic's unethical behavior. I would also write a letter to Kenny, informing him of Wells', and Lelecas', and Philpott's misconduct.[163] I would send it by registered mail, so that Kenny would be obligated to act on it in the same way that Nic should have acted on the evidence binder I gave him. I also would have filed a complaint with the Highway Patrol, the OSBI, and the FBI (remember, the violent quadruple felon at the center of this mess crossed state lines after the shooting), and any other agency I could get to listen.

---

attorney client confidence I put in him, giving the Bar Association yet more reason to disbar him and giving me more damages for a potential lawsuit.

[163] I also would have made a video recording of my sealing the letter in an envelope and sending it through registered mail.

On February 4, 2019, Nic responded to my complaint, which is Appendix H. Like Winston, he drew attention to the fact his accuser (me) was himself being accused of a crime to discredit me. But three things I've learned about corrupt people that apply to both of these two is:

1. Generally speaking, they are not very smart. If they were, they would achieve their success honestly.
2. When people in positions of authority for a long period of time get away with crossing ethical boundaries on occasion, they become emboldened. They start to believe that their (in their minds, excusable) transgressions are actually for the greater good.
3. Once these people become comfortable with these transgressions as a standard business practice, they let their guards down and talk too much.

Both Nic and Winston inadvertently provided evidence in their responses which can be used against them. Before I detail some of the ways Nic mislead and lied to the Bar Association, consider Nic's obligations to other members of the Oklahoma Bar:

From "The Lawyer's Creed",[164]

In all dealings with members of the Bar, I will be guided by a fundamental sense of integrity and fair

---

[164] "Lawyers Creed," Oklahoma Bar Association (OBA Board of Governors , February 14, 2019), https://www.okbar.org/ec/lawyerscreed/.

play. ... In my dealings with the Court and with counsel, as well as others, my word is my bond. ... I recognize that my conduct is not governed solely by the Code of Professional Responsibility, but also by standards of fundamental decency and courtesy. Accordingly, I will endeavor to conduct myself in a manner consistent with the Standards of Professionalism adopted by the Board of Governors.

On page 3, Nic states,

It is alleged that there has been a violation of the Rules of Professional Conduct, 5 O.S. Ch.1, App. 3-A:

Rule 3.3(a)(3}. Rule 3.3(a)(3) provides that "[a] lawyer shall not knowingly: offer evidence that the lawyer knows to be false. If a lawyer, the lawyer's client, or a witness called by the lawyer, has offered material evidence and the lawyer comes to know of its falsity, the lawyer shall take reasonable remedial measures, including, if necessary, disclosure to the tribunal. A lawyer may refuse to offer evidence that the lawyer reasonably believes is false."

Note there are two parts to Rule 3.3- the first forbids an attorney of knowingly offering false evidence and the second parts directs an attorney to take remedial measures upon learning of its falsity.

Nic continues on page 4, "Mr. Turlington's grievance against me appears to be based solely on the exchange between Mr. Connor and Mr. Philpott regarding misdemeanors involving moral turpitude." But **this is a lie**. My very first grievance states,

> 1. *Nic Lelecas accepted perjury in court*, and now, after being informed, *knowingly refuses to seek remedy* for that falsehood. The perjury is indisputable. When asked directly about his criminal history, on the stand, under oath, Darrell Philpott first evaded, and then lied on the record.

> A) *Philpott's first provable perjury was in the opening minutes of the hearing when Philpott testified his initial drug felony was for "Possession"*, specifically denying "Trafficking" (lines 21-23, p. 29, preliminary transcripts). See page 3, CRIMES tab for Philpott's **Possession w/ purpose to Deliver Controlled Substance felony** (to which he pled Guilty).

> B) Philpott's second provable perjury was when he testified that he had been in **no trouble** with the law other than his initial drug felony...

> 2. *Nic Lelecas is violating his **first and third** duty as an attorney* according to 5 OK Stat § 5-3[165]

---

[165] From 5 OK Stat § 5-3, Duties of Attorneys and Counselors: First. To maintain, while in the presence of the courts of justice... the respect due to the said courts and judicial officers... Third.

See Appendix H for a page and a half explanation how Nic violated the 1ˢᵗ and 3ʳᵈ duties as an attorney. None of it had anything to do with crimes of moral turpitude. The last paragraph of my complaint states:

> In conclusion, I want to point out that I did not come to you first. I tried to resolve these falsehoods before the court directly with Nic Lelecas. On 23 July 2018, I waived my right to an attorney and went to Nic Lelecas in person, with a copy of the hearing transcripts, as much of Philpott's criminal record as I could find, the detailed color photos that the Undersheriff withheld, and more. I was accompanied by my brother, Lance Britton Turlington, who is a member of the Oklahoma Bar Association (member #19959) and a Colonel in the Army JAG Corps. In front of my brother, Nic denied Philpott's perjury that I put in front of his face, in writing (the preliminary hearing transcripts). I thought Nic would do something to address these falsehoods, but he refuses, **which is why I appeal to you to at least take this as an ethical complaint about Nic Lelecas consenting to falsehoods presented to the court, and refusing to make the falsehoods known to the judge or otherwise remedy the falsehoods in any way.**

To... never to seek to mislead the judges by any artifice or false statements of facts or law

Clearly, my grievance against Nic Lelecas was not "based solely the exchange between Mr. Connor and Mr. Philpott regarding misdemeanors involving moral turpitude."

> *Nic lied to the Bar when he told them* my *grievance appeared to be based solely on an exchange regarding misdemeanors involving moral turpitude. Nic completely evaded the subject of my complaint, which was "...**about Nic Lelecas consenting to falsehoods presented to the court and refusing to make the falsehoods known to the judge or otherwise remedy the falsehoods in any way.**"*

Under the title "Preliminary Hearing", on page 3, Nic Writes:

> Much of the grievance is focused on Darrell Philpott's testimony at the preliminary hearing regarding his criminal history. At the preliminary hearing, the victim testified during cross-examination that he was a convicted felon for possessing a half a trash bag of weed in Benton County, State of Arkansas about 30-35 years ago and that he had not been convicted of any misdemeanors involving moral turpitude or dishonesty. ...

When Darrell Philpott was questioned further during the course of cross-examination regarding "trouble" he had been in, Mr. Philpott testified he had traffic violations. When asked if he remembered anything else, Mr. Philpott responded with "Well, not a whole bunch."

Nic responds to his failure to address his witness's perjury[166] on page 3,

> The case file maintained by the District Attorney's Office at the time of the preliminary hearing did not contain a criminal history record for Mr. Philpott and there were no conversations between myself and Mr. Philpott in preparation for the preliminary hearing regarding Mr. Philpott's criminal record.

NOTE: If Nic and Philpott had no conversations at all prior to the hearing, then Nic would have simply stated, "We had no conversation". But by Nic admitting that "...there were no conversations between (he) and Mr. Philpott in

---

[166] <u>Rule 3.3, Rules of Professional Responsibility</u> "(If a) a witness called by the lawyer, has offered material evidence and the lawyer comes to know of its falsity, the lawyer shall take reasonable remedial measures, including, if necessary, disclosure to the tribunal."

preparation for the preliminary hearing *regarding Mr. Philpott's criminal record*," Nic was admitting there *were* conversations about *something,* **off the record**.

Nic then states:

> A review of the Oklahoma Supreme Court Network for any criminal records involving Darrell E. Philpott in Delaware County reveals the following history:
>
> (1) Case No: CRM"1991-00955 was dismissed/settled on March 12, 1997.
> (2) Case No: CM~2001-00339 was a misdemeanor Public Intoxication charge that resulted in a journal entry of judgment against Mr. Philpott on April 26, 2001.
> (3) Case No: CM-2001-00802 was a misdemeanor Public Intoxication charge that resulted in a journal entry of judgment against Mr. Philpott on September 18, 2001.
> (4) Four (4) [*sic*} traffic citations/tickets having been filed against Mr. Philpott in 2003.

What Nic didn't mention while explaining his alleged ignorance of Philpott's 40 year crime spree was that Nic had prosecuted Philpott for crimes in the past; Nic failed to mention that to the Bar. He also failed to mention that both Lance and I had given him government records of Philpott's Arkansas and Missouri misdemeanors and felonies.

At this point Nic should not be portraying Philpott as a non-felon. Doing so is deception by omission. Deception by omission, or lying by omission, is also known as exclusionary detailing. It takes place when information is left out in order to mislead or to further a misconception. Lying by omission includes the failure to correct pre-existing misconceptions. As shown in this chapter, Nic Lelecas left out material evidence multiple times to the Oklahoma Bar and even failed to correct the Judge's misconceptions from the multiple falsehoods that took place during my Preliminary Hearing.

THE STATE OF OKLAHOMA, TO ANY SHERIFF, CONSTABLE, OR POLICEMAN IN THIS STATE:

WHEREAS, an Information having been filed on 07-25-2003, in the District Court of Delaware County, State of Oklahoma; Charging

DARRELL E PHILPOTT

with crime of   **ORIGINAL**

(NO INSURANCE)

BENCH WARRANT: FAILURE TO PAY

you are hereby commanded forthwith to arrest the above named:

Bench warrants are only issued for crimes. Nic Lelecas knows this. "Failing to Appear" is a crime regarding the administration of justice. The fundamental nature of Failing to Appear is that of contempt. For the record, the Court lists Nic Lelecas as prosecutor in all four violations, Failures to Appear charges, and subsequent arrest warrants. So Nic knew that Philpott had committed crimes other than traffic, both during the hearing, and when he replied to the Bar complaint. Nic deceived the court by letting the Judge (and any potential jury) believe that Philpott's crimes were limited to traffic violations and a single felony. Note the images for this case are restricted.

Parties Involved

Agency	OKLAHOMA HIGHWAY PATROL *of Vinita OK*
DA	LELECAS, NICK *of Jay OK*
Judge	JUDGE LITTLEFIELD
Officer	EBERLE, ROGER
Defendant	PHILPOTT, DARRELL E *of Maysville AR* ‖ Monitor this person

Calendar events

Date	Time	Description
09/26/2003		CST:BEGS Completed : 01/02/2004 Code: X
12/18/2003		CST:MAIL FINE AND COST LETTER
12/31/2003		CST:EXTEND PAYMENT Completed : 06/08/2004 Code: X
01/07/2004		BENCH WARRANT: FAILURE TO PAY Completed : 06/02/2004 Code: X

Case entries

🏛 Images for this case are restricted and may only be viewed at the court.

Date	Description
07/25/2003	FILE AND ENTER CITATION
	LAW LIBRARY FEE
	ARREST FEE
	DPS REVOLVING ASSESSMENT
	FINE
	AUTOMATED FINGERPRINTING INFORMATION SYSTEM
	CLEET ASSESSMENT
	FORENSIC SCIENCE IMPROVEMENT ASSESSMENT
	10% ASSESSMENT OF DPS
	10% ASSESSMENT OF AFS1

The four 2003 traffic tickets that Nic admitted Philpott had were for Taxes Due State, No Insurance, Operating a Motor Vehicle in a Manner not Reasonable and Proper and Failure to Wear Safety Belt. Even though Nic was listed as the prosecutor for those violations, Philpott's Delaware County Snitch Immunity didn't work as usual for those violations because the arresting officer was a Highway Patrolman, not Delaware County Sheriff's Deputy Gayle Wells.

Possession w/ purpose to Deliver Controlled Substance is a felony, as is perjury. When Philpott denied the nature of his felony, he committed a felony. When Philpott denied being in any "trouble" other than one felony and "traffic tickets", he perjured another felony.

Nic lied to the Bar Association when he stated my griev- ance against him "appears to be based solely on misde- meanors of Moral turpitude."

On page 4, Nic states, "In preparation for this response, an Interstate Identification Index (triple "I") criminal history record for Darrell E. Philpott was obtained", and lists the following four crimes:

1. An arrest on January 27, 1981 by the Benton County Sheriff, State *of* Arkansas for the charge of Theft by Receiving. No disposition indicated.

2. An arrest on February 9, 1981 by the Benton County Sheriff, State of Arkansas for the charge of Criminal Mischief. No disposition indicated.

3. A one (1) year sentence in 1981 from Benton County, State of Arkansas, for what appears to be for Possession of a controlled substance with intent to deliver.

4. A one (1) day sentence in 1997 from Sulpher [sic] Springs City Court, for the charge of Fleeing and the charge of DWI.

None of this was news to Nic. As for the theft "charge", it was more than that, it was a conviction for a felony. Both Lance and I gave Nic the Judgement for that felony, and on the same record was Philpott's felony conviction for Burglary. Nic is pretending like he didn't know the outcome, but he did. *Once again, Nic is being untruthful.*

The 1981 Criminal Mischief confirms once again, Philpott's troubles with the law were not merely traffic tickets. And Nic knew this.[167]

As "*for what appears to be for Possession of a controlled substance with intent to deliver* [sic]", even here Nic tried to downplay Philpott's conviction by saying "*for what appears to be*". This is dishonest. Using terms like *appears to be, may*

---

[167] Philpott's blood alcohol limit that when he was arrested that day was over twice the legal limit. See Chronology, page 350

be or *allegedly* is unnecessary and misleading. Once again, Nic is trying to soften the edges of Philpott's felonies. The record is conclusive and not subject to interpretation. This is a drug dealing conviction, not mere possession, and Nic knew this. He was given the record in person and by email. To be clear, the record states the charge as, "Possession of Controlled Substance W/ Intent to Deliver".

Next, Nic lists a 1997 conviction "from Sulpher [sic] Springs City Court, for the charge of Fleeing[168] and the charge of DWI". Fleeing from the Police and DWI are not mere traffic tickets. That is a mischaracterization. These are serious and dangerous crimes.

Nic continues:

> Second, additional research would be required into the facts of Mr. Philpott's DWI arrest, and the Arkansas DWI statute/ordinance he was convicted of, before the possible application of the *Bunn* decision can be made. Without further examination, it is impossible to determine if Mr. Philpott's answer to Mr. Connor was false, thus requiring further examination to determine *Bunn's* applicability and a

---

[168] This 1997 Arkansas conviction for Fleeing Arrest shouldn't be confused with Philpott's 14 April 2001 Fleeing Arrest, or his 2014 Fleeing Arrest shortly before I shot him. These are all separate incidents.

determination if any remedial measures
are needed.

To be clear, and to give Nic the benefit, it is possible that
Nic may have been honestly ignorant of the law despite having been a prosecutor for almost 20 years in a county adjacent to Arkansas.

In some jurisdictions, such as Oklahoma, a DUI charge de-
notes a greater degree of impairment than a DWI for a driver
charged with drinking and driving. In other jurisdictions,
such as Arkansas, a DWI is the "worse" of the two charges.
The titles of the charges and their definitions are the same;
they are just swapped. To wit: In Oklahoma, a DUI is .08
BAC (Blood Alcohol Content) or more, or any amount of a
Schedule I chemical or controlled substance. [169] A BAC level

---

[169] <u>47 O.S. § 11-902</u> **Persons Under the Influence (DUI) of Alcohol or Other Intoxicating Substance or Combination Thereof** A.
It is unlawful and punishable as provided in this section for any
person to drive, operate, or be in actual physical control of a motor
vehicle within this state, whether upon public roads, highways,
streets, turnpikes, other public places or upon any private road,
street, alley or lane which provides access to one or more single or
multi-family dwellings, who:

1. Has a blood or breath alcohol concentration, as defined in
Section 756 of this title, of eight-hundredths (0.08) or more... 3.
Has any amount of a Schedule I chemical or controlled substance... D. Any person who is convicted of a violation of driving
under the influence with a blood or breath alcohol concentration

of .15 or higher is considered "aggravated DUI" in Oklahoma. Aggravated DUIs are felonies. Every one of Philpott's blood alcohol tests throughout his drunk driving career were .15 and over.

In Arkansas, anything over .08 BAC is DWI and anything between .05 and .08 is DUI.[170] In other words, a DWI in Arkansas is a DUI in Oklahoma, and a DUI in Oklahoma is a DWI in Arkansas. So, when the Oklahoma courts rule that a DWI is a Crime of Moral Turpitude, they are ruling that a DUI in Arkansas is a Crime of Moral Turpitude.

Keep in mind I researched and gave documentation for at least nine separate arrests and convictions for DWI in Arkansas and gave this to Lelecas. So, when Nic plays like he doesn't know that the State's only witness is morally bankrupt and is not credible, he is simply perpetuating his dishonest character.

And for the final straw on this camel's back, keep in mind, that Philpott had 2 warrants for his arrest when he assaulted me. One was for a 2009 DWI, and the other a 2009 poaching offense. 2 years later in 2016 , when Arkansas authorities arrested Philpott for yet another DWI (and a meth felony),

---

of fifteen-hundredths (0.15) or more pursuant to this section shall be deemed guilty of aggravated driving under the influence.

[170] AR Code § 5-65-103 (a) (2) **Driving or Boating While Intoxicated (DWI)** It is unlawful and punishable as provided in this chapter for a person to operate ... a motor vehicle if at that time the alcohol concentration in the person's breath or blood was eight hundredths (0.08) or more ....

Philpott was convicted on the 2009 DWI warrant. Philpott was also convicted on the 2016 meth felony and DWI.

> *Oklahoma courts have determined that a simple DUI (which is anything over .08 Blood Alcohol Content) is a crime of moral turpitude. When Nic told the Bar about the III criminal report and the criminal report from Philpott's police file, he was implying those were the only crimes he knew about. This is a lie by omission. Nic knew about Philpott's 4 decade career of crime, including at least 9 such charges, (including* **two convictions since Philpott assaulted me in 2014),**[171] *multiple methamphetamine charges and convictions, theft, burglary and drug dealing felonies, resisting arrests, committing assault and battery on women in at least two separate instances, threatening to kill police officers, multiple instances of fleeing from arrest, multiple instances of assaulting police officers and at least one instance of assaulting EMTs, and other dangerous and violent crimes, using firearms while a felon, countless failures to appear for court, and over a decade of being a wanted fugitive and more.*

> *However, Nic claims more research is needed before he can admit that Philpott has a moral turpitude problem.*

---

[171] According to 47 OK Stat § 47-11-902,(C) (2), **Persons Under the Influence of Alcohol:** Any person convicted of (drunk driving in) this state or another state or having a prior conviction within ten (10) years of the date following the sentence shall, upon conviction, be guilty of a felony. Philpott has committed multiple felonies drunk driving alone.

Nic continues:

> I have attempted to visit with Darrell Philpott re-
> garding the testimony he provided regarding his
> criminal history, but communicating with Mr.
> Philpott has been challenging. Mr. Philpott has
> neither a telephone **or** vehicle of his own, nor does
> he have a reliable mailing address as he moves fre-
> quently. After speaking with Mr. Philpott utiliz-
> ing a phone of an acquaintance of his earlier this
> year, an appointment was scheduled in my office
> for January 10, 2019. Mr. Philpott failed to attend
> this appointment.

In fact, court records show the DA and Sheriff tried *six*
times to subpoena Philpott in the five years they were trying
to build a case based on his testimony and were unable to locate him a single time.

> *Once again, Lelecas deceives by omission. The simple*
> *truth is Philpott is a criminal fugitive. Why doesn't Nic*
> *just admit this?*

Nic closes his Bar response by what appears to be
giving me legal advice:

Should Mr. Turlington desire to attack the credibility of Darrell Philpott at trial, he would have to overcome the hurdles presented by 12 O.S. §2609-Impeachment by Evidence of Conviction of Crime. Mr._ Turlington, in addition to convincing the trial court that the probative value of admitting evidence of the 1997 DWI outweighs its prejudicial effect to the accused, he would first need to establish that the 1997 DWI was a crime punishable in excess of 1 year pursuant to the law under which the witness was convicted required by 12 O.S. §2609(A)(l) and overcome the ten (10) year limitation found in 12 0.5. §2609(8).

Nic never addressed my charges that he violated his oath of office,[xxxiii] or that he violated his first and third duty as an attorney. [172]

---

[172] 5 OK Stat § 5-3, Duties of Attorneys: It is the duty of an attorney and counselor: First. To maintain, while in the presence of the courts of justice... the respect due to the said courts and judicial officers, and at all times to obey all lawful orders and writs of the court... Third. To employ for the purpose of maintaining the causes confided to him such means only as are consistent with truth, and **never to seek to mislead the judges by any artifice or false statements** of facts or law.

Nic lied about not knowing about Philpott's 2017 felony. Not only did I hand Nic a copy of Philpott's judgement for the 2017 felony, but Lance emailed it to him, as well as links to Philpott's RAP video I made,[173] and Philpott's 2017 drunk driving charges. Of course, Lance's emails can be proven. In closing, Nic wrote what appeared to be legal advice on what I would have to do if I wanted to impeach Philpott. By this time, it was obvious that I understood Oklahoma impeachment rules better than Nic did.

---

[173] www.RapeOfDelco.com/RAP.mp4

State Representative (later State Senator) Rick Littlefield[xxxiv] and Ed Turlington sr, circa 1977. Rick was best friends with Grove football coach (later Superintendent) Tommy Steen when Ed was GHS principal in the 70s. Ed became friends with Rick and campaigned for him. Rick was appointed interim Sheriff in 2011 after the Delaware County jailhouse mass rape. Sheriff Littlefield restored order and respect to the Delaware County Sheriff's office. Regrettably, it was not a job he wanted to keep.

Littlefield was an old fashioned, rural democrat. Harlan Moore wanted to replace him, so he ran as a Democrat. Once Moore won that election, he saw this was a very socially conservative area, so he ran as a Republican. Moore obviously had no party loyalty one way or another. The important thing is that he is not from here and he does not share our values.

[8]

IT'S OVER, BUT IT ISN'T FINISHED

Is the best of the free life behind us now?
Are the good times really over for good?

— Merle Haggard, Son of Indian Territory Pioneers

I would have to agree that most of these folks were better
than any of today's people. They took care of their own and
dealt with those that weren't. Many things they did weren't
legal, but I don't recall ever fearing the ones I knew when I
was a kid. Some were friends, some were only
acquaintances, some were family. It didn't seem abnormal
at the time because backroom deals were commonplace in
those days.

— Cherokee Mounted Brave descendant and 6th
generation Delaware District, Indian Territory / Delaware
County, Oklahoma citizen Steve Martin[xxxv]

Edwin Hardee Turlington is with Ed Turlington and 44 others.   [•••]
May 12 · 🌐 ▾

Thank you for letting me tag you. Please share and repost and discuss.

District Attorney Kenny Wright wants to be the State AG someday. Okies do not need someone in that position, much less as an assistant prosecutor, who believes its ok to put a patriot and his family through hell for five years after a false arrest.

Below is the Roots1 clip is from the forthcoming fully featured DVD on my false arrest on 14 April 2014, over FIVE years ago.
lg
It is a 7-minute video on family in Oklahoma's Ottawa and Delaware Counties (formerly Indian Territory's Delaware District)

If you are kin to the people in the video or know them and we haven't talked please let me know.

As you can see from the introduction I am moving away from discussing the despicable quadruple felon and violent career criminal wife beater who attacked me 5 years ago who the Delaware County Sheriff covered for because he is a police informant (and the Sheriff assumed I was his snitch's drug customer) and moving on to the prosecution team.

I will have some true and accurate, documented and very embarrassing videos about each of them shortly if my case isn't dropped soon.

When I shot the drug dealer in self-defense, he had already been convicted for felony drug dealing, felony theft, and felony robbery. Since he attacked me with a glass bottle, he's been convicted on another meth felony. He will be impeached at any trial, if there is one, and he decides to show up, which he won't, since he currently has warrants for his arrest and is dying from kidney failure (from almost 40 years of hard drug use), and he says he will not die in jail and won't be taken alive.

He will kill someone soon and you will be able to thank Sheriff Harlan Moore, Deputy Gayle Wells, DA Kenny Wright and Prosecutor Nic Lelecas.

If my case isn't dropped my mid may I will have another DVD on proprietorial misconduct in my case. According to my little brother Lance Turlington, a full bird Colonel in the Army JAG corps, who has fifty Lawyers and paralegals working under him (the prosecutors who work for him are *two* supervisory levels beneath him), the prosecutor in my case engaged in a pattern of conduct that could get him disbarred, if not convicted. Lance also said he would formally charge the prosecutor if my false charges were not dropped. What makes my case unusual from most police and prosecutorial misconduct cases is not only the level of evidence but the fact it came out prior to trial.

I am looking at ten years for something everyone involved in my prosecution knows I didn't do, which is shoot the convicted felon drug dealer, convicted felon thief, and convicted felon burglar Darrell Philpott in the back as Philpott claimed.[xxxvi]

UNDER FALSE PRETENSES, the DA motioned to dismiss my charges on 2 July 2019. Any review of Darrell Philpott's record shows that he has been a fugitive from justice most of his adult life. This is important to acknowledge because the District Attorney Kenny Wright still refuses to admit this on the record. Whatever the District Attorney's *real* reason, the one he gave was that the victim was unable to testify. This is yet another lie by omission. Darrell Philpott is not unavailable, in the sense that most people would use the word. The DA's position is that Darrell Philpott is a credible witness, who they simply can't get ahold of for some unknown reason. The truth is, they can't get ahold of Philpott because he is a criminal fugitive, actively hiding from the law, and they know this. For years prior to his trespass, Philpott had warrants for his arrest. He had warrants for his arrest when he assaulted me and when he testified against me. He now has new warrants stemming from his 2018 arrest when he assaulted responding medics and threatened to murder an Arkansas deputy .

District Attorney Kenny Wright and Prosecutor Nic Lelecas claim that Philpott is unavailable because he "failed to maintain meaningful contact". This is a deceptive omission. Philpott is unavailable and actively avoiding contact because he is once again a criminal fugitive, and Kenny Wright and Nic Lelecas know this.

Philpott knows the Oklahoma District Attorney can't protect him from *Arkansas* prosecution and that is why he is hiding from *all* law enforcement now. DA Kenny Wright's abuse of prosecutorial discretion that protects Philpott won't save him in Arkansas.

The only subpoena actually served on Philpott was the one sent certified mail on 30 September 2014. According to court records, the Prosecution was "Unable to serve Darrell Philpott" on any of the following seven attempts. Despite this, Philpott knew to appear at my Preliminary Hearing on 8 December 2015. According to court records, the DCSO served the other six witnesses for the Preliminary Hearing. Only Philpott was to be served by the District Attorney.

The point is the DA's office will not admit this on the record because it shows their only witness has an absolute lack of moral turpitude and credibility. If the DA's office admits that Philpott has no credibility, then **they have to admit they shouldn't have charged me to begin with.**

SUBPOENA

STATE OF OKLAHOMA, COUNTY OF DELAWARE:

To: Darrell E. Philpott, P.O. BOX 11, MAYSVILLE, AR 72747 *DA to serve*
    Brandon Houston, Delaware County Sheriff Office, P.O. Box 476, Jay, OK 74346 *DCSO to serve*
    M.G. Wells, Delaware County Sheriff Office, P.O. Box 476, Jay, OK 74346 *DCSO to serve*
    Bill Hobbs, Jay Police Department, P.O. Box 348, Jay, OK 74346 *DCSO to serve*
    Frank Miller, Delaware County Sheriff Office, P.O. Box 476, Jay, OK 74346 *DCSO to serve*
    James Morgan, Jay Police Department, Jay, OK 74346 *DCSO to serve*
    Jack Thomas, *DCSO to serve*

You are hereby commanded to appear before the District Court of Delaware County in the City of Jay on the **8th day of December, 2015 at 10:30 AM**, then and there to testify on behalf of the State of Oklahoma as a witness in the above entitled case wherein the State of Oklahoma prosecutes the said EDWIN HARDEE TURLINGTON JR and you

Apparently, the District Attorney believed Philpott would be more responsive to contact from their office than the Sheriff's office. Maybe this is because of the relationship between Lelecas and Philpott that dates to 1991. We will never know.

> *The fact the DA still wanted Philpott to testify against me 5 years after my arrest demonstrates their intent. The DA was given all the copies of Philpott's documentation in this book: his endless criminal record to include his currently active arrest warrant number, his perjuries, and his inability to even identify me in court. Yet, they would still prosecute me today, based on Darrell Philpott's "credibility", if they had the chance. They cannot or will not admit they are wrong.*

FILED¹

IN THE DISTRICT COURT OF DELAWARE COUNTY
STATE OF OKLAHOMA

JUL ~ 2 2019

CAROLINE M. WEAVER
DELAWARE CO. COURT CLERK

THE STATE OF OKLAHOMA,
        Plaintiff

No. CF-2014-224

-vs-

EDWIN HARDEE TURLINGTON, JR.
        Defendant.

MOTION TO DISMISS

I, **KENNY WRIGHT**, District Attorney of said County, in the name and by the authority of the State of Oklahoma, moves the Court to dismiss the above entitled cause without prejudice for the following reason, to wit:

VICTIM HAS FAILED TO MAINTAIN MEANINGFUL CONTACT/COMMUNICATION
WITH THE DISTRICT ATTORNEY'S OFFICE

WHEREFORE, Kenny Wright, District Attorney, moved the court dismiss the above entitled cause without prejudice.

DATED this ___/___ day of July, 2019.

KENNY WRIGHT
District Attorney

By: _____
NICHOLAS P. LELECAS
ASSISTANT DISTRICT ATTORNEY

Delaware County District Attorney Kenny Wright and assistant prosecutor Nic Lelecas can't admit the truth: their "victim" is a wanted fugitive who now refuses to enter a courtroom.

FEAR AND LOATHING IN DELAWARE COUNTY

Typically, people do not want to believe their local law enforcement officers could be corrupt, especially country people. But remember, these people aren't from the country. District Attorneys Eddie Wyant and Kenny Wright, Prosecutor Nic Lelecas, Sheriff Harlan Moore and criminal defense attorney / multiple felony defendant Winston Connor are all city boys, despite what they might like for the voters here to believe.[174]

To be clear, I believe most law enforcement officers are honest people, including most law enforcement officers in our area. As detailed earlier in the book, several Delaware County deputies went out of their way to include the exculpatory evidence in the investigation (although it was withheld from the PC Affidavit). Still, what happened to me is not an isolated incident.

I included an article in Appendix MM titled "The Rape of Delaware County".[175] The subtitle of this book comes from that article. The article centers on an actual mass rape of Delaware County jail inmates by Law Enforcement Officers, but also mentions Sheriffs of two other Oklahoma counties

---

[174] See page xvi

[175] William Norman Grigg, "The Rape of Delaware County - LewRockwell LewRockwell.com," LewRockwell.com, May 24, 2012, https://www.lewrockwell.com/2012/05/william-norman-grigg/copification/.

who were convicted for raping inmates. As you read about the other two Sheriffs, note not just the depth of their depravity, or the length of time they had spent as Oklahoma Law Enforcement officers, but how many decades they spent *in charge* of Law Enforcement Departments. And as you read, remember Gayle Wells was demoted from the Chief of Grove Police Department to patrol officer after he sexually harassed a Police Department employee.

Melvin Holly, former Sheriff of Latimer County and *a Law Enforcement Officer of forty years*, was charged with raping four inmates, having sexual contact with four others, and improperly touching three employees and the teenage daughter of an employee. A jury found Holly guilty on 14 of 15 charges, including 7 felonies. In addition to the sexual assault charges, Holly was found guilty of threatening to kill an inmate if she told authorities about Holly's relationship with her. Holly was sentenced to 25 years in prison, with no chance for parole.

On 16 April 2008 Sheriff Mike Burgess of Custer County was "... charged with 35 felony counts involving an alleged sex-slave operation at his jail. The allegations include(d) having sex with female inmates and threatening to have a drug court participant in his custody sent to prison if she didn't comply with his demands."[176] Prosecutors also charged Burgess with threatening an inmate "... that if she didn't perform

---

[176] Tony Thornton, "Sheriff Resigns in Sex Scandal," Oklahoman.com (The Oklahoman, April 17, 2008), https://oklahoman.com/article/3231081/sheriff-resigns-in-sex-scandal.

his required sexual favors, she would not ever be able to see her children until after they had grown up." Burgess was also charged with Bribery for asking a drug court participant to recover incriminating DNA evidence from a victim's home. In exchange, Burgess would get the victim's brother released from prison. Burgess was sentenced to 79 years in prison. *Burgess had been Custer County Sheriff since 1994.*

You would think after a 13 million dollar law suit, that the Delaware County Sheriff's Office would reform itself, but they didn't. One of the problems in Delaware County is that the District Attorney's office is complicit in the rampant police misconduct. If victims of local police abuse complain to the DA about law enforcement officers engaging in illegal behavior, all they get in response are flat denials.

The problem of Delaware County Law Enforcement Officers abusing their power continues because, even in the face of overwhelming evidence, the District Attorney chooses to deny police misconduct instead of prosecuting it.

AFTERWORD

ABUSE OF POLICE AND PROSECUTORIAL DISCRETION

BLACK'S LAW DICTIONARY DEFINES *WANTON MISCONDUCT* as "an act, or a failure to act, when there is a duty to do so, in reckless disregard of another's rights, coupled with the knowledge that injury will probably result." Black's defines "administrative discretion" as "A public official's or agency's power to exercise judgment in the discharge of its duties," and "prosecutorial discretion" as "A prosecutor's power to choose from the options available in a criminal case, such as filing charges, prosecuting" (or not prosecuting, or offering immunity to a snitch...). Likewise, police discretion is a law enforcement officers power to choose whether or not to arrest someone, or write a ticket, etc. *By its very nature, the discretion to ruin people's lives can easily lead to the abuse of power.* When deciding to make an arrest or a prosecution, honest police and honest DAs consider the probability that a particular suspect did what he is accused of doing,[177] the   citizen's rights,[178] and the likelihood of a

---

[177] If there is a contradiction in testimony between -Is it more likely that a college educated disabled veteran in his 40s shot a violent drug addict with three felony convictions (including one for burglary) in his back for burning trash? Or is it more likely the triple felon (including one for dealing drugs) was cooking meth on what he believed was on foreclosed land (as reported by the Sheriff)? Would a reasonable person give the benefit give the benefit of the doubt to the family man or the felon?

[178] Does a citizen in Oklahoma have the right to make an arrest? Does he have the right to defend himself?

successful prosecution.[179] This last consideration is based on governmental priorities[180] and government resources.

Police and Prosecutors can abuse their discretion in more than one way. The most common way is to arrest and prosecute citizens in the absence of probable cause (or, as in my case, with manufactured probable cause). In Delaware County, the more common abuse of discretion is the refusal to arrest protected criminals, even in the face of clear and convincing evidence. In the first instance, the victims are limited to the abused individuals and the people who care about them. However, the second form of prosecutorial abuse affects the entire community. When there is a snitch to protect, the welfare of the general public is just collateral damage.

In Delaware County drug addicts get treated better by the Sheriff and District Attorney than honest working people. Worse yet, poor people who have no value as an informant, and can't afford a lawyer, effectively have no protection under the law at all.

---

[179] Would a Delaware County jury composed of citizens who are likely crime victims or know people who are crime victims be likely to convict a veteran and family man for shooting a known violent drug addict and thief? Regardless of the circumstances?

[180] Does the 13th Judicial District want to put disabled veterans in prison or pursue the rampant theft committed by violent drug addicts?

pussy (slang): a weak or cowardly man or boy : WIMP, SISSY
- Merriam Webster Dictionary, 2020

puss: 1. A cat. 2. Archaic A girl or young woman. Used as a term of endearment. 3. A man regarded as weak, timid, or unmanly.
- The American Heritage Dictionary, 2020

pusillanimous pussies:

...Grove Police Chief Mark "Titties" Morris, Grove Cop " Jerrybear" Bohannon, former Delaware County Sheriff Harlan "Outsider" Moore and his Undersheriff Melvin Gayle "Slower, Softer, Less" Wells, District Attorney Kenny "Homewrecker" Wright, Former District Attorney Eddie "Child Porn" Wyant, Prosecutor "New England" Nic Lelecas, and all the other government employees in our community who protect criminals at the expense of law abiding citizens.

Pervert Gayle Wells' (p.228) protégé Grove Police Chief Mark "Titties" Morris impersonating a police officer in a Tulsa establishment, while gripping his victim so hard that the folds of her flesh bunch up in his hand. Note that "Titties" has no more police authority in Tulsa than a prison inmate does, but that doesn't keep him from flashing his badge and gun to impress a young woman to pose for a picture with him in her underwear- which he circulated among his Police Department without her permission. At the time the photo was taken, open carry was illegal in Oklahoma.

LANCE'S TRAILER

For instance, after I was on the wrong side of a confrontation with their snitch Darrell Philpott, my family could not get the most basic police responses to other problems. My brother Lance's trailer was stolen from my farm by a local drug addict, who I will refer to as *"Dick"*.[181] This was a $5000 double-axle diamond plate steel car hauler that Lance had left with me prior to his last deployment. I called Lance when I found the trailer parked behind *Dick*'s house. Since it was Lance's property, he would have to be the one to report it to the police.

Lance phoned Delaware County Deputy Hendricks[xxxvii] and provided him with a copy of the trailer title, so Hendricks could verify the trailer's serial number. Hendricks went to the addict's home where he saw the trailer. *Dick* admitted the trailer belonged to Lance, that *Dick* took it from my property when I wasn't there, and he would only return it if I were to exchange it for a trailer that *Dick* had left on my property. The problem with that deal was that *Dick* had also stolen the trailer he had left on my property from someone who had hired him to do construction work. I learned the trailer *Dick* left at my house belonged to John Rowley of

---

[181] "Dick" was a successful businessman before his meth addiction, and his family is still respected in Grove. "Dick" was born and raised in California.

Bartlesville, so I contacted Rowley and arranged for him to get it back.

Lance called District Attorney Wright, Sheriff Moore, and Grove Police Chief Mark Morris multiple times. None would return his calls. Lance suspected they were avoiding him for some reason, so wrote them all certified letters with copies of his trailer title. He told each of them that Detective Hendricks had spoken to *Dick*, obtained a confession, and that the trailer was on *Dick's* land. He even told them that *Dick* had stolen farm equipment from his own mother to support his meth habit. Lance told them he was an active duty Lieutenant Colonel about to be promoted, a member of the Oklahoma Bar, and a former prosecutor. Lance closed by explicitly asking them to acknowledge receipt of his letter. So, DA Kenny Wright, Sheriff Harlan Moore, and Chief Morris each had a certified letter from an Army officer who works in law enforcement, who is from the area but serving his country on the east coast, a trailer title, and a confession from a known thief. This should have been easy. But in Delaware County, you never know if the drug addict has an off the record relationship with local law enforcement.

Neither Wright nor Morris responded at all. Sheriff Moore had *Gayle Wells* (of all people) call Lance to tell him that *Dick* was dying of cancer, as though that made him immune from arrest.

The official response from Delaware County Law En-forcement administration to a victim of crime, who was serving his country on active duty out of state, was a collective shoulder shrug. Dick is now dead, and Lance's trailer is gone. Lance's letter, as well as the police report with Dick's mother explaining how he stole her tractor to feed his meth addiction, is in Appendix NN.

GROVE POLICE SERGEANT "JERRYBEAR" BOHANNAN PROTECTS TONY "METH IN YOUR PANTIES" ROHMAN

When I asked Brian Elder to recommend a contractor, he suggested Josh Shaddon[xxxviii] and said that Josh had done work for Elder Real Estate since the Nineties. I liked Josh and his work so much, I had him build an addition onto our home. Josh took another construction job while the wood floor was being laid, so I had to find someone else to trim in the windows and floors.

About that time, meth addict Tony Rohman[xxxix] posted on Facebook: "You dream it we build it!", along with several pictures of what (in hindsight) was probably not his work. Tony took measurements for the trim and the desk at my house. When I asked why he wasn't writing them down, he said he could remember them. After giving him a $400 advance, Rohman picked up $900 worth of materials I paid for at Lowes. The following day Rohman told me he would be unable to finish the job but would send someone else to do it. I explained to him that was unacceptable and that he needed to get out to my house and do the job,[182] to which he agreed. Rohman gave me excuses for weeks until I texted him:

Date : 03/09/2018 02:00:41 PM

Tony do you realize you dopers spend more energy cheating and lying and BSing and making excuses and complaining and putting off the inevitable than you would working an honest job?

If you made that desk in the pictures then youre good enough to crank something like that every other day and sell it on Facebook. And still have time for recreational activities.

I'm guessing you sold or traded my baseboards and window trim for dope, and are trying to get them back.

That was all the excuse Rohman needed to feign offense and text the following:

To All from : Tony Rohman
Date : 03/09/2018 02:45:56 PM

---

[182] I did not use those exact words.

*...I have however lost all interest in installing any-
thing for you. ... Idk where you are getting all this
crap, but the level of disrespect and judging another
human being based upon your false assumptions se-
riously makes me regret the amount of time I put
into this project perfecting every single detail. ...*

Based on the desk pictures Rohman texted me, I decided
it was worth the $400 I had fronted him. We planned for me
to get my hardware he had, and I texted back the following:

To : Tony Rohman
Date : 03/09/2018 03:50:18 PM
*If everything is there I will be satisfied with the turn
of events and keep the legal system out of it... If so
we will call it even*

Rohman and I had an agreement until the last text above.
According to Delaware County prosecutor Nic Lelecas,
Rohman breached the contract through fraud by embezzle-
ment.

Two days later Rohman's girlfriend texted me that their
family dog had bitten Tony in his crotch, so she was going to
meet me instead of him and sent me a false address. I didn't
hear from either Rohman or his girlfriend until 16 March
when I texted Rohman that I was going to the DA that day.

I called Delaware County Sheriff's Deputy Travis Goodman, [183] who went to school with Lance and me in Afton. I explained the situation to Travis and that Rohman's girlfriend had already sent me a false address to meet her. I asked Travis if he could meet us at that address. Travis said he was unable to unless I got an Affidavit of Assistance at the Courthouse. Travis is not lazy. He is honest and a hard worker, so I knew he was not lying to get out of anything. Travis explained it was Sheriff Harlan Moore's new policy. The courthouse only issues affidavits of assistance to parties in an active court case. This effectively prevents the deputies from being involved in the community as peace keepers.

Old fashioned policing involves officers of the peace helping to resolve issues before they become cases. Instead of preventing problems, Sheriff Harlan Moore thrives on them. The constant conflict of snitching and heavy handed police tactics keeps our jails overflowing and the court house doors swinging. Good lawmen like former Delaware County deputies Travis Goodman, Frank Miller and Hendricks could absolutely serve as officers of the peace, and would, had Sheriff Harlan Moore let them.

Next, I stopped at the Grove Police Department to get an escort to Rohman's false address. I showed police Sgt

---

[183] Travis has since left DCSO.

Bohannan[xl] the text messages and the agreement between Rohman and me to cancel the contract. The texts proved unlawful conversion of property, which is a crime, so I asked Bohannan for an escort to go with me in case there was a problem while I retrieved my property.

After looking at the texts and asking me if I had consulted an attorney, Bohannan stated it was a matter of contract law, thus a civil matter, and I would not get an escort. I explained that Rohman's failure to fulfill his obligations was a material breach of that contract, physically pointing to the text showing we cancelled the contract. It didn't matter. Bohannan was either too stupid to understand the law, or too lazy, cowardly, or corrupt to go with me to the felon's house.[184]

So, I went to what I knew was a false address without a police escort. There was no storage facility of any sort at the address. A nearby resident pointed to a house down the street that *did* have a large 4 car garage. He said the people who owned it were constantly moving furniture and appliances and other goods into and out of that at all hours of the day and night and my belongings were probably in it. About that time, I received a call from Rohman's girlfriend that she was at the garage that was just pointed out to me. Tony Rohman was absent from the exchange. Ever the gentleman, Rohman sent his girlfriend to handle the potentially hostile situation. I retrieved my hardware, desk, and shelving with the help of Tony's cousin. The cousin politely explained he had a "past",

---

[184] When I showed those same texts to Delaware County Prosecutor Nic Lelecas, Nic agreed the texts showed the crime of embezzlement.

got out of that lifestyle and wanted me to understand that he had *no* part in any of Tony's prior dealings with me. When I got home, I learned that the desk was not made for me, in fact it wasn't a desk. It was an L shaped cabinet, and the two pieces were so long that neither fit into the addition. They were just some (probably stolen) furniture Tony Rohman had stashed in the garage prior to ever meeting me. His routine of taking measurements in my house, but not writing them down, was just an act.

Once again, I had to resolve a criminal problem my-self. The exchange of my stolen property went well; but I hate to imagine what might have happened had Tony the courage to show up and try to stiff me again. It is almost as though the law enforcement administration in our area prefers criminal conflict over peace in our community.

Remember earlier, when I texted my assumption to Rohman that he was a drug addict and how it offended him? Well, at that time, Rohman had already been charged with a meth felony. On July 31, 2016, Grove police officers caught Tony Rohman driving around Grove with meth, drug para-phernalia, without insurance and taxes owed the State. Al-ways the gentleman, Tony had his girlfriend hide his meth in the underwear she was wearing.

Here is the chronology of Tony's expedited handling by the DA:

16 December 2016 – Arrest Warrant issued for Failure to Appear at court

2017:

31 March: Another warrant for Rohman's arrest was issued for Failure to Appear.

28 April: Rohman pleads guilty to counts 3 and 4

26 October: Rohman released from jail

27 October: Rohman FTA

17 October: Failure to pay court fees; arrest warrant issued

2018:

19 September: Rohman Fails To Appear; bond forfeited

28 November: Rohman sends a 'kite' (request) to be released on his own recognizance

14 December: Lelecas motions to accelerate Rohman's sentence, Rohman pleads guilty on 2 misdemeanor counts, and he is released from jail.

On 5 February 2018, Rohman's sister[xli] sold meth to an undercover State narcotics officer in a Grove Dollar Store parking lot. She jumped bail and is currently wanted by authorities.

Rohman's father, Timothy Rohman, is currently in prison for Domestic Assault By Strangulation, 2 counts of Burglary and Carrying Weapon/Drugs/Alcohol Into

Jail. Timothy's father brought the Rohmans to Grove from Kansas City in 1990. [185]

The most basic duty of an honorable man is to protect his woman. But Tony Rohman's first instinct upon getting arrested is to have his baby mama put his dope in her underwear because he would rather her go to prison than him. This is exactly the kind of man who gets protected by snitch immunity; a guy who will get others in trouble so he can get a reduced sentence.
We don't know what made Tony Rohman decide to plead guilty to two of his charges more than two years after his arrest, but we do know Rohman is a meth addict and that he was set free into our community the same day he plead guilty. His meth felony charge is ongoing as of the date of this publication.

---

[185] The Rohman family's criminal records, and complete text messages for the above conversations are at:
www.13thjudicialdistrictok.us/tonyrohman.htm and
www.RapeOfDelco.com/tonyrohman.htm

"Peeping Tom" Spradling
and Delaware County's Dirty Little Secret

Gabriela Chavez
May 31

If anyone was in Wal-Mart around 5pm and went to try clothes on . I want you to be aware of this pervert! A man named Thomas Spradling was sticking his phone under the dressing room crack recording! I personally confronted him and saw the video of my friend !!! Cops were called and he was taken to jail! Smh! Sad world!!

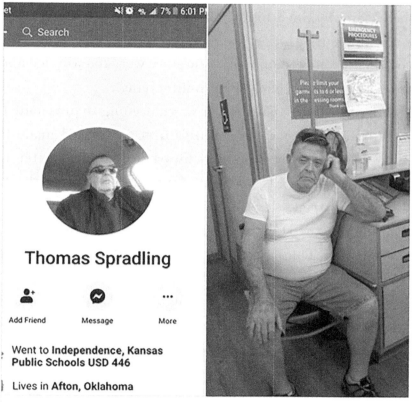

Victoria Lynn Slifer, Charlynn Savage and 124 others   168 Comments

Another outsider blesses our community.
Kansan "Peeping" Tom Spradling gets caught taking
pictures of a woman undressing.

KANSAN "PEEPING" TOM SPRADLING, a Delaware County resident, was caught taking pictures of a woman changing clothes in a Walmart dressing room on 31 May 2019. Spradling's victim was trying on different bathing suits when she noticed a hand holding a cell phone reach under the dressing room partition wall. Gabriela Chavez, the victim's *female* friend snatched the phone out of Spradling's hand and detained him until store security arrived. Chavez and the security officer executed a citizen's arrest. I can only assume the male shoppers in the store were too worried about getting arrested themselves to intervene.

After learning that the DA was not going to prosecute the case "because it was Spradling's first offense", I made this the focus of my community awareness efforts. After two weeks of phone calls, social media posts, posting to the 13th Judicial District sex offender registry and making a lot of phone calls, the DA filed charges against Spradley.

"Peeping Tom" Spradling was convicted on 29 October 2019 of <u>21 OK Stat § 21-1171</u> (c), "Peeping Tom – Use of photographic, electronic or video equipment", given a deferred 1-year sentence (probation) with a fine and "victim compensation assessment" fee totaling $300 (payable at $40.00 a

month). Prosecutor Nic Lelecas was present for the State.

Peeping Tom is a serious crime based on sexual deviancy. If Spradling had been caught peeping on Mrs. Kenny Wright, he would have been sentenced to $5000 and a year in jail, the maximum penalty under the statute.

To the Delaware County DA's office, it is much more important who a criminal is than what he is accused of doing. "Peeping" Tom Spradling's victim lives in Craig County and her friend who snatched the phone out of Spradling's hand is from the Oklahoma panhandle. These victims are outsiders. There is no political gain for protecting them.

Spradling, on the other hand, was married to a prominent local businesswoman for several decades in Delaware County. Spradling's wife was well known and respected in the community. There was a political risk in alienating her friends.

Almost two years after Spradling's conviction, he still isn't listed on the Delaware County Sheriff's sexual offender online registry.

Bottom line: If I hadn't made it a community awareness issue through social media, Spradling wouldn't have been prosecuted.

Sexual deviancy is a problem with the Spradlings. "Peeping Tom" Spradling's son, William (a former Grove city employee), [186] and William's son, "William jr" [187] are registered as 1st degree Child Molesters in Missouri. Peeping Tom's nephew, Jimmie Spradling, is registered as a sex offender in Kansas. [188]

---

[186] "Missouri State Sex Offender Registry," Sex Offender Details for William Joseph Spradling Sr" (Missouri State Highway Patrol, April 01, 2016),

https://www.courts.mo.gov/casenet/cases/header.do   Convicted 10 Jan 2008, Conway, Missouri, Case 17AO-CR00761-01

[187] "Missouri State Sex Offender Registry," Sex Offender Details for William Joseph Spradling" (Missouri State Highway Patrol,   September   10,   2008), http://www.mshp.dps.missouri.gov/CJ38/OffenderDetails?page=0&column=name&id=67014044 Convicted 10 Sep 2008, Conway, Missouri, Case 07LA-CR01061-01

[188] "Sex Offender Details for Jimmie Ray Spradling," Oklahoma Sex & Violent Offender Registry (The Oklahoma Department of Corrections , October 30, 2017),

https://sors.doc.state.ok.us/svor/f?p=119:216:::NO:RP,216:O, P216_REG_ID:040A4843A913608985741F8E50AA9C2A,1&fb clid=IwAR2HSJQ9zzaWjJLfw9i1kKcM-guDrCDRgenBjtgsvQqTNxV2Mi9o-kxDQRtk) Convicted 9 July 2004 for Lewd or Indecent Acts/Proposals to a Child, Wilson County, Kansas, Case 2003-263

Edwin Hardee Turlington
💬 Conversation Starter · June 2 at 1:12 PM

William Patton Spradling born 28 August 1964, last address 26007 FAISON LN JOPLIN, MO was convicted in Missouri in 2017 for Child Molestation. Case Number 17AO-CR00761-01

 Wanda Jackson, Geneva Brogdon and 9 others   75 Comments

 Janet Bruckner I know if my dad had ever molested me or my kids I'd want him in prison then Hell. And I wouldnt be sticking up for him. Child molestation is the lowest of the low. I worked with a man who's great granddaughter age 18 months old was raped by her moth... See More

 6

Like · Reply · 4d

 ████████ I'll just Add this I'm a Victim of Child Molestation for 6 Years from Ages 5 to 11 by a Family Member, I would Never become a Molester, I Call Them Soul Stealers, I'm 39 Years Old and I'll Never Forget What that Man Did to Me. Child Molesters are Lowest of Low, Some Things Happened with My Son's and the Women Conducting the Investigation Was taking up for The Predator Saying We Don't Know What Happened in His Childhood, I said Ma'am, It's More than a Sickness Your Looking at a Victim of Molestation I

At first glance it may seem there isn't much in common between Dick's theft and meth background, Tony Rohman's fraud and meth background, and sex offender "Peeping" Tom Spradling's public perversion. But the similarity in each case is: there is obviously a crime committed and there is really nothing left for police to solve in that crime (just show up and make an arrest). Yet local law enforcement seems to take no interest pursuing these cases.

One other similarity in these cases is that each case involved a single bad actor, so there was little- to- no snitch benefit to local law enforcement.

Epilogue

Turlington speaking on police and prosecutorial misconduct, Oklahoma State Capitol Rotunda, Oklahoma City, Oklahoma 14 March 2019

In my case, the bottom line is the Delaware County Sheriff's Office never had the Probable Cause they needed to make an arrest. Gayle Wells was summoned *at home* to take over the investigation from the honest and experienced detectives at the scene. Wells then manufactured the Probable Cause he needed to make an arrest by altering witness testimony, withholding exculpatory evidence, and feeding optimal answers to Philpott, the felon with active arrest warrants. Sheriff Harlan Moore ran the disinformation campaign to the public through misleading statements and outright lies to newspaper journalists.

The word of a resident should always be taken over the word of a trespassing felon unless evidence shows otherwise. What should have been a simple case of a crazed drug addict with a nearly 40 year long string of felonies being shot in self-defense by a family man military retiree, turned into a perverted circus.

Philpott was unable to name whose land he claimed he was on the night he assaulted me. **To this day, the Prosecution has yet to produce a witness to testify Philpott was on their land, much less produce a witness to testify that Philpott had permission to be on their land.** Philpott was a triple felon with active warrants for his arrest the night he assaulted me in 2014 and as of this writing (25 December 2019), Philpott is a quadruple felon, with new warrants for his arrest. Those warrants stem from an incident in which he physically assaulted EMTs and threatened to murder a police officer. He is a wanted fugitive as of the date of publication of this book.

Sheriff Harlan Moore has decided to not run for a third term, either as a republican or a democrat. However, he has thrown his support behind Tracy Shaw who moved to Delaware County from the city in the 90s.

> Today, we are committed to the concept of Community Policing therefor, we are no longer the sole guardians of law and order. All members of our community become active allies in the efforts to enhance the safety and qualify of life we enjoy here in Delaware County.
> I am proud to be your Sheriff and am equally proud of the successes we have had through the last couple of years. It is only because of the cooperative effort of all of you who call Delaware County home.
>
> Harlan M. Moore, Sheriff
> *From Delaware County Sheriff's Office Facebook page*

Obviously, by referring to "Community Policing" by "active allies", Harlan Moore isn't referring to the right of Delaware County citizens to make arrests and stop crime. Moore is referring to neighbors snitching on each other.

Of course, in Harlan Moore's way of thinking, anyone can call Delaware County "home". But for most of us, we don't have to *call* Delaware County our home, because it *is* our home. Only move-in politicians like Moore, "Country Kenny" Wright, [189] Nic Lelecas, Gayle Wells, and Winston "Back Door" Connor, show up and feel the need to start

---

[189] See page xvi above

claiming they are from here. For honest people, your hometown is where you're from.

Gayle Wells has plagued our community for over thirty years. According to the Vietnam Veterans at the American Legion hall in Jay, Gayle Wells dodged the draft and hates veterans because of a cowardly jealousy. Gayle Wells is not merely indifferent towards veterans, he is hostile toward them. In addition to everything he did to frame his case against me, remember that when Wells was Chief of Police at Grove, he sexually harassed a subordinate. *The harassment was so bad that Wells was demoted from Chief of Police to patrol officer.* This is public knowledge. Imagine the innocent people Wells has put in prison, the citizens he has sexually harassed, and the lives of his victims' families he has ruined.

In our faces: "Harder, Faster, Longer & MORE", Gayle
Wells' life motto. This is what Wells puts on social media for
women and children to read. This was **after** Wells was demoted from Police Chief to Patrol officer for sexual harassment.

Darrell Philpott had active arrest warrants that were almost 5 years old when he assaulted me. Because Wells protected his snitch instead of enforcing the law, these warrants
would be over seven years old by the time Arkansas authorities caught him. In the time since Delaware County Sheriff
Harlan Moore ordered my arrest, Philpott has been convicted
of another felony, two more DWIs, and jumped bail from a
2018 arrest. Philpott has spent 9 of the last 10 years hiding

as a fugitive from the law (or being protected by Delaware County law enforcement).[xlii] The entire case against me is based on the credibility of this man.

I don't need to repeat his remarkable criminal history here, but any rational person would consider him a menace to society. This is why countless locals including two uniformed law enforcement officers told me my biggest mistake was not shooting him in his head. A relative of Philpott's told me that Philpott is now dying from kidney failure and is determined to not die in jail. That same relative said that Philpott stated he would not be taken alive.

4 October 2016: Bentonville County, Arkansas Deputy Justin Crane has no problem 'getting ahold' of Darrell Philpott. Crane found Philpott parked in the middle of the road, with his foot on the brake pedal and the engine running, passed out drunk. Crane's arrest resulted in Philpott's fourth felony conviction and another DWI conviction. Video of Crane's arrest at RapeOf-Delco.com/rap.mp4

Winston "Crime Pays Me" Connor, the former Delaware County Assistant District Attorney still retains his license to practice law, despite currently awaiting trial on ten felonies (including Solicitation of Murder, Solicitation of a Prostitute, and Pandering), and having two attorneys accuse him in court of soliciting the murder of one man and threatening the murder of another (with the solicitation recorded on a wiretap). [190]

East coast liberal and former Delaware County Assistant DA Winston Connor making the news

However, Mr. "Crime Pays Me" is finally getting his just rewards. His wife has divorced him, and his reputation is ruined. His empire of death threats, hookers, drug dealer

---

[190] Available at www.RapeOfDelco.com/wiretap.mp3

immunity, backstabbing his own clients and *exploiting poor people* is crumbling around him.

Nic Lelecas: I warned Nic that if he proceeded with a baseless prosecution against a disabled veteran, from a local family, despite being shown the exculpatory evidence that Sheriff Moore and Deputy Wells withheld, that it would ruin Nic politically here. I told Nic would write a book so that Delaware and Ottawa County citizens could see the exculpatory evidence that he saw, as well as his courtroom lies, and how he and the DA and Sheriff's office deceived the public. Nic, like the other Delaware County officials, thought he was above reproach. So, when Nic runs for office someday, go to chapter 7 and read how he allowed a violent multiple felon, with active warrants for his arrest, to commit perjury against a local patriot and family man. Read how Nic entered a falsehood before the court multiple times and then lied to the Oklahoma Bar Association.

Nic was given records of every arrest, every conviction, every failure to appear, and every protective order and sworn statement that is in this book, *and more*. The only reason that Nic doesn't want his witness impeached is that **the entire foundation of snitch immunity is the testimony of criminals.** If we admit that the testimony of impeached criminal witnesses lacks credibility, then his entire house of cards comes down.

Of course, the public can bring down this house of cards in the next election. It is important to know who is running.

Harlan Moore's handpicked establishment candidate is Tracy Shaw. Shaw is not from here. Moore imported him. Matt North, a former Delaware County deputy has also announced his candidacy. He says that Gayle Wells is the cop that he wanted to be. Several have announced their candidacy, and others have told me their intention to run. The important thing is that we need to pick someone whose character we know and trust. We need a change in leadership in local law enforcement.

In conclusion, always remember Oklahoma law authorizes the following:

1. Citizen's arrest
2. Stand your ground
3. Open carry of firearms for law abiding citizens without a permit
4. Concealed carry of firearms without a permit
5. Castle Doctrine for Homeowners

The problem never was the law. The problem was, and is, out of state opportunists moving in to our community and importing their foreign values into our law enforcement. Oklahoma authorizes Citizen's Arrest, but Nic Lelecas doesn't like it. Oklahoma authorizes self-defense shooting, but Sheriff Harlan Moore doesn't like it. Oklahomans have always been welcoming and hospitable as part of our Southern culture. We just have to ensure that the move-ins adopt our culture and not the other way around.

Conclusion

I wrote this book to clear my name. Most people simply haven't experienced an arrest, so they don't really understand what is happening. When a person is arrested, he experiences two things off the bat: stress and humiliation. Of course, there are career criminals with no conscience and no shame (like the one I shot), but for most ordinary people, the experience is defined by stress and humiliation.

The immediate stress is from the danger of your surroundings. One of my cellmates was a schizophrenic murderer[xliii], and the other cellmate was a flamboyant homosexual who lived on the floor under the murderer's bunk. Beyond the typical jailhouse stress, is the uncertainty of the future, and thinking about how a prison sentence would impact your family. For me, that meant the ability to be a father and husband, worrying about how it will affect my pregnant wife, and my sons (aged 2 ½ and 5 at the time), and later, their little sister and a new brother. For me, knowing what I would and wouldn't do to survive in prison, there was also the serious possibility that I would never see them again. Then I wondered if my elderly parents would even be alive after a potential 10 year sentence. This stress is almost unbearable for any man, even the guilty ones. Not being able to fall asleep until the early hours of the morning, then once asleep, jolting awake from nightmares that your children grew to adults without you, and having to run and check on them while they sleep becomes normal. Hair turning white and huge dark bags under the eyes become normal. If this happens to you, be prepared to spend your life savings on an attorney. Be prepared to become unemployable as your name is trashed in the newspaper. In my case, living in a remote area infested with drug addicts and dealers, I had to think about the accomplices of the man I shot knowing where I live, and what could happen to my family when I am not home. These are the types of things that cause an almost insurmountable amount of stress for someone who actually committed the crime. I didn't, so I had even more on my mind.

Once in jail and learning that the drug dealer I shot is a protected informant, made me start to wonder if I was even going to get a fair investigation. Being a former law enforcement officer, I understood what a simple case mine should have been: a disabled veteran catches a violent felon with active arrest warrants trespassing on his family's land and arrests the violent felon; the felon attacks the veteran, so the veteran shoots the trespasser in self-defense. That should have been the end of it. But sitting in jail, knowing it is taking days[xliv] to write a simple PC Affidavit, and assuming they were manufacturing a case against me, caused more stress. A lot more, because then I knew the problem wasn't me vs. a trespassing drug dealer; the problem was me vs. the local Sheriff and the almost unlimited power of government.

Obtaining proof that the lead investigator withheld evidence and altered evidence throughout his biased investigation, and that the drug dealer I shot is a triple felon and had warrants for his arrest the night I shot him, was the first sense of relief since the arrest. But then, after having been handed a slam dunk case, my attorney presented none of this evidence to the court. Then that same attorney was charged with ten felonies and was discovered to have ties to the leader of a local drug ring. Then, the prosecutor knowingly entered false information three times in the court record. At this point, the weight of the world was on my shoulders, because it was me vs. the entire legal system, and the system was corrupt. It starts to feel like no matter what you prove, it just doesn't matter. It feels like you can't possibly "win". Of course, having your life ruined for 5 years before charges are finally dropped can hardly be considered winning.

But just because my attorney wouldn't show the Court the exculpatory evidence, it didn't mean that I couldn't. After waiving my right to an attorney and approaching the prosecutor in multiple face-to-face meetings with the evidence, I was met with what appeared to be a lack of concern, and an unwillingness to even consider the witness perjury that had been entered into the court record.

Then there is the humiliation. In a small town, people know everyone, and they tend to talk about everyone. In Afton, where I went to school, every high school senior knew every kindergartener and their parents. My mother went to the same school in the 50s and 60s, and it was the same then. Also, I am a junior named after my father. Upon meeting Walt Jennings, a Grove banker, and disabled Marine at the Grove DAV chapter (where I am a life member), he exclaimed, "Your father was a legend!" Over a 30 year period my father was either high school principal or superintendent in 4 towns in our judicial district. Only one of those towns (Grove) has a population of over a thousand. So, when any of my father's scores of former students, teachers, or peers, in the area hear my name on tv or read it in the papers, they know who I am regardless of if they ever met me. Remember, I left this area in the 80s to join the Army.

When I came home, it should have been a good homecoming, where everyone knew me or my family. But, within a week of returning, the first thing most people had heard of me was that I had shot someone over a property dispute (which of course wasn't true) and I was charged with felony "shooting with intent to kill".

The local TV channels and newspapers ran my mugshot. When the court scheduled my disposition docket almost two years later, the local newspapers actually ran my mugshot *again*, reminding its readers that I "... was charged in 2014 with assault and battery with a dangerous weapon". The frustrating thing was that the same media sources had also run a story titled "Turlington Honored",[191] about me receiving national recognition as a Noncommissioned Officer in the Army Reserves. The newspaper could have run that photo of me, in uniform, with my family at Washington DC, but

---

[191] "Turlington Honored." 2011. The Miami News-Record. The Miami News-Record. June 5, 2011.
https://www.miamiok.com/news/article_c8a69398-a42f-569e-9874-120a95033cbb.html.

instead they ran the mugshot provided by the Sheriff that made me look like a criminal.

So, that was the image my community had of me. My two oldest sons were attending cub scout meetings, my wife was teaching in a local school,[192] my elderly mother was attending church in the same town, and everyone they came into contact with was seeing my mugshot in the news, just like the Sheriff wanted. At the time of this writing, my firstborn son Hardee, who is 10, has spent over half his life wondering if he would have to grow up without his father. You really can't appreciate what this does to you, your wife, children, and elderly parents, unless it has happened to you. I pray it never does. It shouldn't have happened to me.

---

[192] The school custodian brought Julie the *second* newspaper article that ran my mugshot.

Before and after five years of looking at a life sentence in prison

Hardee, 10 and Hoss, 8 on White Water Creek bank,
2019

Appendix A

Philpott's June 1981 Theft and Robbery Felonies

IN THE CIRCUIT COURT OF BENTON COUNTY, ARKANSAS

STATE OF ARKANSAS   PLAINTIFF

    VS.   NO. CR-81-60

DARRELL EUGENE PHILPOTT   DEFENDANT S
and TROY DILL

ORDER OF PROBATION

NOW on this 8th day of June , 19 81 , appeared the State of Arkansas by David Clinger, Prosecuting Attorney, and the Defendant s , Darrell Eugene Philpott and Troy Dill in person and by their attorney s , Don Huffman and Paul L. Davidson Defendant s , Darrell Fugene Philpott and Trov Dill XXXXXXXXXXXXXXXXXXXXXXXX/changed their plea of not guilty to guilty to the charge of Burglary - Class B Felony and Theft of Property - Class C Felony,

and announced ready for sentencing. The Court determined that Defendant s' plea XXX/were voluntary and that there is a factual basis for the plea.

WHEREUPON the Court noted the Defendants' plea and placed Defendants on probation for 3 years, conditioned as follows:

    1. Defendant s shall not commit an offense punishable by imprisonment.

    2. Defendant s shall work faithfully at suitable employment.

    3. Defendant s shall have no firearms in their possession at any time.

    4. Defendant s shall comply with all other conditions specified in their written probation agreement.

CIRCUIT JUDGE

ENTERED: June 8/ 1981

Appendix B

Philpott's November 1981 Drug Dealing Felony

IN THE CIRCUIT COURT OF BENTON COUNTY, ARKANSAS

STATE OF ARKANSAS   PLAINTIFF

VS.   NO. CR-81-257

DARRELL E. PHILPOTT   DEFENDANT

JUDGMENT AND COMMITMENT

NOW on this 23rd day of September, 1981, appeared the State of Arkansas by David Clinger, Prosecuting Attorney, and the Defendant, Darrell E. Philpott, in person and by his attorney, Stephen P. Sawyer. Defendant, Darrell E. Philpott, changed his plea of not guilty to nolo contendere to the charge of Possession of Controlled Substance W/Intent to Deliver, and announced ready for sentencing. The Court determined that Defendant's plea was voluntary.

Defendant comes on now on this 30th day of October, 1981, ready for sentencing.

IT IS, THEREFORE, CONSIDERED, ORDERED AND ADJUDGED BY THE COURT that the Defendant, Darrell E. Philpott, is guilty as charged, and that he be and hereby is sentenced to confinement with the State Department of Correction for five years, four years of which are suspended on the following conditions, pursuant to Act 378 of 1975:

1. Defendant shall not commit an offense punishable by imprisonment.

2. Defendant shall work faithfully at suitable employment.

3. Defendant shall have no firearms in his possession at any time.

4. Defendant shall comply with all other conditions specified in his written suspended sentence contract.

IT IS FURTHER ORDERED AND ADJUDGED that the Defendant, Darrell E. Philpott, be continued on his present bond until eight a.m. on Friday, 6 November 1981, at which time he shall surrender to the Sheriff of Benton County, Arkansas, to be by him safely and speedily delivered to the Department of Correction for imprisonment during said term, and that the State of Arkansas have and recover from said Defendant all its costs of this prosecution and have execution therefor.

IT IS FURTHER ORDERED that the Clerk of this Court deliver a certified copy of this Judgment and Commitment to said Sheriff to be by him delivered to the authorized representative of the Department of Correction as authority to receive and confine the Defendant at the State penitentiary.

F I L E D
At 10 35 O'Clock ___ M.

NOV 4 1981

CIRCUIT JUDGE

ENTERED: Nov 3, 1981.

Appendix C
Philpott's 2017 Meth Felony Conviction

SENTENCING ORDER

ELECTRONICALLY FILED
Benton County Circuit Court
Brenda DeShields, Circuit Clerk
2017-Jun-20 14:19:17
04CR-16-1813
C19WD02 : 5 Pages

IN THE CIRCUIT COURT OF __BENTON__ COUNTY, ARKANSAS,
__19th__ JUDICIAL DISTRICT __II__ DIVISION

On __June 7, 2017__ the Defendant appeared before the Court, was advised of the nature of the charge(s), of Constitutional and legal rights, of the effect of a guilty plea upon those rights, and of the right to make a statement before sentencing.

Offender / Court Info

Defendant [Last, First, MI]	Philpott, Darrell Eugene		DOB ▓▓▓▓	Sex Male	Total Number of Counts 3
SID #	AR515899	Race & Ethnicity	White		

Supervision Status at Time of Offense

Judge Brad Karren   File Stamp

Prosecuting Attorney/Deputy Carly Marshall

Defendant's Attorney Public Defender- Jay Saxton ☐ Private ☒ Public Defender ☐ Pro Se ☐ Appointed

Change of Venue ☐ Yes ☒ No
If yes, from:

Legal Statement

☐ Pursuant to A.C.A. ☐ §§16-93-301 et seq. or ☐ §§_____ this Court, without making a finding of guilt or entering a judgment of guilt and with the consent of the Defendant defers further proceedings and places the Defendant on probation.

There being no legal cause shown by the Defendant, as requested, why judgment should not be pronounced, a judgment:

☒ is hereby entered against the Defendant on each charge enumerated, fines levied, and court costs assessed. Defendant was advised of the conditions of the sentence and/or placement on probation and understands the consequences of violating those conditions. The Court retains jurisdiction during the period of probation/suspension and may change or set aside the conditions of probation/suspension for violations or failure to satisfy Department of Community Correction (D.C.C) rules and regulations.

☐ of conviction is hereby entered against the Defendant on each charge enumerated, fines levied, and court costs assessed. The Defendant is sentenced to the Arkansas Department of Correction (A.D.C.) for the term specified on each offense shown below.

Defendant made a voluntary, knowing, and intelligent waiver of the right to counsel. ☐ Yes ☒ No

Offense #1

A.C.A. # of Offense+ / Name of Offense+	5-64-419(a)(b)(1)(A) ~ POSSESSION OF A CONTROLLED SUBSTANCE			Case # 2016-1813-2
A.C.A. # of Original Charged Offense	5-64-419(a)(b)(1)(A)	ATN BTN0065 7982 1	Offense was ☐ Nolle Prossed ☐ Dismissed ☐ Acquitted	
		Appeal from District Court ☐ Yes ☒ No	Probation/SIS Revocation+ ☐ Yes ☒ No	

Offense Date 10/04/2016	Offense is ☒ Felony ☐ Misd. ☐ Viol.	Offense Classification ☐ Y ☐ A ☐ B ☐ C ☒ D ☐ U

Number of Counts: 1	Criminal History Score 0	Seriousness Level 3	Defendant ☐ Attempted ☐ Solicited ☐ Conspired to commit the offense

Presumptive Sentence ☐ Prison Sentence of _____ months ☒ Community Corrections Center ☒ Alternative Sanction

Defendant Sentence* (see Page 2) Imposed ☐ ADC ☐ Jud.Tran. ☐ County Jail	if probation or SIS accompanied by period of confinement, state time: __70__ days or ___ months
_____ Months	Sentence was enhanced _____ months, pursuant to A.C.A. §§_____
Probation 60 Months	Enhancement to run: ☐ Concurrent ☐ Consecutive
SIS _____ Months	Defendnat was sentenced as a habitual offender, pursuant to A.C.A. §5-4-501, Subsection
Other ☐ Life ☐ LWOP ☐ Death	☐ (a) ☐ (b) ☐ (c) ☐ (D)

Victim Info* (see page 2) ☒ N/A [Multiple Victims ☐ Yes ☐ No]	Age	Sex ___ Male ___ Female	Race & Ethnicity ☐ White ☐ Black ☐ Asian ☐ Native American ☐ Pacific Islander ☐ Other ☐ Unknown ☐ Hispanic

Defendant voluntarily, intelligently, and knowingly entered a	Defendant:
☒ Negotiated plea of ☒ guilty or ☐ nolo contendere.	☐ Was sentenced pursuant to ☐ §§16-93-301 et seq., or ☐ other §§_____
☐ Plea directly to the court of ☐ guilty or ☐ nolo contendere	☐ Entered a plea and was sentenced by jury.
	☐ Was found guilty by the court & sentenced by ☐ court ☐ jury.
	☐ Was found guilty at a jury trial & sentenced by ☐ court ☐ jury.
	☐ Was found guilty of a lesser included offense by ☐ court ☐ jury.

Sentence is a Departure ☐ Yes ☒ No	Sentence Departure is ☐ Durational or ☐ Dispositional. If durational, state how many months above/below the presumptive sentence:

Departure Reason (See page 2 for a list of reasons)	Sentence will run ☐ Consecutive ☒ Concurrent
Aggravating # _____ or Mitigating # _____ . For Agg.#16 or Mit. #10.	To offense # 2, 3
Or if departing from guidelines, please explain:_____	Case # _____

Appendix D
Philpott's Active Arrest Warrants
When He Assaulted Turlington
Philpott's June 2009 Missouri Arrest for Poaching

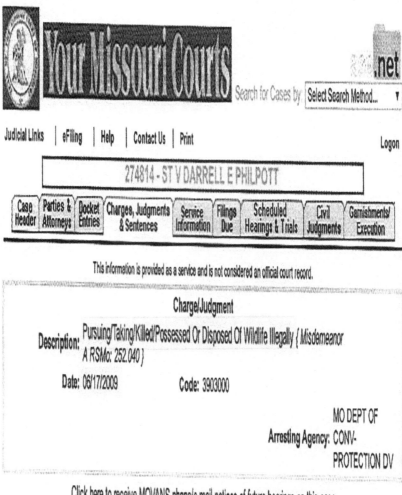

Your Missouri Courts

Search for Cases by: Select Search Method... ▼

Judicial Links | eFiling | Help | Contact Us | Print

Logon

274814 - ST V DARRELL E PHILPOTT

Case Header | Parties & Attorneys | Docket Entries | Charges, Judgments & Sentences | Service Information | Filings Due | Scheduled Hearings & Trials | Civil Judgments | Garnishments/ Execution

This information is provided as a service and is not considered an official court record.

Charge/Judgment

Description: Pursuing/Taking/Killed/Possessed Or Disposed Of Wildlife Illegally { Misdemeanor A RSMo: 252.040 }

Date: 06/17/2009   Code: 3903000

Arresting Agency: MO DEPT OF CONV- PROTECTION DV

Click here to receive MOVANS phone/e-mail notices of future hearings on this case

Case.net Version 5.13.12.0   Return to Top of Page   Released 04/04/2016

Appendix D *(Continued)*
Philpott's Active Arrest Warrants
When He Assaulted Turlington
Philpott's October 2009 Missouri Arrest Warrant
For Failing to Appear on Poaching Charge

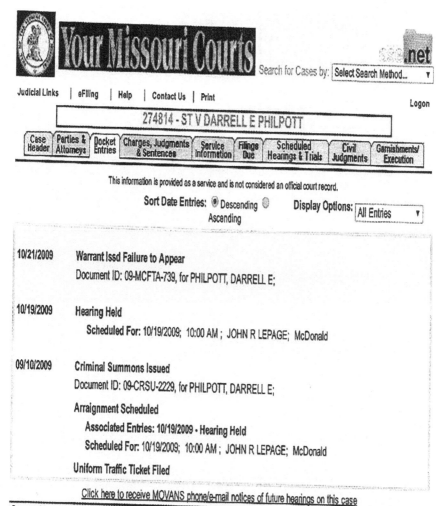

Your Missouri Courts

Search for Cases by: Select Search Method... ▼

Judicial Links | eFiling | Help | Contact Us | Print

Logon

274814 - ST V DARRELL E PHILPOTT

Case Header | Parties & Attorneys | Docket Entries | Charges, Judgments & Sentences | Service Information | Filings Due | Scheduled Hearings & Trials | Civil Judgments | Garnishments/ Execution

This information is provided as a service and is not considered an official court record.

Sort Date Entries: ⦿ Descending ○ Ascending   Display Options: All Entries ▼

10/21/2009	**Warrant Issd Failure to Appear** Document ID: 09-MCFTA-739, for PHILPOTT, DARRELL E;
10/19/2009	**Hearing Held** Scheduled For: 10/19/2009; 10:00 AM ; JOHN R LEPAGE; McDonald
09/10/2009	**Criminal Summons Issued** Document ID: 09-CRSU-2229, for PHILPOTT, DARRELL E; **Arraignment Scheduled** Associated Entries: 10/19/2009 - Hearing Held Scheduled For: 10/19/2009; 10:00 AM ; JOHN R LEPAGE; McDonald **Uniform Traffic Ticket Filed**

Click here to receive MOVANS phone/e-mail notices of future hearings on this case

Case.net Version 5.13.12.0   Return to Top of Page   Released 04/04/2016

Appendix D (*Cont.*)
Philpott's Active Arrest Warrants When He Assaulted
Turlington *Philpott's September 2009 Missouri DWI Arrest*

12/7/2018   Case.net: 09MC-CR01292 - Charge Information

Your Missouri Courts   .net

Search for Cases by: Select Search Method... ▼

Judicial Links | eFiling | Help | Contact Us | Print   Logon

09MC-CR01292 - ST V DARRELL PHILPOTT

| Case Header | Parties & Attorneys | Docket Entries | Charges, Judgments & Sentences | Service Information | Filings Due | Scheduled Hearings & Trials | Civil Judgments | Garnishments/ Execution |

This information is provided as a service and is not considered an official court record.

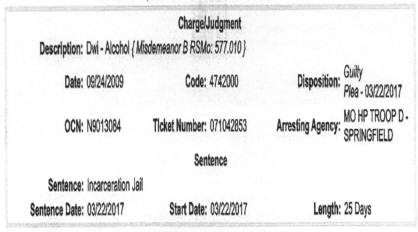

Charge/Judgment

Description: Dwi - Alcohol { *Misdemeanor B RSMo: 577.010* }

Date: 09/24/2009   **Code:** 4742000   **Disposition:** Guilty Plea - 03/22/2017

OCN: N9013084   **Ticket Number:** 071042853   **Arresting Agency:** MO HP TROOP D - SPRINGFIELD

Sentence

Sentence: Incarceration Jail

Sentence Date: 03/22/2017   **Start Date:** 03/22/2017   **Length:** 25 Days

Click here to receive MOVANS phone/e-mail notices of future hearings on this case

Case.net Version 5.13.19.3   Return to Top of Page   Released 11/05/2018

Appendix D (*Cont.*)
Philpott's Active Arrest Warrants When He Assaulted
Turlington *Philpott's September 2009 Missouri Arrest Warrant For Failing to Appear on DWI Charges*

12/7/2018

Case.net: 09MC-CR01292 - Service Information

Judicial Links | eFiling | Help | Contact Us | Print

Logon

09MC-CR01292 - ST V DARRELL PHILPOTT

| Case Header | Parties & Attorneys | Docket Entries | Charges, Judgments & Sentences | Service Information | Filings Due | Scheduled Hearings & Trials | Civil Judgments | Garnishments/ Execution |

This information is provided as a service and is not considered an official court record. Further information may be available in the docket entries portion of Case.net. Because service of process may establish legal obligations, you may want to examine the original case file in the clerk's office.

Displaying 1 thru 1 of 1 service records returned for case **09MC-CR01292**.

Issuance

Issued To: PHILPOTT , DARRELL E

Date Issued: 11/04/2009

Document Issued: Warrant Arrest Failure Appear

Document ID: 09-MCFTA-780

Bond Text: cash only

Bond Amount: $1,500.00

Return

Type Of Service: Warrant Served

Service/Attempt Date: 02/25/2017

Served To: PHILPOTT, DARRELL E

10650 SHADY LN CIR
GRAVETTE , AR 72736

Service Text: ARRESTED BY CO10 TAKEN TO MCSO JAIL

Displaying 1 thru 1 of 1 service records returned for case **09MC-CR01292**.

Click here to receive MOVANS phone/e-mail notices of future hearings on this case

Case.net Version 5.13.19.3

Return to Top of Page

Released 11/05/2018

Appendix E
Philpott's 2017 Conviction on 2009 DWI etc.

Report: CZR0026 v18.0	40TH JUDICIAL CIRCUIT MCDONALD CIRCUIT COURT DOCKET SHEET	Date: 10-Dec-2018 Time: 3:12:13PM Page: 1

09MC-CR01292	ST V DARRELL PHILPOTT	Security Level: 1 Public

Case Type:	AC Misdemeanor	Case Filing Date:	15-Oct-2009
Status:	Defendant Sentenced		
Disposition:	Guilty Plea	Disposition Date:	22-Mar-2017
OCN#:	N9013084		
Arresting Agency:	MOMHPDD00		

		Release/Status Change Date	Reason
Judge	**JOHN R LEPAGE (31362)**		
Defendant	**DARRELL E PHILPOTT (PHIDE0697)**		
REPRESENTED BY: Public Defender	CHARLES G OPPELT (56826)		
Prosecuting Attorney	**BILL DOBBS (49493)**		
Prosecuting Attorney	JANICE LYNNE DURBIN (53604)	31-Dec-2010	No Longer in Office/Position
Prosecuting Attorney	JONATHAN PIERCE (59964)	31-Dec-2014	No Longer in Office/Position

Officer Badge No.:	874

	Charge #	Charge Date	Charge Code	Charge Description
Original Charge:	1	24-Sep-2009	4660800	Operated Vehicle On Hwy Without Valid License - 1st Or 2nd Offense **(Misdemeanor A RSMo: 302.020)**
	Ticket No: 071042855			
Disposition:	22-Mar-2017		Dismissed by Prosec/Nolle Pros	
Original Charge:	2	24-Sep-2009	4737700	Oper A Motor Vehicle In A Careless And Imprudent Manner, Involving An Accident **(Misdemeanor A RSMo: 304.012)**
	Ticket No: 071042854			
Disposition:	22-Mar-2017		Dismissed by Prosec/Nolle Pros	
Original Charge:	3	24-Sep-2009	4742000	Dwi - Alcohol **(Misdemeanor B RSMo: 577.010)**
	Ticket No: 071042853			
Disposition:	22-Mar-2017		Guilty Plea	
Order Date:	22-Mar-2017		Sentence or SIS :	Incarceration Jail
Length :	25 Days		Start Date :	22-Mar-2017
Original Charge:	4	24-Sep-2009	4736700	Driver/Front Seat Passenger Fail To Wear Properly Adjusted/Fastened Safety Belt **(Infraction RSMo: 307.178)**
	Ticket No: 071042853			
Disposition:	22-Mar-2017		Dismissed by Prosec/Nolle Pros	

Filing Date	Description
15-Oct-2009	Information Filed
	Arraignment Scheduled
	Scheduled For: 02-Nov-2009;10:00 AM; JOHN R LEPAGE; Setting: 0; McDonald
02-Nov-2009	Hearing Held
	Scheduled For: 02-Nov-2009;10:00 AM; JOHN R LEPAGE; Setting: 0; McDonald
04-Nov-2009	Warrant Issd Failure to Appear
	Document ID: 09-MCFTA-780, for PHILPOTT, DARRELL E. , Bond Amount: 1,500.00, Bond Text: cash only
	Service/Attempt Date: 25-Feb-2017
28-Feb-2017	Warrant Served

Appendix F
Preliminary Hearing Transcripts, Page 20
Philpott Arms Himself With A Bottle

20

1   A   -- it was --

2   MR. CONNOR: Since we're not using a projector --

3   THE COURT: -- you may approach.

4   A   It was at the trash [indicating].

5   Q   [By Mr. Lelecas] The trash that's in the middle of

6   the photograph?

7   A   Yeah.

8   Q   And where was the defendant when you were walking over

9   towards the trash?

10   A   When I was at the trash, he was standing right over

11   here [indicating].

12   Q   When you say 'standing right over here' --

13   A   -- he was to my left when I was at the trash.

14   Q   Approximately how close was he to you when you were at

15   the trash putting the smoulder out?

16   A   Ten, 12 feet.

17   Q   What did you do when you got to the trash pile that's

18   shown in Exhibit No. 1?

19   A   I tried to put it out.

20   Q   And what did you do --

21   A   -- instead of reaching in there and burning my hand, I

22   seen a beer bottle, so I walked around there and picked it

23   up to see if it had anything in it.

24   Q   Where did you --

25   A   -- to see if it had any water in it, because it had

Appendix F (*Cont.*)
Preliminary Transcripts, Page 21
Philpott Arms Himself With A Bottle

1   been raining.

2   Q   Where did you see the --

3   A   -- at the back side.

4   Q   Let me ask you question before you answer.

5   A   Okay.

6   Q   In State's Exhibit No. 1, can you show me the

7   approximate location of that bottle that you checked for

8   water?

9   A   Back here [indicating].

10   Q   When you say 'back here', you're looking at the far

11   left-hand corner -- lower corner -- of the pallet, is that

12   correct?

13   A   Yeah.

14   Q   Did you check the bottle?

15   A   Yeah.

16   Q   Was there anything in it?

17   A   Nothing.

18   Q   What did you --

19   A   -- I put it back down.

20   Q   What did you do after you checked the bottle and put

21   it back down.

22   A   [Indecipherable]

23   THE REPORTER: Slow down and say that, again.

24   A   I walked back around the trash, to the front of the

25   pallet, raised it up a little bit, and just squeezed the

Appendix G

Probable Cause Affidavit (PC Affidavit)

IN THE DISTRICT COURT OF DELAWARE COUNTY
STATE OF OKLAHOMA
Page 1 of 17

STATE OF OKLAHOMA)
Plaintiff,)
)
vs.)   Case No. 2014-0478B
)
TURLINGTON JR, EDWIN HARDEE)
Defendant.)

PROBABLE CAUSE AFFIDAVIT FOR ARREST WITHOUT WARRANT

Comes now the undersigned Affiant, and states upon Oath or Affirmation that the following information and facts ar correc to the best of the Affiant's knowledge and belief. The undersigned believes that probable cause exists for th detention of the below named ARRESTEE for the below listed crimes committed on the below listed date, in Delaware County , Oklahoma.

Subject Name	TURLINGTON JR, EDWIN HARDEE		
SSN	245983981	**DOB**	10/10/1968
Sex	Male	**Race**	White
Hair	Brown	**Eye**	Brown
Ethnicity	Not Hispanic Origin	**Build**	Muscular
HGT	5 Ft. 11 In.	**WGT**	240 lbs.
Address	910 SUNSET STRIP		
City	MIAMI		
State	Oklahoma 74354		

Date Of Arrest 04/14/2014 **Time Of Arrest** 20:30
Arrest Location NORTH MAIN ST. (DELAWARE COUNTY)
Arrest City JAY
Offense Location .3 mile east of 68296 E. 370 Road, .3 east of 68296 E. 370 Road
Offense City JAY

Offense(s) Committed / Anticipated Charge(s)
1. 21 O.S. § 652(C) • Any assault and battery upon another by means of any deadly weapon, c by such other means as is likely to produce death, or in any manner attempts to kill another, or i resisting the execution of any legal process
2. 21 O.S. § 1289.16 • Points a shotgun, rifle or pistol or any deadly weapon with the intention · discharging the weapon or with malice or for any purpose of injuring.

Facts & Circumstance that support probable cause to arrest the above named person are
On April 14, 2014 at approximately 1947 hours, I, Deputy Chris Hardison with

Appendix G

Probable Cause Affidavit (Cont.)

IN THE DISTRICT COURT OF DELAWARE COUNTY
STATE OF OKLAHOMA
Page 2 of 17

Case No. : 2014-0478B
Defendant : TURLINGTON JR, EDWIN HARDEE

Facts & Circumstance that support probable cause to arrest the above named person are
the Delaware County Sheriff Department was dispatched to 68296 E. 370 Road in
Delaware County, Oklahoma on a disturbance with shots fired. Before my arrival the
suspect, later identified as Edwin Hardee Turlington DOB 10/10/1968 left the area,
westbound, in a black Ford extended cab truck. The alleged victim, later identified as
Darrell Eugene Philpott DOB 02/16/1961 also left prior to my arrival and was allegedly
taken to a hospital in Gravette, Arkansas. Upon arrival at approximately 2037 hours, I
met with James Steven Barrett DOB 11/04/1982. James Barrett stated he and Darrell
Philpot had gone east of the residence to cut some firewood on the south side of the
road. After cutting some wood, they decided to burn some trash they found by the road.

Another neighbor, Joseph Bradley DOB 05/12/1980 was driving westbound past James
Barrett and Darrell Philpot. Joseph Bradley stated he was stopped by a white male later
identified as Edwin Turlington driving a black Ford truck. Edwin Turlington asked if he
was on his property and Joseph Bradley stated "no". Joseph Bradley stated he observed
Edwin Turlington pull up next to James Barrett and Darrell Philpot on the passenger side
of their truck. Joseph Bradley stated approximately 20 minutes later, James Barrett
pulled in and stated Edwin Turlington had just shot Darrell Philpott. Joseph Bradley
stated he gave Darrell Philpot a ride to Jack Thomas' residence.

I asked James Barrett to come with me and show me where this all happened. James
took me approximately 1/4 mile east of 68296 E. 370 Road. James Barrett stated they
were cutting wood and when they were leaving, they decided to burn a pile of trash.
When they decided to leave, A black Ford truck driven by Edwin Turlington cut them off
in the roadway. After both vehicles came to a stop, James Barrett stated Edwin
Turlington pointed a small pistol at his head and questioned them about trespassing.
After things seemed to calm down, James Barrett and Darrell Philpott backed up to put
the fire out. James Barrett stated he stayed in the truck as Darrell Philpott got out of the
passenger side of his truck to walk over to put the fire out. James Barrett stated he was
parked in the roadway facing westbound. Darrell Philpott and Edwin Turlington walked
over to the fire.

James Barrett stated Darrell Philpott began walking fast to the truck as Edwin Turlington
was advancing after him. James Barrett stated as Darrell Philpott reached the passenger
side of his truck that Edwin Turlington shot at him and struck him in the right leg. James
Barnett stated they drove eastbound toward Joseph Bradley's residence and Edwin
Turlington drove westbound.

I located several drops of blood in the middle of the roadway approximately 12' north of
the south edge of the roadway and approximately 9' west of the

Appendix G

Probable Cause Affidavit (Cont.)
IN THE DISTRICT COURT OF DELAWARE COUNTY
STATE OF OKLAHOMA
Page 3 of 17

Case No. : 2014-0478B
Defendant : TURLINGTON JR, EDWIN HARDEE

Facts & Circumstance that support probable cause to arrest the above named person are

tree at the SE of the driveway. I located an empty 380 caliber casing 36' south of the blood drops and approximately 8' west of the tree. After Detective Houston arrived, he collected the evidence. After he processed the scene, he drove to the residence where James Barrett's truck was parked to process the scene there.

Edwin Turlington was located by Jay police. He was detained and transported to the Sheriff Office and waited until he spoke to Detective Frank Miller.

ON MONDAY 04/14/2014 AT 2000 HRS. I, CAPT. M.G. WELLS, WAS ADVISED OF A SHOOTING WHICH HAD JUST OCCURRED NEAR THE OAK CHAPEL COMMUNITY IN THE EAST CENTRAL PORTION OF DELAWARE CONTY. ACCORDING TO INITIAL INFORMATION ONE MAN WAS SHOT. FIELD DEPUTIES WERE ON THE WAY TO THE SCENE.

I MADE CONTACT WITH DET. BRANDON HOUSTON AND REQUESTED HE RESPOND TO A LOCATION ALONG THE COUNTY ROADWAY AT S690 AND E370 AND BEGIN A FOLLOW UP INVESTIGATION.

AT 2038 HRS. DET. HOUSTON CALLED ME AND TOLD ME THE CIRCUMSTANCES SURROUNDING THE SHOOTING WAS "SPREAD OUT." THE VICTIM WAS TAKEN TO THE HOSPITAL AT GRAVETTE, AR. THE WITNESSES WERE BEING LOCATED IN THE AREA AND NEAR SOUTHWEST CITY, MO. AND THE VICTIM LEFT THE SCENE AND WAS JUST LOCATED AND DETAINED AT JAY, OK. HE TOLD ME THERE WERE AT LEAST TWO VEHICLES INVOLVED AS WELL WHICH HAD TO BE PROCESSED.

DET. HOUSTON TOLD ME THERE WAS EVIDENCE TO BE PROCESSED AND RECOVERED AT THE SCENE OF THE SHOOTING.

I LEARNED DET. FRANK MILLER WAS RESPONDING TO ASSIST DET. HOUSTON.

I TOLD DET. HOUSTON I'D GO TO GRAVETTE AND LOCATE THE VICTIM.

I LEFT MY RESIDENCE AND DROVE TO GRAVETTE HOSPITAL. I MADE CONTACT WITH THE EMERGENCY ROOM CHARGE NURSE AND ACTIVATED MY PERSONAL RECORDER.

WITNESS: RENZIL REARDON, R.N. EMERGENCY ROOM, GRAVETTE

Appendix G

Probable Cause Affidavit (Cont.)

IN THE DISTRICT COURT OF DELAWARE COUNTY
STATE OF OKLAHOMA
Page 4 of 17

Case No. : 2014-0478B
Defendant : TURLINGTON JR, EDWIN HARDEE

Facts & Circumstance that support probable cause to arrest the above named person are
ARKANSAS

I INTRODUCED MYSELF AND TOLD NURSE REARDON I NEEDED TO TALK WITH THE SHOOTING VICTIM FROM DELAWARE COUNTY. HE WAS MOST COOPERATIVE AND LEAD ME TO A TREATMENT ROOM.

WITNESS: I ALSO MET THE CERTIFIED NURSE ASSISTANT AND IDENTIFIED HIM AS: LEIF GARRETT.

ON CONTACT WITH A MALE IN THE ER I IDENTIFIED MYSELF. THERE WERE SEVERAL RELATIVES IN THE TREATMENT ROOM. I ASK THEM TO STEP OUTSIDE WHILE I TALKED WITH THE VICTIM BY HIMSELF. THEY ALL COMPLIED.

I ALSO IDENTIFIED A GRAVETTE POLICE OFFICER WHO CAME INTO THE EMERGENCY ROOM TO ASSIST.

WITNESS: PTLM. JACK SANDERS GRAVETTE POLICE DEPT. 479 787 5911

I OBTAINED BIRGRAPHICAL INFORMATION FROM THE MALE IN THE HOSPITAL BED:

VICTIM: DARRELL EUGENE PHILPOTT W/M DOB 02/16/61 SSN 430 29 7908 UNEMPLOYED RES: LIVING WITH COUSIN JACK THOMAS; OAK CHAPEL AREA.

I OBSERVED MR. PHILPOTT TO HAVE HIS RIGHT LEG EXPOSED FROM THE SHEET. THERE WAS AN ACE BANDAGE AROUND HIS THIGH ABOUT MID WAY BETWEEN HIS THIGH AND HIS KNEE.

AS I TALKED WITH MR. PHILPOTT, I ASKED HIM IF HE'D BEEN DRINKING EARLIER IN THE DAY. HE SAID, "YES, BUT ONLY A HALF PINT." I ASK HIM WHAT HE WAS DRINKING AND HE TOLD ME, "1/2 PINT OF WHISKEY." I COULD NOT SMELL ALCOHOLIC BEVERAGE ON OR ABOUT HIS BODY AT THE TIME OF CONTACT. PHILPOTT APPEARED TO BE SOBER.

I TOLD PHILPOTT I WAS INVESTIGATING THE SHOOTING INCIDENT WHICH OCCURRED

Appendix G

Probable Cause Affidavit (Cont.)

IN THE DISTRICT COURT OF DELAWARE COUNTY
STATE OF OKLAHOMA
Page 5 of 17

Case No. : 2014-0478B
Defendant : TURLINGTON JR, EDWIN HARDEE

Facts & Circumstance that support probable cause to arrest the above named person are

EARLIER. HE INDICATED HE UNDERSTOOD. HE WAS COOPERATIVE. I ASKED IF HE KNEW WHO SHOT HIM. HE TOLD ME, "NO, I THINK THE GUY MAY LIVE A COUPLE OF HOUSES EAST."

I ASK HIM TO EXPLAIN WHAT HAPPENED. PHILPOTT TOLD ME HIM AND STEVE BARRETT WERE CUTTING WOOD NEARBY. PHILPOTT TOLD ME HIS COUSIN, JACK THOMAS, SENT H IM AND BARRETT TO GET THE WOOD FOR HIS WOOD STOVE.

I ASKED MR. PHILPOTT WHO OWNED THE PROPERTY WHERE THEY WERE CUTTING WOOD. HE TOLD ME, "WE WERE ON PROPERTY OWNED BY MICHAEL RAINEY'S BUDDY." IN RESPONSE TO MY QUESTIONS, PHILPOTT WAS UNABLE TO HE COULD NAME THE "BUDDY." HE JUST CONFIRMED HIS COUSIN, JACK THOMAS SENT THEM TO THE LOCATION TO GET WOOD.

PHILPOTT TOLD ME THEY STARTED A SMALL FIRE TO BURN DEBRIS. AS THEY WERE LEAVING THE WOOD LOT, STEVE BARRETT WAS DRIVING HIS CHEVROLET PICKUP TRUCK AND PHILPOTT WAS A PASSENGER. HE SAID THERE WAS ABOUT A HALF LOAD OF WOOD IN THE BED.

THEY TURNED WEST ONTO THE COUNTY ROADWAY (E370). PHILPOTT SAID, "A GUY PULLED UP IN A BLACK FORD AND PULLED A GUN ON US."

I ASKED HIM TO BE MORE SPECIFIC ABOUT WHAT HAPPENED. HE SAID, "AT FIRST HE PASSED US AND TURNED IN FRONT OF STEVE, FORCING US TO STOP. THE GUY CAME RUNNING BACK AND POINTED A SMALL HANDGUN RIGHT AT STEVE'S HEAD THROUGH THE WINDOW. HE WAS YELLIN', "YOU'RE TRESPASSIN." "WE TRIED TO TELL HIM WE WEREN'T BUT HE WAS YELLIN' "I AIN'T AFRAID TO PUT A CAP IN YOUR ASS MOTHERFUCKER."

PHILPOTT SAID, " WE HAD A LITTLE TRASH FIRE. THE GUY WAS YELLING FOR US TO PUT IT OUT. HE WAS STILL YELLIN', "I AIN'T AFRAID TO PUT A CAP IN YOUR ASS MOTHERFUCKER WHO WAS TRESPASSIN'." "SO I WALKED ACROSS THE ROAD AND STOMPED IT OUIT."

I ASKED PHILPOTT WHY THE MAN SHOT HIM. HE SAID, "HE SHOT ME FOR TELLING HIM HE WAS A PUNK FOR PULLING A GUN ON US."

I ASKED IF EITHER HIM OR BARRETT HAD A GUN OR ANY WEAPON. HE SAID, "NO."

Appendix G

Probable Cause Affidavit (Cont.)

IN THE DISTRICT COURT OF DELAWARE COUNTY
STATE OF OKLAHOMA

Page 6 of 17

Case No. : 2014-0478B
Defendant : TURLINGTON JR, EDWIN HARDEE

Facts & Circumstance that support probable cause to arrest the above named person are

I ASKED PHILPOTT WHEN HE GOT SHOT. HE TOLD ME HE WAS WALKING BACK TO BARRETTS TRUCK. HE SAID, "I TOLD HIM, HE WAS A PUNK MOTHERFUCKER...IF YOU REALLY WANT TO DO SOMETHING PUT YOUR GUN DOWN." PHILPOTT SAID, "HE THREW A BEER BOTTLE AT ME. I TOLD HIM THAT JUST PROVES YOUR A PUNK MOTHERFUCKER."

PHILPOTT SAID HE WALKED AROUND THE MAN WITH THE GUN WHO WAS STANDING IN THE ROADWAY. HE SAID, "AS I GOT TO STEVE'S TRUCK, I WAS JUST ROUNDING THE FRONT OF THE TRUCK, HE SHOT ME FROM BEHIND, IN THE BACK OF THE LEG."

WHILE TALKING WITH MR. PHILPOTT I ASKED HIM TO SIGN A "RELEASE OF MEDICAL RECORDS FORM." OFFICER SANDERS LEFT THE TREATMENT ROOM AND RETURN SHORTLY WITH THE NECESSARY FORM. MR. PHILPOTT READ THE FORM AND SIGNED IT.

THE HOSPITAL LATER PROVIDED ME WITH A COPY OF HIS MEDICAL RECORDS AND AN XRAY COMPACT DISC. THERE WERE LATER PLACED IN THE CASE FILE.

I TALKED WITH CNA GARRETT. I ASKED HIM IF HE WAS GOING TO RE-DRESS AND WRAP MR. PHILPOTT'S INJURY. HE TOLD ME HE WAS. AS I WATCHED, GARRETT REMOVED THE BANDAGE. I TOOK PHOTOS OF THE EXPOSED INJURY.

THE WOUND APPEARED TO BE A THROUGH AND THROUGH SMALL CALIBER GUNSHOT TO THE RIGHT THIGH FROM BACK TO FRONT.

I ALSO TOLD MR. PHILPOTT I WAS GOING TO PERFORM A GUNSHOT RESIDUE KIT ON HIS HANDS AND FACE TO CHECK TO SEE IF HE'D FIRED A WEAPON RECENTLY. HE SAID, "NOT TODAY ANYWAY," AND AGREED. I FOLLOWED THE DIRECTIONS ON THE GSR KIT; DOING BOTH HANDS IN ORDER AND THEN HIS FACE. I SECURED THE SAMPLES IN THE INDIVIDUAL VILES AND RETURNED THEM TO THE KIT ENVELOPE. THEY WERE SEALED WITH EVIDENCE TAPE.

I ALSO TOLD MR. PHILPOTT I WAS GOING TO DO SWABS OF THE INSIDE OF HIS CHEEKS TO OBTAIN A DNA SAMPLE. HE AGREED. I MADE TWO SWABS OF BOTH CHECKS AND THE INSIDE OF HIS MOUTH. BOTH SWABS WERE PLACED IN SEPARATE PLASTIC BAGS AND LATER SEALED AS EVIDENCE.

I CONCLUDED MY CONTACT WITH MR. PHILPOTT. I OBTAINED HIS MEDICAL RECORDS FROM STAFF AND LEFT THE HOSPITAL.

Appendix G
Probable Cause Affidavit (Cont.)

IN THE DISTRICT COURT OF DELAWARE COUNTY
STATE OF OKLAHOMA
Page 7 of 17

Case No. : 2014-0478B
Defendant : TURLINGTON JR, EDWIN HARDEE

Facts & Circumstance that support probable cause to arrest the above named person are

Det. Brandon Houston; Supplemental Report.

Narrative

1- On Monday, 04/14/2014 at 19:47 hours, Delaware County Deputy Chris Hardison received a radio dispatch to 68296 E. 370 Road; reference to a gun-shot victim. Captain M.G. Wells contacted me by phone. Wells assigned this case to me further investigation.

WITNESS: DEPUTY CHRIS HARDISON, DELAWARE COUNTY SHERIFF DEPARTMENT, JAY, OKLAHOMA.

2- I arrived on scene and spoke with Deputy Hardison. Deputy Hardison told me when he arrived, the victim, Darrell Philpott, had already left the scene in a private vehicle to seek medical attention.

3- Deputy Hardison told me he was directed by witness, Stephen Barrett, to a section of County Road E. 370; where Philpott was reportedly shot. This location is located .5 miles west on County Road E. 370 from the intersection of County Road S. 690.

Appendix G
Probable Cause Affidavit (Cont.)

IN THE DISTRICT COURT OF DELAWARE COUNTY
STATE OF OKLAHOMA
Page 8 of 17

Case No. : 2014-0478B
Defendant : TURLINGTON JR, EDWIN HARDEE

Facts & Circumstance that support probable cause to arrest the above named person are
WITNESS: JAMES "STEVEN" BARRETT, DOB: 11/04/1982, W/M, ADDRESS
S. 655 ROAD, GROVE, OKLAHOMA.

4- Deputy Hardison told me he observed, what appeared to be blood residue or
graveled surface of the roadway; as well as a spent shell casing approximately
south of the blood. The shell casing was described as a .380 cal. Pistol cartridg

5- Deputy Hardison placed evidence markers near the observed shell casing ar
residue prior to my arrival. I observed a marker labeled "1" placed within the mic
County Road E. 370.

6- At this evidence marker, I observed what appeared to be blood residue on th
of the gravel and dirt roadway. I photographed the blood residue.

7- Then using a D.N.A. swab, I collected a sample of the blood residue. The blc
sample residue sample was completed using two swabs. Each swab was place
evidence and attached to this file.

8- Approximately 36 feet south of the observed blood residue observed on the s
County Road E.370, I observed an evidence marker labeled "2". I observed this
placed near a spent .380 cartridge.

9- I observed the cartridge to be labeled "SPEER". The cartridge was photograr
tagged, and then collected into evidence.

10- As I photographed the .380 cartridge, I observed James Steven Barrett spe
with Deputy Hardison. I approached Deputy Hardison and Barrett. I observed B
giving Deputy Hardison a written statement.

11- I spoke with witness, Stephen Barrett. Stephen told me he and Philpott wer
wood along the County Road E. 370; and burning trash. Blood residue and spe
casing were located near the location described.

12- Stephen said, "We were leaving and a guy in a black Ford pickup cut us off.
out and stuck a gun to my head and was trying to take the keys out

Appendix G

Probable Cause Affidavit (Cont.)

IN THE DISTRICT COURT OF DELAWARE COUNTY
STATE OF OKLAHOMA
Page 9 of 17

Case No. : 2014-0478B
Defendant : TURLINGTON JR, EDWIN HARDEE

Facts & Circumstance that support probable cause to arrest the above named person are
of the ignition." Stephen said, "He was pissed off because he thought we were (
land."

13- In a written statement, Stephen wrote: "Philpott and me was cutting firewoo
burning trash. We went to leave and were pulling onto the dirt road. A male in a
truck cut in front of us. He stopped, jumped out and came to the driver side win
put his gun to my head and tried to pull my keys out of the truck and then we st;
back up. He kept following us on foot." "He (Turlington) told Philpott to get out a
the fire out so he (Philpott) walked over and put out the fire. Then he (Philpott) ;
walking back to get in the truck, and that's when the guy shot him in the leg. We
backing down the road. Turlington's vehicle was last seen westbound on the co
towards Jay, Ok."

14- After speaking with Barrett, I returned to processing the crime scene. I did n
observe any further items of evidentiary value. No further items collected. I left t
scene.

15- Deputy Hardison and I followed Barrett to a residence .3 miles west of the c
scene. Barrett pointed to a white Chevrolet pickup and said, "That's my truck. T
truck I brought him to the house in after he was shot." I asked Barrett for consei
process the Chevrolet pickup. Barrett consented in writing.

16- Upon first observation of the Chevrolet pickup, operated by Barrett I, obsen
vehicle not having an Oklahoma tag to the rear of the vehicle. I observed the Ve
Identification Number as the following: 1FTRX14W55FA89169.

17- I opened the driver side door of Barrett's vehicle. I observed, what appearec
blood, on the passenger seat. The blood was soaked into the fabric of the seat,
as along the side and front of the seat. The material along the front and side of
was observed as leather or similar to. I photographed this observation.

18- Using a D.N.A. collection swab, I swabbed the blood and tagged it as evide
used three swabs, one for each sample collected. Each swab was signed, date
timed. Each swab was then tagged as evidence.

19- I did not observe and other items of evidentiary value. Concluding my

Appendix G

Probable Cause Affidavit (Cont.)

IN THE DISTRICT COURT OF DELAWARE COUNTY
STATE OF OKLAHOMA
Page 10 of 17

Case No. : 2014-0478B
Defendant : TURLINGTON JR, EDWIN HARDEE

Facts & Circumstance that support probable cause to arrest the above named person are
search of the vehicle.

20- As I processed the Barrett's vehicle, Detective Frank Miller collected items f
within the residence. Refer to Detective Miller's report for further. 21- After a prc
Barrett's vehicle I left the residence and returned to the Sheriff Department.

22- Upon arrival of the Sheriff Department, I contacted the Delaware County Di:
Center and Spoke with Garry Youngblood.

23- At 20:07 hours, Dispatcher Garry Youngblood received a 911 call. The calle
identified himself as Ed Turlington. Youngblood told me Turlington said, "His mc
a contract on the land where the two men were cutting wood and burning trash.
Youngblood asked Turlington, "Are you the one that did the shooting?" Turlingtc
replied, "Yes."

24- At 20:30 hours, Jay Police Officer Bill Hobbs stopped the suspect vehicle w
city limits of Jay, Oklahoma. He made personal contact with the driver, Edwin T

WITNESS: OFFICER BILL HOBBS, JAY POLICE DEPARTMENT, JAY, OKL/

25- I spoke with Officer Hobbs about his contact with Turlington. Hobbs told me
approached the operator, Edwin Turlington. Officer Hobbs told me he asked Tu
of any weapons in his possession for officer safety.

26- Officer Hobbs told me Turlington said, "I have a gun in the glove box."

27- Turlington was detained and transported to the Delaware County Sheriff De
for further investigation.

28- The vehicle driven by Turlington; a black Ford, 2005, pickup, was towed to t
Delaware County Sheriff Department parking lot; awaiting search by warrant. Tl
vehicle was secured by Deputy James Morgan. Dep. Morgan stayed with the Ti
truck until the search warrant was obtained.

Appendix G

Probable Cause Affidavit (Cont.)

IN THE DISTRICT COURT OF DELAWARE COUNTY
STATE OF OKLAHOMA
Page 11 of 17

Case No. : 2014-0478B
Defendant : TURLINGTON JR, EDWIN HARDEE

Facts & Circumstance that support probable cause to arrest the above named person are
On Tuesday, 04/15/2014 at 01:37 hours, a search warrant was granted by Judg

29- At 02:19 hours, the search warrant was posted and executed on Turlington'

30- During the search of the vehicle I observed a black, semi-auto, Kel Tec, .38
handgun (SERIAL# K8Q61) as I opened the glove box of the vehicle. I photogra
firearm as I observed it. The firearm is consistent with the description given by E

31- I removed the firearm from the glove box. I observed the firearm to be missi
ammunition magazine. The firearm was photographed and tagged as evidence.

32- I observed an ammunition magazine within the center console of the vehicle
magazine contained four live cartridges. I photographed the magazine before re
the live cartridges.

33- I examined the live cartridges. I observed the first three cartridges to be labe
"SPEER". This label is consistent with the spent cartridge recovered from the cr
scene on County Road E. 370. I tagged the four live cartridges and magazine a
evidence.

34- I observed a green case near the gear shift. I opened the green case and ol
black handcuffs within the case. I photographed the case and handcuffs, and th
tagged the pair as evidence.

35- I observed a "Galaxy III" Samsung cell phone. I photographed the cell phon
then collected it as evidence.

36- I concluded my search finding no further items of evidentiary value.

37- I will reflect the items collected from the Turlington vehicle, onto a Search W
Return. I will forward the return to Judge Denny for his review and signature.

Appendix G
Probable Cause Affidavit (Cont.)

IN THE DISTRICT COURT OF DELAWARE COUNTY
STATE OF OKLAHOMA
Page 12 of 17

Case No.   : 2014-0478B
Defendant : TURLINGTON JR, EDWIN HARDEE

Facts & Circumstance that support probable cause to arrest the above named person are

Det. Frank Miller Supplemental Report.

On April 14, 2014, I responded to 68296 E. 370 Rd, Rural Jay, Oklahoma, in De
to assist in the investigation of a shooting.

<u>Suspect: Edwin Hardee Turlington, DOB ██████</u>

<u>Victim: Darrell Eugene Philpott, DOB 2/16/1961</u>

Upon arrival, after obtaining a consent to search from the home owner, I was at
clothing that was allegedly worn by the victim at the time of the shooting.

Near the entry way to the kitchen, was:

#1, blue shirt, soiled;

#2, billfold;

#3, comb;

In the bathroom was:

#4 & #5, Left foot and Right foot matching camouflage boots;

Appendix G

Probable Cause Affidavit (Cont.)

IN THE DISTRICT COURT OF DELAWARE COUNTY
STATE OF OKLAHOMA
Page 13 of 17

Case No. : 2014-0478B
Defendant : TURLINGTON JR, EDWIN HARDEE

Facts & Circumstance that support probable cause to arrest the above named person are
#6, red O.U. shirt, later determined not to be related to the investigation;

#7, underwear soaked with what appeared to be blood;

#8, blue jeans soaked with what appeared to be blood;

#9, pair of socks with what appeared to be blood transfer on them;

#10, rag with what appears to be blood;

#11 & #12, two red spots on the floor later determined not to be related to the investigation.

I photographed the scene and gathered items #1, #2, #3, #4, #5, #7, #8, #9, #10 as evidence.

The blue jeans had a small hole in the front right thigh and the rear right thigh. The hole in the front was approx. 2 1/4 inches lower than the hole in the back.

I later went to the county jail and interviewed the suspect, Ed Turlington. .

Suspect: Edwin Hardee Turlington, DOB 10/10/1968

Victim: Darrell Eugene Philpot, DOB 2/16/1961

On April 14, 2014, at approx. 2305 hrs, at the Delaware County Jail, 327 S. 5th St, Jay, Oklahoma, in Delaware County, I Det. Frank Miller, spoke with Mr. Turlington. I read him his rights under Miranda, and he said that he understood them, and agreed to speak with me. Mr. Turlington signed indicating such.

I utilized a gunshot residue collection kit upon Mr. Turlington, with his

Appendix G

Probable Cause Affidavit (Cont.)

IN THE DISTRICT COURT OF DELAWARE COUNTY
STATE OF OKLAHOMA
Page 14 of 17

Case No. : 2014-0478B
Defendant : TURLINGTON JR, EDWIN HARDEE

Facts & Circumstance that support probable cause to arrest the above named person are
        cooperation.

        Mr. Turlington told me, "My mother just bought 10 acres I'm going to rent from her." He told me that 370 Rd travels through section #8, and his brother just bought that from Vernon Moss. He said that his brother just signed a contract for deed with Mr. Moss, but then said that he hadn't purchased it yet. The property is located 1/2 mile west of the intersection of 370 Rd and 690 Rd. Mr. Turlington said that there is a driveway that goes south off of 370 Rd at that location that travels through his brother's property, to his mother's property, where he is renting a home and 10 acres from his mother. Mr. Turlington has been in the process of moving in. Prior to moving in, he said that someone had stripped and stolen the wiring from the home.

        Mr. Turlington told me that as he drove up to the property owned by his brother, to go to his own property, he saw a fire on his brother's property, and 4 men nearby. Mr. Turlinglington described them as "3 white men and a Mexican". He also saw a white pickup truck and a blue Nissan Sentra. The man described as "a Mexican" was in the blue Nissan Sentra.

        Mr. Turlington said that he confronted the 3 men and told them that they were trespassing, and that they committed arson by starting the fire, and told them they were under arrest, "Citizen's Arrest". The men went over to the area where the fire was burning, and one of them (later determined to be Darrell Philpot) went to stomp out the fire. Mr. Philpot picked up a bottle, so Mr. Turlington showed him that he had a gun, a Kel-Tec .380. Mr. Turlington said that Mr. Philpot then started calling him a "mother fucker". Mr. Turlington told Mr. Philpot to put it down. Mr. Turlington said that he (Mr. Turlington) picked up a bottle because he would rather hit him with a bottle than shoot him. Mr. Philpot kept saying "C'mon mother fucker! C'mon mother fucker!" and then "...He came at me and I threw the bottle at him."

        At that point Mr. Turlington said that there were 2 guys in the truck, and Mr. Philpot was about 3 meters in front of the truck, and that Mr. Turlington was between Mr. Philpot and the truck. He said that he heard the truck door open behind him, and that it was about to be 2 on 1. Mr. Turlington said, "I had already decided I wasn't going to shoot anyone in the head ..." so when the door opened behind him he turned to look back, "... and I heard this guy lunge forward at me and that's when I ... 'pop' ..."

        Mr. Turlington said that when he pulled the trigger he was "probably arm's reach, if not it was very close, an arm and a half reach" away from Mr. Philpot. Mr. Turlington said that he still had the bottle in his hand when he

Appendix G

Probable Cause Affidavit (Cont.)

IN THE DISTRICT COURT OF DELAWARE COUNTY
STATE OF OKLAHOMA
Page 15 of 17

2014-0478B
TURLINGTON JR, EDWIN HARDEE

:umstance that support probable cause to arrest the above named person are
shot him. Mr. Turlington said that "he was coming to me, and I heard someone else
coming up from the back, so ..."

Mr. Turlington said that the only verbal commands he gave Mr. Philpot were that he was
under arrest. He did not giving any other verbal warnings prior to shooting him.

I began to ask Mr. Turlington some follow up questions for clarification. When I asked
Mr. Turlington if he had made it down to the house this evening, he told me "... I don't
want to discuss it a whole lot more without a lawyer ... I came in to make a statement,
and that's my statement." I did not ask any further questions.

I asked if he was willing to give me his statement on paper, and he said that he would. I
provided a pen and paper. A copy of the written statement is attached to this report.

IN REVIEW OF THIS INVESTIGATION; I HAVE EXAMINED THE STATEMENTS OF
THE VICTIM; WITNESSES AND THE SUSPECT. I HAVE REVIEWED DESCRIPTIONS
OF THE SHOOTING FROM ALL INVOLVED AND CHECKED THE EVIDENCE AND
PHOTOS MADE BY INVESTIGATORS.

BASED ON MY REVIEW I DETERMINED EDWIN HARDEE TURLINGTON WAS THE
PRIMARY AGGRESSOR IN THIS INCIDENT. AS RESULT OF HIS ACTIONS I
REQUEST THIS PROBABLE CAUSE AFFIDAVIT BE FORWARDED TO THE
DISTRICT ATTORNEY FOR REVIEW AND FILING OF CHARGES ON
TURLINGTON.AS DESCRIBED ABOVE.

/ Yes ☐   Times (1) ☐ (2) ☐ or _____

declare that the above information is true and correct to the best of my knowledge and belief.
ne   Badge No.

(Signature of Affiant)

Appendix G

Probable Cause Affidavit (Cont.)

IN THE DISTRICT COURT OF DELAWARE COUNTY
STATE OF OKLAHOMA
Page 16 of 17

Case No. : 2014-0478B
Defendant : TURLINGTON JR, EDWIN HARDEE

Subscribed and sworn before me this 4-16-14

My commission number 04000672

My commission expires 1-23-16

_____
Notary Public

☐ Yes   ☑ No   Sheriff's Affidavit Required

☐ Bond Posted   ☐ Appear in Court

BOND POSTED
A probable cause determination is not necessary, the arrestee bonded out of jail on the _____ at

_____

APPEAR IN COURT
The undersigned Judge of this Court having conducted a probable cause determination for the above named person's arrest without warrant by sworn testimony and/or affidavit finds:

☐ This affidavit/testimony contains sufficient facts showing probable cause for the person's arrest existed at the time of the arrest. Arraignment before a court is ordered on _____ at _____

    ☐ The Court sets an appearance Bond in the amount of $ _____
    ☐ Bond in the amount of $_____   For the crime of _____
    ☐ Bond in the amount of $_____   For the crime of _____
    ☐ Bond in the amount of $_____   For the crime of _____
    ☐ Bond in the amount of $_____   For the crime of _____
    ☐ Bond in the amount of $_____   For the crime of _____
    ☐ The Court denies Bond at this time.

☐ This affidavit/testimony contains insufficient facts to show probable cause for the person's arrest existed at the time of arrest. The arrestee is ordered released from custody immediately.
Date _____   Time _____

    The undersigned Judge of this Court, upon sworn testimony and/or Affidavit, hereby determines there to be probable cause to detain the defendant(s).

_____   _____
          Judge   Date

Appendix G

Probable Cause Affidavit (Cont.)

IN THE DISTRICT COURT OF DELAWARE COUNTY
STATE OF OKLAHOMA
Page 17 of 17

Case No. : 2014-0478B
Defendant : TURLINGTON JR, EDWIN HARDEE

_____

Judge's Signature

Appendix G
Probable Cause Affidavit (Cont.)

2014-0478

EASTERN SHAWNEE TRIBAL POLICE DEPARTMENT
70501 E. 128 ROAD
WYANDOTTE, OK 74370

PERSONAL STATEMENT

NAME: Edwin Hardee Turlington   TRIBE: _____   PHONE: 405 612 8933

ADDRESS: 910 Sunset Strip   CITY: MIAMI   STATE: OK

DATE OF BIRTH: 100768   SSN: 245983981   DRIVER LIC. #: K10020490   STATE: OK

PLACE OF OCCURRENCE: ~~Hwy 59~~ Driveway east   CITY: JAY   STATE: OK

INDIAN TRUST LAND: YES (NO)   of Gated Dr. yours on Vernon Moss/Gene Turlington property Co Rd 370 Jay.

PERSON(S) INVOLVED: EDWIN TURLINGTON   TRIBE: _____

Driver of Truck   TRIBE: _____

Passenger of front seat Passenger rear   TRIBE: _____

TIME OF OCCURRENCE: Approx 18-1830   AM / (PM)   DATE OF OCCURRENCE: _____

PLEASE EXPLAIN AS COMPLETELY AS POSSIBLE EXACTLY WHAT HAPPENED

Approx 18-1830 I was traveling west on Co. rd 370 between Oak Chapel and the hence I am moving into ~~Aubrey Turlington~~ I saw three men trespassing and burning my brother's land. When I approached them, one assaulted

EOS

THE ABOVE INFORMATION AND STATEMENT IS TRUE AND CORRECT TO THE BEST OF MY KNOWLEDGE.

SIGNED: _____

DATE: 14 APR 14   TIME: 23:26

WITNESS: _____

TITLE: INVESTIGATOR

NOTE: *Sheriff Harlan Moore ordered Detective Miller to arrest me as I was just beginning to make the above statement. Moore wasn't interested in my testimony; he had already made his mind up before the investigation began.*

Appendix G
Probable Cause Affidavit (Cont.)

Radio Log - ODIS ... Page 1 of 2

2014-04

DELAWARE COUNTY SHERIFFS OFFICE
Radio Log Record

CALL INFORMATION

Agency:	Delaware County Sheriffs Office	Date / Time:	04/14/2014 19:47
Call Type:	911 CALL	Disposition:	
Final Call:	shots fired		
Entered by:	HARRELL, PENNY		
Location:	68296 E 370 RD		
Tag Number:			

Notes: DEBBIE THOMAS 918-854-5128 AT 68296 E 370 RD ADV SHOOTING JUST HAPPENED UNKNOWN MALE SHOT HER COUSIN IN THE LEG AND HELD A GUN TO THE HEAD OF ANOTHER MAN /// R/P REQ AMB & DEPUTIES BE SENT /// 1950 D16 ADV & ENRT /// 1950 GROVE PD ADV FOR EMS & FR AND ASKED TO STAGE UNTIL DEPUTY ON SCENE /// 1952 D17 ADV & ENRT AS BACK UP /// 1953 D1 ADV /// 1954 D2 ADV /// (GY) 2003 ED TURLINGTON 405-612-8933 CALLED ON 911 AND ADV HIS MOTHER CLOSED ON PROPERTY OUTSIDE SW CITY AND BROTHER BOUGHT LAND AND THERE WERE THREE PEOPLE OUT THERE COMMITTING ARSON /// 2005 D3 ADV P/S D6 WOULD BE ENRT SHORTLY /// 2006 D2 10-8 ENRT /// (GY) 2007 P/S ED TURLINGTON ASKED IF ANYONE WAS STILL AT SCENE OF SHOOTING HE ADV NO /// ASKED IF HE KNEW SHOOTERS NAME AND HE ADV YES ED TURLINGTON HE CONFIRMED HE WAS THE SHOOTER /// MR TURLINGTON ADV 3 MEN WERE STARTING ARSON ON HIS BROTHERS LAND AND THEY WOULD NOT STOP /// ED ADV HE WAS ENRT TO COURT HOUSE IN BLACK TRUCK AND WAS APPROX FIVE MILES NORTH OF JAY /// R/P ADV HE WAS TRAINED IN LAW ENFORCEMENT AND THE GUN WAS UNLOADED AND PIN IN CHAMBER AND NOT ON HIS PERSON /// ALL UNITS ADV /// 2014 D17 10-97 WITH R/P /// 2017 D2 ADV P/S TO SHOOTER WENT STRAIGHT TO VOICEMAIL /// 2018 D6 10-8 ENRT /// 2029 JORDAN WITH BENTON COUNTY SO ADV OFFICER ON-SCENE AT GRAVETTE HOSPITAL REQ NAME OF VICTIM (DARRYL PHILPOT) /// (GY) 2030 VICTIM 10-97 @ GRAVETTE HOSPITAL /// (GY) 2030 D4 10-97 DCSO WITH JAY PD WHO ARE 10-12 WITH SUSPECT SHOOTER / D 4 OUT AT SO /// 2037 D16 10-97 WITH WITNESSES COLLECTING STATEMENTS /// 2038 D16 REQ 43-44 R080409770 PRINT & HOLD /// D 3 ENRT TO GRAVETTE /// 2041 D17 ADV VICTIM CALLED R/P AND ADV HE WAS SHOT IN THE ROAD NOT IN THE WOODS /// 2042 D16 REQ 43-44 G082421716 PRINT & HOLD /// ADV D16 NEG 44 NCIC & LOCAL ON BOTH /// 2044 D6 10-97 /// 2044 D3 ADV ENRT TO GRAVETTE HOSPITAL REQ BENTON COUNTY HAVE OFFICER ON STAND BY UNTIL HE ARRIVES /// (GY) 2044 D 17 44 L999488831 NEG 44 /// 2057 BENTON COUNTY ADV VICTIM HAS ALREADY CHANGED CLOTHES BEFORE HEADING TO HOSPITAL /// D6 ADV /// 2105 D17 REQ D5 TO RELEAVE HIM FROM SCENE /// 2115 D 5 10-97 /// 2118 D16 & D6 10-8 FROM SHOOTING SCENE ENRT TO VICTIMS RESIDENCE /// 2120 D5 10-97 /// 2123 D17 10-8 /// 2131 D16 10-8 /// 2140 D5 & D6 STILL WORKING SHOOTING SCENE /// (GY) 2145 LANCE TURLINGTON, BROTHER OF SUSPECT ASK IF HIS BROTHER WAS GOING TO BE HELD. ADV D 6 AND HE SAID HE WOULD CALL HIM AFTER THE INTERVEIW /// 2206 D6 ENRT TO SO /// 2211 D6 ADV CR 690 & CR 370 .5 MILES WEST ON CR 370 IS CRIME SCENE AND CR 690 & CR 370 .3 MILES WEST ON CR 370 EVIDENCE COLLECTED /// 2221 D3 10-8 FROM GRAVETTE HOSPITAL ENRT TO DCSO /// 2226 D4 10-8 FROM S.O. /// 2227 D5 OUT AT 2700 /// 2232 D6 OUT AT S.O. /// 2238 D6 REQ D17 TO STAY WITH VEHICLE UNTIL SEARCH WARRANT SIGNED /// 2239 D2 10-8 /// 2239 D6 REQ 10-28 OKLA 452ALY PRINT & HOLD /// 2244 D3 OUT AT 2700 /// 2245 D5 CLEAR 2700 OUT AT S.O. /// 2248 D6 OUT AT 2700 /// 2337 D3 REQ COPIES BE MADE OF ALL 911 TAPES REGARDING THIS CALL /// 04/15/2014 D5 10-8 FROM S.O. OUT AT 2700 /// 0110 D3 & D6 10-8 /// 0111 D5 10-8

CALLER INFORMATION

Name:	THOMAS, DEBBIE
Phone Number:	(918)854-5128
Location:	68296 E 370 RD

PARTY INFORMATION

1 MILLER, FRANK (DELAWARE COUNTY SHERIFFS OFFICE)
Called : 04/14/2014 21:05   Arrived : 04/14/2014 21:20   Completed : 04/15/2014 01:11
Notes :

Appendix G
Probable Cause Affidavit (Cont.)

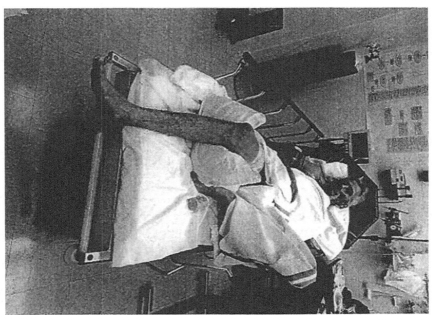

This photo, which tells nothing about the bullet wound, is the same size as the one DCSO scanned in with the PC Affidavit documents, making it appear as though it was part of the Affidavit. The photograph that was made to look like it was part of the PC Affidavit, was also black and white. Not only is it not numbered like the rest of the Affidavit documents (1/17, 2/17, etc.), according to the prosecutor, it was not among the PC Affidavit documents he received
(see Appendix H, page 1, para. 3). The preceding two pages and the following black and white photo of Philpott's leg were also scanned into the PC Affidavit PDF file the prosecutor gave me during "Discovery" were also unnumbered but made to look as though were part of the PC Affidavit.

Appendix G
Probable Cause Affidavit (Cont.)

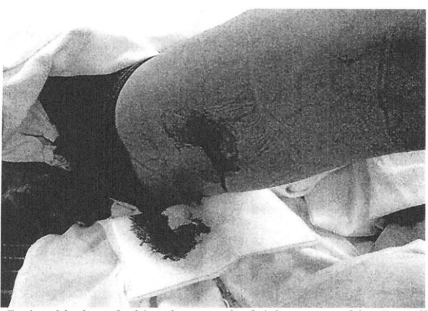

Grainy, black, and white photograph of violent career felon Darrell Philpott's leg that was scanned into the PC Affidavit file I received on CD from the prosecutor during Discovery, making it appear as though it was part of the PC Affidavit submitted to the Court (it was not, according to the prosecutor, see preceding page). Like the photograph in the preceding page, it does nothing to tell the viewer anything about the nature of the wound. In a through and through bullet wound, such as the one above, the wounds must be compared with each other to tell which the entrance is, and which is the exit. In my case, I reported to Deputy Frank Miller that I shot Philpott in the front of his leg, as he was committing armed assault against me. Wound Specialist Renzil Reardon, RN, wrote in his medical report that Philpott was shot in the front of his leg, and the bullet exited through the front. Not only did the Lead Investigator, Deputy Gayle Wells, make the conclusory statement in the PC Affidavit that the wound "appeared to be... from the back to the front", but he withheld the report from the PC Affidavit altogether.

Appendix H
Prosecutor Response to Bar Complaint

OKLAHOMA BAR ASSOCIATION
Attn: Gina Hendryx
P.O. Box 53036
Oklahoma City, OK 73152-3036

RE: Grievance by Edwin Hardee Turlington Jr., DC-18-258

Dear Ms. Hendryx:

I am in receipt of the above-referenced grievance which contains therein an allegation that there was a violation of the Rules of Professional Conduct, 5 O.S. Ch.1, App. 3-A: Rule 3.3(a)(3). I have been a member in good standing with the Oklahoma Bar Association for twenty years and I deny that I have violated Rule 3.3(a)(3).

As the pending grievance spawned from a criminal case, I believe a brief case history and brief summary of my involvement with this case is necessary for your evaluation. Please note that a more complete case history can be obtained from a review of the court file maintained by the Delaware County Court Clerk.

Case History

1. On July 11, 2014, Winston H. Connor II filed his entry of Appearance on behalf of the Defendant, Edwin Turlington, Jr.

2. On July 3, 2014, a criminal information was filed in Delaware County District Court, Case No. CF-2014-224 which alleged that Edwin Hardee Turlington, Jr., on or about the 14th day of April, 2014, unlawfully, willfully, knowingly, and wrongfully committed the crime of Assault and Battery with a Dangerous Weapon in violation of 21 O.S. §645 against Darrell Philpott. Contained within the Information is the State's Notice of Open File pursuant to Title 22 O.S. §258.

3. Simultaneously with the filing of the criminal information, an eight (8) page Probable Cause Affidavit For Arrest Without Warrant signed by M.G. Wells of the Delaware County Sheriff's Office was filed with the court clerk without any attachments.

4. On December 8, 2015 Edwin Turlington, Jr. and his attorney, Winston H. Connor II, appeared before the Honorable Alicia Littlefield and a preliminary hearing was conducted. During the preliminary hearing, the State of Oklahoma called three (3) witnesses: Darrell Philpott, Frank Miller, and Jack Thomas. At the conclusion of the preliminary hearing, the court overruled the

Appendix H

Prosecutor Response to Bar Complaint (Cont.)

demurrer and found reason to believe that the crime of assault and battery with a dangerous weapon had been committed.

5. On January 6, 2016 Edwin Turlington, Jr. and his attorney, Winston H. Connor II appeared for District Court Arraignment. Mr. Turlington entered a plea of not guilty and waived speedy trial. The court set the case on the felony disposition docket on July 25, 2016.

6. On February 14, 2018, the court signed an Order allowing Winston H. Connor II to withdraw from his representation of Mr. Turlington.

7. On March 16, 2018, Mr. Turlington executed and caused to be filed a Waiver of Right to An Attorney.

8. On January 7, 2019, Jason David Smith filed his limited entry of appearance with limited scope of representation on behalf of Mr. Turlington.

9. The criminal case is currently set for announcement before District Judge Barry V. Denney on July 22, 2019.

10. No criminal history for Darrell Philpott was ever provided by the Delaware County Sheriff's Office prior to the preliminary hearing.

Brief Outline of Contact with Edwin Turlington, Jr.

1. On April 3, 2018, I had my first meeting with Mr. Turlington. After reminding Mr. Turlington that I was not his attorney, we discussed the issue of discovery. Mr. Turlington expressed that he had obtained little documentation from his previous attorney after his withdrawal from representation. After opening our case file with Mr. Turlington present, I made a list of the documents and recordings Mr. Turlington requested a copy of. During this meeting, Mr. Turlington provide me a notebook containing some of his concerns regard the case.

2. On May 3, 2018, I had a meeting with Mr. Turlington at which time I provided him a copy of discoverable material previously discussed on April 3, 2018. Should the Bar Association require a copy of the list of materials/documents provided to Mr. Turlington, it will be made available at your request.

3. On June 14, 2018 I had a meeting with Mr. Turlington and his brother, Lance Turlington, who participated by cell phone. During this brief meeting, Lance Turlington conveyed concerns he had regarding the night of the incident when his brother was interviewed at the Delaware County Sheriff's Office. At this meeting, Edwin Turlington provided me with a two (2) page document containing his concerns and a copy of a witness statement prepared by Joseph Bradley's.

4. On July 19, 2018, I had a meeting with Edwin Turlington and Lance Turlington. Part of the conversation centered on attempts Lance Turlington made to contact Edwin Turlington the night of the incident when Edwin Turlington was interviewed by law enforcement, in addition to a discussion regarding the injury Darrel Philpott received. Lance Turlington provided me with a written timeline regarding his attempts to contact his brother at the Delaware County Jail the night of the incident.

Appendix H

Prosecutor Response to Bar Complaint (Cont.)

5. I have had additional contacts with Lance Turlington since the July 19 meeting that are not outlined herein as I am of the opinion that they are not relevant to the grievance presented. Should the Bar Association request information regarding these contacts, please contact me and the information will be provided.

PRELIMINARY HEARING TESTIMONY

Much of the grievance is focused on Darrell Philpott's testimony at the preliminary hearing regarding his criminal history. At the preliminary hearing, the victim testified during cross-examination that he was a convicted felon for possessing a half a trash bag of weed in Benton County, State of Arkansas about 30-35 years ago and that he had not been convicted of any misdemeanors involving moral turpitude or dishonesty. See: Preliminary Hearing transcript pages 29 – 30 which are attached hereto as Attachment "A".

When Darrell Philpott was questioned further during the course of cross-examination regarding "trouble" he had been in, Mr. Philpott testified he had traffic violations. When asked if he remembered anything else, Mr. Philpott responded with "Well, not a whole bunch." See: Preliminary Hearing transcript pages 75-76 which are attached hereto as Attachment "B".

RULES OF PROFESSIONAL CONDUCT
RULE 3.3(a)(3)

It is alleged that there has been a violation of the Rules of Professional Conduct, 5 O.S. Ch.1, App. 3-A: Rule 3.3(a)(3). Rule 3.3(a)(3) provides that "[a] lawyer shall not knowingly: offer evidence that the lawyer knows to be false. If a lawyer, the lawyer's client, or a witness called by the lawyer, has offered material evidence and the lawyer comes to know of its falsity, the lawyer shall take reasonable remedial measures, including, if necessary, disclosure to the tribunal. A lawyer may refuse to offer evidence that the lawyer reasonably believes is false."

1. Have I knowingly offered evidence that I know to be false?

No, on behalf of the State of Oklahoma I did not offer false evidence, material or otherwise, regarding Mr. Philpott's criminal history. During the preliminary hearing Mr. Philpott's testimony regarding his criminal history occurred during the cross examination by Mr. Connor. It was not offered by the State of Oklahoma.

2. If a lawyer, the lawyer's client, or a witness called by the lawyer, has offered material evidence and the lawyer comes to know of its falsity, the lawyer shall take reasonable remedial measures, including, if necessary, disclosure to the tribunal.

The case file maintained by the District Attorney's Office at the time of the preliminary hearing did not contain a criminal history record for Mr. Philpott and there were no conversations between myself and Mr. Philpott in preparation for the preliminary hearing regarding Mr. Philpott's criminal record.

A review of the Oklahoma Supreme Court Network for any criminal records involving Darrell E. Philpott in Delaware County reveals the following history:

Appendix H

Prosecutor Response to Bar Complaint (Cont.)

(1) Case No: CRM-1991-00955 was dismissed/settled on March 12, 1997.

(2) Case No: CM-2001-00339 was a misdemeanor Public Intoxication charge that resulted in a journal entry of judgment against Mr. Philpott on April 26, 2001.

(3) Case No: CM-2001-00802 was a misdemeanor Public Intoxication charge that resulted in a journal entry of judgment against Mr. Philpott on September 18, 2001.

(4) Four (4) traffic citations/tickets having been filed against Mr. Philpott in 2003.

In preparation for this response, an Interstate Identification Index (triple "I") criminal history record for Darrell E. Philpott was obtained. The criminal history record indicated that at the time of Mr. Philpott's preliminary hearing testimony the following:

1. An arrest on January 27, 1981 by the Benton County Sheriff, State of Arkansas for the charge of Theft by Receiving. No disposition indicated.
2. An arrest on February 9, 1981 by the Benton County Sheriff, State of Arkansas for the charge of Criminal Mischief. No disposition indicated.
3. A one (1) year sentence in 1981 from Benton County, State of Arkansas, for what appears to be for Possession of a controlled substance with intent to deliver.
4. A one (1) day sentence in 1997 from Sulpher Springs City Court, for the charge of Fleeing and the charge of DWI.

Mr. Turlington's grievance against me appears to be based solely on the exchange between Mr. Connor and Mr. Philpott regarding misdemeanors involving moral turpitude. Mr. Connor asked Mr. Philpott if he had been convicted of any misdemeanors involving moral turpitude to which Mr. Philpott answered "no."

Moral turpitude has been most recently defined by the Oklahoma Court of Criminal Appeal in *Tucker v. State*, 2016 OK CR 29, 395 P.3d 1. The Court in *Tucker* cited *Bunn v. State*, 1977 OK CR 52, ¶ 6, 561 P.2d 969, 971., where the Court of Criminal Appeal held that driving under the influence was a crime of moral turpitude because it is inherently dangerous to the public, and "shows a lack of personal integrity and a lack of concern for and respect of the person of others and their property." *Id.* ¶ 7, 561 P.2d at 972.

In the present case it is premature to determine whether or not the holding in *Bunn* can be applied to the Mr. Philpott's 1997 DWI conviction. First, *Bunn* held that the charge of driving under the influence was a crime of moral turpitude, it did not address the crime of DWI. Second, additional research would be required into the facts of Mr. Philpott's DWI arrest, and the Arkansas DWI statute/ordinance he was convicted of, before the possible application of the *Bunn* decision can be made. Without further examination, it is impossible to determine if Mr. Philpott's answer to Mr. Connor was false, thus requiring further examination to determine *Bunn's* applicability and a determination if any remedial measures are needed.

I have attempted to visit with Darrell Philpott regarding the testimony he provided regarding his criminal history, but communicating with Mr. Philpott has been challenging. Mr. Philpott has neither a telephone or vehicle of his own, nor does he have a reliable mailing address as he moves frequently. After speaking with Mr. Philpott utilizing a phone of an acquaintance of his earlier this year, an appointment was scheduled in my office for January 10, 2019. Mr. Philpott failed to attend this appointment. Additional attempts to meet with Mr. Philpott have been made resulting in Mr. Philpott calling me the afternoon of January 31, 2019 where he agreed to visit with me in my office on February 6, 2019.

Appendix H

Prosecutor Response to Bar Complaint (Cont.)

Should Mr. Turlington desire to attack the credibility of Darrell Philpott at trial, he would have to overcome the hurdles presented by 12 O.S. §2609 –Impeachment by Evidence of Conviction of Crime. Mr. Turlington, in addition to convincing the trial court that the probative value of admitting evidence of the 1997 DWI outweighs its prejudicial effect to the accused, he would first need to establish that the 1997 DWI was a crime punishable in excess of 1 year pursuant to the law under which the witness was convicted required by 12 O.S. §2609(A)(1) and overcome the ten (10) year limitation found in 12 O.S. §2609(B).

Should the Oklahoma Bar Association have any further questions or requests, please do not hesitate to contact me.

Sincerely,

NICHOLAS P. LELECAS

Attachments

NPL:lj

Appendix I

Exculpatory Wound Nurse Report that Deputy Wells Withheld from PC Affidavit

Ozarks Community Hospital
ER/Urgent Care Nursing Assessment

Pt Acct #: ▓▓▓   Med. Rec. #: 5002777
Name: PHILPOTT DARRELL E
Date: 041414 Birth Date ▓▓▓ Age: 53 Gender M

ARRIVED BY: ☑ POV ☐ Walk ☐ EMS ☐ Other
Ht & Wt 130 lbs oz 58.97 kg 58967 g 72 in 1.73 m2 0
Ht & Wt New   BMI: 17.63

Vital Signs:

Temperature	Pulse	Respiration	Blood Pressure	O2 Saturation
			/	

Vital Signs: New

Medical Screening By: R REARDON RN
Time of medical screening: 2035
Medical screening Acuity: ☐ C ☑ E ☐ U ☐ N
☐ Recheck Onset of Sx: 1 HR

GSW R FEMUR

ACE WRAP

Meds/Dose/Freq: ⦿ None   ○ See Medication Reconciliation
Allergy
No Known Drug Allergy

Primary Care Provider: NONE
Pharmacy NA
Immunization/Tetanus Up-to-Date: ○ Y ⦿ N ○ Unsure
Advanced Directive: N   Driver Avail: ⦿ Y ○ N
Physician Time in: 2035   Physician Time Out: 2040

Time	BP	Pulse	Resp	Temp	Route	SaO2	Pain
2115	122/84	76	20		Oral	100	
2130	121/84	85	17		Oral	100	
2200	139/91	74	18		Oral	100	
2300	132/84	84	18			100	

Medication / IV Fluids	Dose	Route	Time	Initial
TDAP	0.5	IM	2120	RAR

Physical Assessment:

Neurological
☑ Awake ☑ Alert ☑ Oriented x 3 ☐ Disoriented
Responsive to: ☑ Voice ☐ Pain ☐ Unresponsive

Respiratory
Breath Sounds:
☑ Clear ☐ Wheezes ☐ Rales ☐ Rhonchi
☐ Diminished Location:

Cardivascular
Heart tones: ☑ Normal ☐ Murmur
Rythm: ☑ Regular ☐ Irregular ☐ Paced

Abdominal
Pain: ☑ None ☐ Sharp ☐ Ache ☐ Cramping ☐ Dull
☐ Constant ☐ Intermittent
Bowel sounds: ☑ Active ☐ Hyperactive ☐ Hypoactive ☐ Absent
Last BM: ☐ days ☑ Today ☐ Normal ☐ Diarrhea ☐ Bloody
Last Menstrual Period:

Extremities
☐ No obvious abnormalities ☐ Deformity ☐ Laceration ☐ Abrasion

IV start: ☐ 16G ☐ 18G ☐ 20G ☐ 22G ☐ 24G Attempts:
Time: Location:
Saline Lock Flush: ○ Yes ○ No
O2:   L/M via ☐ mask ☐ cannula ☐ NRB Time:
Telemetry: ☐ Yes ☐ No Rhythm:
Foley: size Output: Time:
NGT: size Output: Time:

Nursing Narrative
Time to Room: 2035   Room #:

Appendix I

Exculpatory Wound Nurse Report that Deputy Wells Withheld from PC Affidavit (Cont.)

Bruising ☑ Bleeding Redness Edema

☑ Bleeding Controlled

☑ Pulses present Pulses Absent

Cap refill: ☑ <3 Seconds >3 Seconds

Skin

☑ Pink Pale Flushed Cyanotic Jaundiced ☑ Warm

Hot to Touch Cool ☑ Dry Clammy Diaphoretic

Identified Barriers	Learning Needs	Social History
Cultural ○ Y ◉ N	Readiness ◉ Y ○ N	Tobacco: 1 PPD
Spiritual ○ Y ◉ N	Motivation ◉ Y ○ N	Alcohol ○ Y ○ N Amount: 1 PINT
Emotional ○ Y ◉ N	Capability ◉ Y ○ N	Illicit Drugs ◉ Y ○ N Type, Freq, Last used: MARIJUANA

```
GSW R UPPER THIGH FROM ANTERIOR TO POST THROUGH
AND THROUGH BLEEDING CONTROLLED---DISTAL
SENSATION/CIRCULATION INTACT---NO DEFORMITY
OBSERVED------------------------------------RAR
2040---XRAY AND LAB COMPLETE----------RAR
2120---TDAP EXP03/18/16--LT #JP44F----RAR
2310---REPORT CALLED TO P BURNETT RN-------RAR
2310---TRANSPORTED TO 350 VIA STRETCHER----RAR
```

T/A

Disposition: ○ DC ○ AMA ○ Transferred
○ OBSERVATION ◉ Admitted to: 350

Physician Decision to Admit (date):

Physician Decision to Admit (time):

Transferred to: 350   Via: ○ EMS ◉ POV

Time of disposition: 2310

Condition: ◉ Stable ○ Improved ○ Worsened ○ Expired

Primary RN:
Relief RN Signature:

Tech Signature:

Relief Tech Signature:

Appendix J
Preliminary Hearing Transcripts, p.52
Philpott Drinks a Full Bottle Prior to Interview

52

1   Q   All right.. Tell me what happened to that bottle of

2   whiskey.

3   A   I drank the rest of it after I got shot.

4   Q   I see, so you drank some swaullers -- up to a quarter,

5   whatever you drank -- while you cut wood, and the next time

6   you drank was when?

7   A   After I got shot.

8   Q   So, right after you got shot, you pulled the bottle

9   out and started drinking?

10   A   A little bit after that.

11   Q   Well, what's 'a little bit'?

12   A   Oh, 30 minutes.

13   Q   All right. Where were you when you started drinking,

14   again?

15   A   At the house.

16   Q   All right. So, after you left the location and went

17   to Joseph Bradley's house, you started drinking?

18   A   Yeah.

19   Q   And did you finish off the rest of the bottle?

20   A   Yeah; on the way to the hospital. But at Joseph's, I

21   had a drink, probably, and then he took me to the

22   house [sic].

23   Q   Was it a full bottle before you opened it and started

24   cutting wood?

25   A   Yeah.

Appendix K
Preliminary Hearing Transcripts, p.53
Philpott Drinks 2nd Bottle of Whiskey Before Police Interview

53

1   Q   And you finished the pint --

2   A   -- half pint --

3   Q   It was a half pint bottle?

4   A   Yeah.

5   Q   So, you finished the half pint bottle after you were

6   shot -- about 30 minutes or so -- after going to Mr.

7   Bradley's house, is that right?

8   A   Yeah.

9   Q   All right.

10   A   I really finished it on the way to the hospital.

11   Q   All right. Tell me this. How much after you drank

12   the whiskey was the first time you were interviewed by law

13   enforcement?

14   A   Probably 15, 20 minutes; 30 minutes.

15   Q   Had you used any other substances?

16   A   No.

17   Q   Did any law enforcement ever ask you for any blood so

18   they could test it to determine what might be in your

19   system?

20   A   No.

21   Q   Okay, let's go back to when the -- Steve lights the

22   fire, you all are pulling out, and tell me what happens

23   right then.

24   A   Right when?

25   Q   The fire's lit and you all are leaving; what happens

Appendix L

Preliminary Hearing Transcripts, page 29
Philpott Commits Perjury by Omitting Theft and Burglary Felonies and Denying Possession with Intent

29

1		8, do either one of these photographs depict where you felt
2		the bullet go into your leg?
3	A	Yeah.
4	Q	Which one?
5	A	Number 7.
6	Q	State's 7?
7	A	Yeah.
8	Q	Did you say anything to the defendant at the time you
9		were going back to the truck?
10	A	No.
11		MR. LELCAS: Pass the witness.
12		THE COURT: Mr. Connor?
13		--
14		CROSS EXAMINATION
15	BY MR. CONNOR:	
16	Q	Mr. Philpott, let's start out with, have you ever been
17		convicted of a felony?
18	A	Yeah.
19	Q	Of what?
20	A	Half a bag full of weed.
21	Q	Possession with intent?
22	A	Possession; yeah.
23	Q	Trafficking?
24	A	No; possession.
25	Q	Where was that at?

Appendix M

Preliminary Hearing Transcripts, page 76

More Perjury, Philpott Changes Clothes and Destroys Evidence

76

```
 1   Q   You don't remember anything else?

 2   A   Well, not a whole bunch.

 3   Q   Well, what do you remember, if anything?

 4   A   I know I've had a lot of tickets.

 5   Q   Traffic tickets?

 6   A   Yeah; back when I was younger.

 7   Q   I could care less about traffic tickets, so let's

 8   eliminate those.  Anything other than traffic tickets?

 9   A   Not that I know of.

10   Q   Poaching?

11   A   No; don't believe in it.

12   Q   Okay.  Why did you go to the house instead of the

13   hospital?

14   A   To check out my wound.

15   Q   And to throw the whiskey bottle into something else to

16   burn?

17   A   I throwed it in the wood stove; yeah.

18   Q   Was the wood stove going?

19   A   A little bit.

20   Q   So, you went and burned that, right?

21   A   Yeah.  And I changed my clothes.

22   Q   Anything else?

23   A   [Indecipherable]

24       THE REPORTER:  Say that, again.

25   A   Went and got in the car and went to the hospital.
```

Appendix N
Deputy Wells Declares Philpott the Victim Prior to Interview 03:02 (entire interview is online at *www.RapeOfDelco/philpott.mp3)*

01:55 WELLS: And your cousin being?

01:57 PHILPOTT: Uh, Jack Thomas

01:59 WELLS: Jack Thomas?

02:01 PHILPOTT: Yeah

02:02 WELLS: Where does Jack live?

02:03 PHILPOTT: Um... hehe, over there? haha, I do not, I don't, I don't know his address.

02:13 WELLS: Does he live out near Oak Chapel?

03:14 PHILPOTT: Yeah.

02:15 WELLS: Does he live on 370 road?

02:16 PHILPOTT: You know where um, the dumpsters are?

02:17 WELLS: Yes, sir.

02:18 PHILPOTT: Alright, take a right and it's the second drive on your left. Or on the right.

02:38 WELLS: Ok. Let me get that first of all make sure we get those clothes recovered. Okay?

02:47 PHILPOTT: I know his home phone.

02:49 WELLS: Oh, good!

02:51 PHILPOTT: It's uh, let me see, 918-854-5128.

02:56 WELLS: 5,1,2,8, Okay!

03:02 WELLS: Hey, Brandon, I'm talking with uh, Mr. Philpott here - the victim, he says that when he changed the clothes, that he was wearing, when he was shot, are in his cousin's vehicle-

03:17 PHILPOTT: Bathroom

03:18 WELLS: I'm sorry, in his cousin's bathroom.

03:32 WELLS: Super deal, the cousin's name is Jack Thomas? Does that match? Okay, alright, that's all I needed, man. I'll (unintelligible) I'll carry on here.

03:46 WELLS: He was talking to him as we spoke.

03:47 PHILPOTT: Amen

03:48 WELLS: Uh, let me get just a little biographical information from you if I can. Are you Daryl or Darrell?

03:57 PHILPOTT: Darrell

03:58 WELLS: And your middle name?

03:59 PHILPOTT: Eugene

Appendix O
Preliminary Hearing Transcripts, page 48
Philpott Plans to Set Fire on "Foreclosed Land" then Abandon it

1   leave?

2   MR. LELECAS: I'm going to object, your Honor.

3   It calls for --

4   THE WITNESS: -- we was just going to go --

5   THE COURT: Time out.

6   THE WITNESS: -- maybe a quarter of a mile --

7   THE COURT: Sir, just --

8   THE WITNESS: -- and come back.

9   THE COURT: What is your objection, Mr. Lelecas?

10   MR. LELECAS: My objection is to the form of the

11   question. Mr. Connor's inferring that there was some sort

12   of plan, but there's been no facts before this Court from

13   this witness --

14   THE COURT: Sustained. Rephrase the question.

15   Q   [By Mr. Connor] Was it your understanding that Steve

16   was lighting the fire and then you all were leaving, right

17   A   Right.

18   Q   And where were you all going to go?

19   A   To the house to unload the wood.

20   Q   Okay. And then what?

21   A   Go back and check on the fire.

22   Q   All right. So, the plan was to light the fire, leave

23   it, unload wood, and then come back to see if it was still

24   burning or spreading or whatever?

25   A   Yeah.

Appendix P

Turlington's Former Defense Attorney

Winston Connor is Arrested on TEN Felonies Charges

The holiday's over! Oklahoma defen: attorney is arrested after arriving home from a Caribbean vacation as is accused of soliciting a murderer t(kill another convicted killer in prisor

- Defense attorney Winston Connor II, 54, was arrested Saturday after havin been secretly indicted by an Oklahoma grand jury in November
- Connor faces charges including solicitation of first-degree murder, racket(and unlawful communication with an inmate
- Authorities said Connor asked convicted murderer Slint Tate to kill anothei while they were behind bars during a tapped phone conversation
- Tate, 36, is serving life in prison for killing a sheriff's deputy when he was 1(
- The attorney was taken into custody after stepping off an airplane from a Caribbean vacation with his wife

By MAXINE SHEN FOR DAILYMAIL.COM
PUBLISHED: 14:45 EDT, 14 January 2019 | UPDATED: 00:00 EDT, 15 January 2019

An Oklahoma defense attorney has been arrested for allegedly asking a convicted murderer to kill another murderer while they were behind bars.

Attorney Winston Connor II, 54, was arrested Saturday in Charlotte, North Carolina, after stepping off an airplane from a Caribbean vacation with his wife.

Connor was said to have been secretly indicted by a grand jury in November, which charged him with solicitation for first-degree murder, racketeering, witness tampering, assault, unlawful communication with an inmate and drug and prostitution offenses, **News OK** reported.

The charges appear to stem from investigations that began in 2016, when authorities heard Connor on the phone with convicted murderer Slint Tate, 36, who was in prison serving a life sentence for fatally shooting a sheriff's deputy when he was 16.

Just last Wednesday, Connor took to Facebook to share photos of himself on a Turks and Caicos getaway with his wife and friends.

Appendix P (Cont.)
Turlington's Former Defense Attorney
Winston Connor is Arrested on TEN Felonies Charges

According to court records obtained by the newspaper, the Oklahoma state narcotics bureau suspected that Tate was running a drug ring out of prison and had been listening in on Tate's cell phone calls.

In May 2016, authorities heard Connor and Tate discussing a reduction in his prison sentence and also Connor's efforts at getting his secretary's car returned.

Tate was sentenced to an additional 20 years on his life-without-parole sentence in September 2018 for running a million-dollar drug ring via smuggled cell phones while in Oklahoma State Penitentiary.

In addition to allegedly putting out a hit on Williams, Connor was investigated following raid on two illicit massage parlors in Tulsa.

In 2017, Connor came under further investigation after a raid on two illicit Tulsa massage parlors which authorities said sexual services and involved at least one juvenile, according to **Tulsa World**.

From:

Dailymail.com, Maxine Shen For. "Oklahoma Attorney Arrested for Soliciting a Murderer to Kill Another Convicted Killer While." Daily Mail Online. January 15, 2019. Accessed August 05, 2019. https://www.dailymail.co.uk/news/article-6590947/Oklahoma-attorney-arrested-soliciting-murderer-kill-convicted-killer-while.html.

Appendix Q
Preliminary Hearing Transcripts, page 13
Philpott is Unable to Identify Turlington 3X
The Prosecutor Enters a Falsehood into the Record 3X

13

1   Q   [By Mr. Lelecas]   So, you and Steve -- you're in

2   Steve's vehicle -- his truck -- and you're stopped because

3   of traffic, and Joseph Bradley drove by, and he was headed

4   east, you said; correct?

5   A   Yeah.

6   Q   And that would be up the hill, as depicted in the

7   photograph, correct?

8   A   Yeah.

9   Q   Does your vehicle move after Joseph Bradley leaves?

10 A   Yeah; we pulled out.

11 Q   What direction do you pull out in?

12 A   We pulled out, turned left, headed west.

13 Q   And what happens next after Steve gets the truck on

14 370 Road heading west?

15 A   A pickup comes flying down the hill and went around us

16 and cut us off.

17 Q   Do you remember what type of pickup it was?

18 A   No.   It was just a full-size pickup.

19 Q   And what happens after you get cut off?

20 A   Guy comes out with a gun.

21 Q   Is that individual that came out with a gun present in

22 the courtroom today?

23 A   I believe that's him [pointing].

24 Q   You believe that's him?

25 A   Yeah.

Appendix Q (Cont.)

Preliminary Hearing Transcripts, page 14
*Philpott is Unable to Identify Turlington **3X**,*
*The Prosecutor Enters a Falsehood into the Record **3X***

14

1   MR. CONNOR: Judge, I'm going to object. Either

2 he knows or he doesn't know, your Honor.

3   THE WITNESS: That's him.

4   MR. CONNOR: Very well.

5 Q   [By Mr. Lelecas] And for purposes of the record, Mr.

6 Philpott, can you describe the clothing of the individual

7 that you identified as the person who pulled the gun out?

8 A   He's wearing a gray jacket with a -- I'd say a white

9 shirt, but it might have kind of a greenish tint to it. I

10 can't tell you from here what color it is; and a tie.

11   MR. LELECAS: I'd ask that the record reflect

12 he's identified the person that pulled the gun, for

13 purposes of preliminary hearing.

14   MR. CONNOR: I don't know that he's done that

15 yet, based on the description, your Honor.

16 Q   [By Mr. Lelecas] Mr. Philpott, you pointed to an

17 individual in the courtroom today as the person that came

18 out of the truck with the gun, correct?

19 A   Yes, sir.

20 Q   Okay. Can you tell me, from his head down, what he's

21 wearing today?

22 A   He's wearing pants and a jacket and a shirt and a tie.

23 Q   What color is the jacket?

24 A   Kind of a gray color.

25 Q   And what about the tie?

Appendix Q (Cont.)

Preliminary Hearing Transcripts, page 15
Philpott is Unable to Identify Turlington 3X,
The Prosecutor Enters a Falsehood into the Record 3X

15

1   A   It's plaid.

2   MR. LELECAS: I'd ask that the record reflect

3   that he's identified the person that pulled the gun as

4   being present in the courtroom today.

5   MR. CONNOR: I'm the only one with a gray jacket

6   and a plaid tie, and I assure you it wasn't me.

7   THE COURT: Just ask him where he's sitting or --

8   THE WITNESS: -- okay, he has a tan coat.

9   Q   [By Mr. Lelecas] Is there anything on his coat?

10   A   A gold button.

11   THE COURT: The record will reflect that he has

12   identified the defendant.

13   Q   [By Mr. Lelecas] You indicated that the individual

14   you just identified came out of the vehicle -- his vehicle

15   -- out of his truck --

16   A   -- yes --

17   Q   -- and did what?

18   A   Pulled a gun -- he had a gun when he got out of the

19   truck.

20   Q   Do you recall what type of gun it was?

21   A   A blue automatic pistol.

22   Q   And how was he holding the pistol when you first saw

23   it?

24   A   When I first saw it, it was in both hands.

25   Q   Both hands?

Appendix R
Preliminary Hearing Transcripts, page 51
Philpott Drinks Whiskey Prior to Shooting

51

1   inches?

2   A   Probably an inch.

3   Q   All right. So, about a quarter of a pint, would you

4   say?

5   A   Oh, not quite a quarter, but close.

6   Q   Well, did you ever say that you drank a quarter of a

7   pint?

8   A   Probably not.

9   Q   Could you have?

10   A   It was just easier to say 'two swaullers'.

11   Q   My question is, not what was easier to say, but do you

12   recall telling law enforcement that you drank a quarter of

13   a pint?

14   A   No.

15   Q   Okay. Tell me this. Was your memory of what happened

16   that day better then or now, or is it the same?

17   A   It would probably be better then.

18   Q   Okay. Now, when did you drink the whiskey?

19   A   While we was cutting wood.

20   Q   And was it in a bottle?

21   A   Yeah.

22   Q   What kind of whiskey?

23   A   R & R.

24   Q   Was it a glass bottle?

25   A   Plastic.

Appendix S
News on 6 Article, April 15, 2014

Fight Over Trespassing Ends In Delaware County Shooting, Arrest

Tuesday, April 15th, 2014, 3:42 PM CDT
by Dee Duren

Turlington Mug Shot

DELAWARE COUNTY, Oklahoma - Delaware County Sheriff's Office said a fight over trespassing led to a shooting and arrest Monday night. It happened just before 8 p.m. in the Oak Chapel community.

Sheriff Harlan Moore said investigators worked through the night trying to piece together details of the incident that left one man wounded.

Moore said two men: Steven Barrett and Darrell Philpott, went to some property near the intersection of E370 and S690 to cut wood at the request of a third man who thought the property was in foreclosure. They also started a fire to burn trash on the property, a news release states.

Appendix S (Cont.)
News on 6 Article, April 15, 2014

Police say as they were leaving the logging road, a man in a black Ford pickup truck veered in front of their vehicle, forcing them to stop. The driver of the pickup, later identified as 45-year-old Ed Turlington, jumped out and approached the men carrying a small handgun.

Barrett, 31, and Philpott, 53, said the man cursed at them and made threats, telling them they were trespassing. Philpott told deputies he got out of the truck and "had an exchange of unfriendly conversation" with Turlington.

Philpott said as he turned away, Turlington shot him in the back of his right leg. Barrett and Philpott drove to a nearby hospital.

"Investigators determined the bullet entered Philpott's leg from the back side," Sheriff Moore said.

Turlington called 911 and identified himself as the shooter, saying the men were committing arson on some property his brother was buying, according to the sheriff.

"I didn't want to do it, but I couldn't get them to stop," he reportedly said.

Deputies took Turlington into custody, impounding his truck and recovering a .380-caliber semi-automatic pistol. They are requesting he be charged with felony assault with a firearm on Barrett and shooting with intent to kill Philpott.

Turlington is in the Delaware County Jail.

Appendix T

Norse Trackmen Win

Northeastern A&M defeated Connors of Warner, 84 to 48, in a dual track and and field Robertson Field.

Busiest performer for Coach Jack Rucker's Norsemen was Ed Turlington, freshman from Satellite Beach, Fla. He anchored the winning 440, 880 and mile relay foursome, placed second in the 100 dash and third in the 220 dash.

The 100 dash, into the wind, was won by Gary Deaton of Connors in 10.1. Deaton and Randy Scott of the Norse tied for first in the 220 at 23.8.

Double winners for the Norse included George Gibbs, 5:05.2 in the mile and 11:20 in the two-mile run, and Guy Owen, 5:11 for the high jump and 112.11 in the discus throw.

Connors Clips

SUMMARY

100 dash — Deaton, Connors 10.1; Turlington, Norse, 10.3; Hanoch, Norse 10.4; Curry, Norse, 10.45.

440 dash — James, C, 53.0; Gray, N, 54.7; Gill, C, 54.8.

220 lo whurdles — Whitefield, C, 27.9; Carter, N; Barbour, C.

440 relay — Norse (Curry, Hanoch, Scott, Turlington), 45.2; Connors (Gill, Barbour, Whiteheat, Deaton), 46.0.

Mile run — Gibbs, N, 5:05.2; James, C, 5:08.6; Watts, N, 5:34.

120 high hurdles — Carter, N, 16.5; Whitefield, C, 17.1; Barbour, C, 17.7; Clingan, N, 17.9.

880 run — Lewis, N, 2:10.0; Worley, C, 2:11.0; Gibbs, N, 2:18.7.

2 mile run — Gibbs, N, 11:20; Deaton, C, Watts, N.

880 relay — Norse (Curry, Moody, Scott, Turlington), 1:35.0; Connors, 1:36.9.

Ed Turlington sr Busiest Performer and 100 Yard Dash in 10 Flat , Turlington anchors winning 880 and mile relays, places second in 100 yard dash at 10.2 seconds, and third in 220 yard dash .

NEO A&M, Miami, Oklahoma, 1964

Appendix T (*Cont.*)

PAGE FOUR

Norse Defeat OMA in Dual Track Events

Northeastern A&M's t r a c k and field team, coached by Jack Rucker, outscored the Cadets of Oklahoma Military Academy, 100 to 32, in a dual meet T u e s d a y afternoon at Claremore.

N e x t competition for the Norsemen will be in Saturday's Arkansas Relays at Fayetteville.

Results at Claremore:

440 relay—1. Norse (Curry, Gray, Scott, Turlington), 45.4.

120 high hurdles—1. Carter, Norse, 15.3; 2. Clingan, Norse, 15.6; 3. King, OMA.

100 dash—1. Turlington, N, 10.0; 2. Hanoch, N, 10.1; 3. Harrison, OMA

Ed Turlington places 1ˢᵗ in 100 yard dash in 10 seconds flat, anchors winning 440 relay.
Miami Daily News Record, Miami, Oklahoma,
March 25, 1964 page4.

Appendix U
Jay Police Officer Bill "Nerves of Steel" Hobbs'
Police Report

Jay Police Department
Supplemental Narrative
Case Number: 2014-

Victim:

Suspect: TURLINGTON, EDWIN HARDEE JR.

April 14, 2014 I overheard radio traffic from the Delaware County Sheriff's Office. The radio traffic was in reference to a shooting in Delaware County near Southwest City, Missouri.

The county sent two deputies east on Highway 20. They also had a domestic in the south end of Delaware County with one deputy attending. The traffic stated that the victim of the shooting was transported to a Gravette Arkansas facility by private vehicle. The traffic reported the shooter left the scene in an older, black, extended cab pickup truck. The vehicle was travelling west.

I was sitting in my patrol vehicle at the Jay family Medical Clinic. This is located at 2485 North Main Street in the City of Jay, the County of Delaware and the State of Oklahoma.

Appendix U (*Cont.*)
Jay Police Officer Bill "Nerves of Steel" Hobbs'
Police Report

The dispatcher at the 911 Center advised the shooter was on 911.

The shooter was north of Jay, three or four miles. He was coming

to the sheriff's office to speak with an officer.

I was sitting broadside to traffic on highway 10-59, also known as

Main Street, in a marked patrol unit. I had my headlights and

taillights on. Any traffic travelling south would see me on the west

side of the road.

I was the only Jay Police Officer on duty in the city limits of Jay.

Not knowing the physical capabilities or mental state of the active

shooter I was steeling myself for the unknown. I was attempting to

determine the best way to gain the tactical advantage for the

citizens of Jay and myself. The sheriff's office had a couple of

officers travelling to the sheriff's office.

At approximately 20:15 a black, extended cab Ford pickup passed

my location travelling south into Jay. The vehicle was in the lane

nearest to me. I immediately pulled out behind the vehicle.

At approximately 20:20 I asked my dispatcher to run the vehicle

tag on this vehicle. The tag number was 452 ALY. This was an

Appendix U (*Cont.*)
Jay Police Officer Bill "Nerves of Steel" Hobbs'
Police Report

Oklahoma tag. The tag number checked to Julie K. and or Edwin Turlington of Afton, Oklahoma. The tag had expired in August of the year 2013.

As I was passing the grade school, I asked my dispatcher if she could confirm if this was the vehicle that was involved in the shooting.

As we neared the four-way stop at 5th Street and Highway 10-59(Main Street), she advised the vehicle was the one involved in the shooting.

The light for southbound traffic was red. I observed Chief Shambaugh on 5th Street at the light.

Chief Shambaugh asked me by radio if this was the vehicle. I replied in the affirmative. He advised me to light him up and make the stop. I activated my emergency lights. I placed the white beam of my spotlight on the driver of the vehicle.

Chief Shambaugh and I conducted a felony stop. The window on the driver side was down. I advised the subject to place his hands out the window where I could see them. The subject had a wallet

Appendix U (*Cont.*)
Jay Police Officer Bill "Nerves of Steel" Hobbs'
Police Report

or other item in his hand. The subject complied with my instructions. He asked to shut the truck off. He was allowed to shut the truck off. He asked to put the truck in park. He was allowed to place the truck in park. I asked him if he had any weapons. He advised "in the glove box". I advised him that he would exit the vehicle and lay on the pavement in a prone position, on his belly. The subject exited the vehicle. His complied and lay on his belly. Chief Shambaugh advised me to handcuff the subject and he would cover me. I place the subject in handcuffs. He was patted down. The subject advised that he had surgery on his left shoulder. I advised him that we would sit him upright and assist him to his feet. I asked his name. He replied Ed Turlington.

Turlington was stood up. He made some conversation about land ownership, a lieutenant colonel, buying, renting land, being in the military police, and taking a private investigator class at Afton with the mayor. I did not make much of this conversation. Chief Shambaugh asked Turlington if he might drive his truck out of the roadway. He advised Turlington that he did not want to

Appendix U (*Cont.*)
Jay Police Officer Bill "Nerves of Steel" Hobbs'
Police Report

search his truck. He merely wished to remove it with his

permission from the road.

Turlington was placed in my unit. Turlington was asked again by

Chief Shambaugh if it was permissible to move his truck.

Turlington again approved.

Turlington was taken to the Sheriff's Office. This was at

approximately 20:30. He was turned over to Deputy Todd Stanley.

I placed his wallet/item in the pocket of his hoodie. He was taken

into the Sheriff's Office and handcuffs were removed by Officer

Stanley. He handed me my handcuffs and placed another set on

Turlington, this time placing them in the front of Turlington.

At the Sheriff's Office Turlington asked me if the "guy was

alright". I advised him that I did not have any knowledge of the

other guy or his condition. Turlington stated that he had seen the

guy driving around.

I left the office. This was approximately 20:40.

Appendix V

Jay Police Chief Mike Shambaugh's Police Report

JAY POLICE DEPARTMENT

TYPE OF REPORT- <u>OFFICER REPORT</u>

On 04-14-14 I was advised of a shooting which occurred in Delaware County. No information on the suspect other than he had left in a black extended cab pickup. Officer Hobbs advised that he was possibly behind the suspect, coming into town from the North. I set up at the stop light in Jay and waited for them to arrive. I asked Hobbs if he was sure it was the suspect's vehicle and he got confirmation that it was. The suspect was supposedly on his way to the sheriff's office to turn himself in. The light controlling traffic on Highway 59 turned red and the suspect came to a stop to my immediate left, with Hobbs directly behind him. I sat there for a short time on 5th Street and decided that this was the best time from a tactical standpoint to make contact with the suspect. There was no other traffic at the time nor were there anyone at the businesses in the immediate area. Officer Hobbs safety as well as the suspects safety became my concern and being that we were all in a well lighted area, I advised Hobbs to light him up and make the traffic stop. I didn't want a suspect in a shooting to dictate the terms upon which we were to make contact with him. Hobbs engaged his overhead lights and did shine his spotlight onto the suspect. We both exited our patrol units and advanced toward suspect, Hobbs coming from the driver's side back of the truck while I advanced from the front of the suspect's vehicle. Hobbs was directing suspect to place his hands out of the window and he did so. Suspect asked if he could shut the vehicle off and put it in park, and was advised in the affirmative, so he did so. Hobbs asked suspect if he had any weapons and he stated in the glove box. Suspect was asked to exit the vehicle and lay on the pavement in a prone position, and he did so. I advised Hobbs that I would cover suspect while he handcuffed him. Hobbs went back to his unit to retrieve his cuffs and I advised the suspect that I appreciated his cooperation and that this is just the way things had to be done for his safety and ours. I advised suspect that I didn't want any misunderstandings to happen, and as you can see, I'm not pointing my weapon directly at you. Suspect advised me he understood and that he knew we were just doing our jobs and he didn't want any misunderstandings either, and finished by saying thank you. Hobbs returned and cuffed the suspect and then patted him

Appendix V (*Cont.*)
Jay Police Chief Mike Shambaugh's Police Report

down. Suspect advised his left shoulder was hurt and we assisted him to his feet using his right arm to help him stand. Hobbs asked him his name and he advised it was Ed Turlington. Suspect was mumbling about some land, being a military policeman and being in a private investigator class in Afton. I then asked suspect what he wanted to do with his truck. I advised him I would be willing to drive it to the sheriff's office if he would give me permission to do so. I advised him that I would not search his vehicle, simply drive it to the sheriff's office. He said that would be great. I had a brief conversation with undersheriff Carl Sloan and Turlington was placed in Hobbs unit and I again asked his permission to drive it to the sheriffs office. Again, suspect gave me permission to drive his truck to the sheriffs office. I drove suspect's vehicle to the sheriffs office, turned the truck off, exited the vehicle and handed the keys to Carl Sloan. I advised him it was unlocked. Sloan then locked suspect's vehicle. I then advised him that the suspect had said there was a weapon in the glove box. I advised Sloan I didn't know what kind weapon it was. I left with officer Hobbs a short time later. All above events, occurrences and conversations did occur within the City Limits of Jay, Delaware County, State of Oklahoma.

Mike Shambaugh

MIKE SHAMBAUGH

Appendix W
Former DA Eddie Wyant Defends
Admitted Child Porn Criminals
Asks for probation in case involving 5 to 10 year old victims

Enid News & Eagle

Serving Enid and Northwest Oklahoma | enidnews.com

☰ Menu 🏠 E-Paper App Celebrations Text Alerts Obituaries Public Notices

EDITOR'S PICK TOPICAL FEATURED

Enid teen sentenced in child porn case

By Cass Rains Staff Writer Oct 3, 2017

Drake Edward Swanson

Drake Edward Swanson pleaded guilty June 2 to the charges, which are punishable up to 20 years in prison and/or a fine of up to $25,000 and up to five years in prison and/or a fine of up to $5,000, respectively. Those charged with possession of child pornography are not eligible for deferred sentences.

"These images are absolutely horrific," he told the judge. Jennins said the images that were downloaded depicted children between the ages of 5 and 10.

"These offenders create a market for this type of material," he told the court.

Swanson's attorney, Eddie Wyant, asked the judge for 15 years probation for his client.

Cass Rains Staff Writer, "Enid Teen Sentenced in Child Porn Case," Enidnews.com, October 03, 2017, accessed August 04, 2019, https://www.enidnews.com/oklahoma/news/enid-teen-sentenced-in-child-porn-case/article_e23b0aec-1da4-5ede-9ae3-a7a804150799.html.

Appendix X
Local Rancher Doug Gibson Becomes Hero
by Killing Cattle Rustler
The Seattle Times, June 26, 1994

Friday, July 19, 2019 | 🚗 TRAFFIC

The Seattle Times
Winner of Ten Pulitzer Prizes

Search

Home | News | Business & Tech | Sports | Entertainment | Food | Living | Homes | Travel | Opinion

Sunday, June 26, 1994 - Page updated at 12:00 AM

✉ E-mail article   🖨 Print

Rancher Becomes Hero By Killing Apparent Cattle Rustler

By Scott Parks
Dallas Morning News

AFTON, Okla. - Doug Gibson counted on hard work and luck to bring him success as a cattle rancher.

Instead, Gibson said, this year ushered in a plague of cattle rustlers and no solution from an undermanned sheriff's department.

So, he picked up a shotgun and took matters into his own hands.

Under a full moon at 11:30 p.m. March 30, Gibson killed one of two men walking across his pasture. The other man escaped unharmed and was charged with attempted cattle rustling. Gibson was charged with second-degree manslaughter.

Instantly, at age 32, Gibson became a reluctant hero, and his case spawned a new political movement to fight crime in rural areas.

"All during this thing, I never felt like a hero," said Gibson, who makes a living as a tree trimmer for a rural

Appendix X (Cont.)
Local Rancher Doug Gibson Becomes Hero by Murdering Cattle Rustler

electric co-op and ranches on the side. "A lot of people rallied around me because, finally, the good guy got back."

Gibson's friends and neighbors formed the Doug Gibson Legal Assistance Fund. As donations poured in, Gibson had a decision to make: He could go to trial or accept a plea bargain.

On May 19, Gibson took the deal. He pleaded no contest to the manslaughter charge in return for an 18-month, unsupervised probation. If he doesn't get into trouble during that time, he will go back to court, and his record will be wiped clean.

An Oklahoma statute, commonly called the "make my day" law, says a resident can use deadly force to protect people in imminent bodily

danger. But the law says one cannot use deadly force to protect livestock or other property.

The leaders of the Doug Gibson Legal Assistance Fund say they want the Oklahoma statute to be amended to conform with Texas law, which allows residents to use deadly force to protect their property at night.

"Doug has been the rallying point," said Dr. Wiley Hough, a veterinarian in Miami, Okla.

Gibson lives with his family in a non-air-conditioned farmhouse just off Interstate 44.

Appendix X (Cont.)
Local Rancher Doug Gibson Becomes Hero
by Murdering Cattle Rustler

Gibson arrived home at 5:30 p.m. from a 10-hour shift trimming trees. Before dinner, he drove off to do the chores that sustain his dreams of someday becoming a full-time cattle rancher.

On this day, he was preoccupied with a cow that gave birth to a dead calf the night before, the result of a breech birth. Antibiotics for the cow rested on the seat next to him. As he pulled up to the pasture gate, Gibson was clearly shaken as he spotted the cow lying dead in a pen.

"I really liked that old cow," he said in a slow drawl.

After a moment, he added: "I made $80 at work today. That cow and calf were worth about $1,250. I guess it's just the business."

After two years of part-time ranching, Gibson has built his herd to 26 cows and 16 calves. During a two-week period in March, he said rustlers stole four calves. He had no insurance.

The sheriff's department, he said, would not investigate.

"They just told me to come into town and file a report," he said. "I was afraid I was gonna be out of business if it kept up."

Appendix X (Cont.)
Local Rancher Doug Gibson Becomes Hero by Murdering Cattle Rustler

Sheriff Jim Ed Walker, in response, said he has six deputies to patrol 640 square miles of Ottawa County. He acknowledged not having the manpower to investigate most nonviolent rural crimes.

So, Gibson said he decided to sleep in the barn loft and catch the rustlers if they struck again. On the fifth night of his stakeout, Gibson said he saw two men coming across the pasture. He said he yelled and fired three shots from his Remington 12-gauge shotgun. Gibson said he climbed from the loft and ran the 60 yards to where Robbin Irwin, 42, lay wounded, but still conscious. One pellet had pierced his side. The second man, Daniel Wyrick, was hiding behind a haystack. Gibson said he admonished the men to stay put. Then, he said, he ran 300 yards down the road to his house and called 911.

According to court records, Wyrick and Irwin, both of Joplin, Mo., told investigators their pickup had overheated and stalled on a road near the pasture. They said they were heading for a stock pond to get water for the radiator when Gibson fired.

"The problem was that they didn't have a bucket or anything to carry water," Walker said. "I also checked the engine, and it was OK. Nothing wrong with that truck."

Appendix X (Cont.)
Local Rancher Doug Gibson Becomes Hero
by Murdering Cattle Rustler

Walker also reported investigators found five pieces of nylon rope at the scene and in the pickup. A piece of plywood covered the pickup's bed.

The next day Gibson learned Irwin had died after surgery in Joplin. "It's hard for me to accept that someone actually died," Gibson said. T. Logan Brown, an attorney who is defending Wyrick against the cattle-rustling charges, is one of the few people in Ottawa County who openly challenges what Gibson did that night.

"It was premeditated," Brown said. "He went and bought double-ought buckshot that could stop big game. He laid in wait in a second-story window, and he shot someone. It's taking the law into your own hands."

Wyrick is awaiting trial and could be sent to prison for five years if convicted. Some members of the defense-fund organization, which is searching for a new name, want to use part of the money to hire private detectives to investigate high-profile rural crimes such as cattle rustling.

As the spotlight on his case dims and the organization takes up new causes, Gibson says he hopes his life will return to normal.

"I guess everyone has to know their limitations," he said, "and I'm not one to be in the public eye."

Appendix Y
Joseph Bradley's Sworn Statement

DELAWARE COUNTY SHERIFF'S OFFICE

WITNESS STATEMENT

CA. NO: 2014-0478

DATE 04/14/2014 TIME: _____ NAME: Joseph Bradley
ADDRESS 70200 E 370 Rd   CITY: Jay   STATE: OK
ZIP CODE: 74346   (MALE)/FEMALE   RACE: _____   DOB 05/12/1980
SSN# 429-55-5654 HGT 5'9" WGT 200 EYES Green HAIR Brown
EMPLOYMENT: Contech   CITY Broken Arrow STATE OK
HOME PHONE 918 854-3584 WORK PHONE _____ CELL PHONE 918 353-3788

I UNDERSTAND THAT THE CONTENTS OF THIS STATEMENT ARE TRUE AND CORRECT TO THE BEST OF MY KNOWLEDGE. I HAVE MADE THIS STATEMENT ON MY OWN FREE WILL WITHOUT ANY PRESSURE OR COERCION OF ANY KIND USED AGAINST ME

1. I HAVE THE RIGHT TO REMAIN SILENT.
2. ANYTHING I SAY CAN AND WILL BE USED AGAINST ME IN A COURT OF LAW.
3. I HAVE THE RIGHT TO TALK TO A LAWYER AND HAVE ONE PRESENT WITH ME WHILE I AM BEING QUESTIONED.
4. IF I CANNOT AFFORD TO HIRE A LAWYER, ONE WILL BE APPOINTED TO REPRESENT ME BEFORE ANY QUESTIONING, IF I SO WISH.
5. IF I DECIDE TO MAKE A STATEMENT, I MAY STOP AT ANY TIME.
6. I UNDERSTAND EACH OF THESE RIGHTS.
7. I UNDERSTAND I CAN TERMINATE THIS INTERVIEW AT ANY TIME.

I left from Jack Thomas's house going back to my house on E370 Rd. I seen Steve and Darrel coming out from the logging Road. I stopped and talked to them for a few minutes. When I started to go on home a newer black ford pickup was coming down the hill. He stopped me about 75 to 100 yards from where the Steve and Darrel were at. He asked me if they were with me, I said no and went on home. As I was going up the hill the I seen Steve pull out onto the county Road. The Black ford pulled to the passenger side of Steve's pickup and stopped them. Approximitly 10 to 15 min after I got home Steve pulled into my house and told me that the man had shot Darrel. I then took Darrel home to Jack Thomas's.

PERSON MAKING STATEMENT: Joseph Bradley   DATE: 04/14/2014

Appendix Z

PC Affidavit for Philpott's 2017 Felony Meth, DWI, etc.

PROBABLE CAUSE TO OBTAIN BOND

STATE OF ARKANSAS

PLAINTIFF

VS.

Darrell Eugene Philpott
W/M DOB 2/16/61
S.S. #

DEFENDANT

FACTS CONSTITUTING PROBABLE CAUSE

Comes now Deputy Justin Crane of the Benton County Sheriff's Office and under oath doth state:

On Tuesday 10/4/16, I, Deputy Crane with the Benton County Sheriff's Office, noticed a suspicious circumstance call on the CAD system. I informed CenCom I would be en route to the call. CenCom informed me there was a car parked in the middle of the road on Ballman Rd, just off Hwy 72. They also said the lights of the vehicle were on.

I proceeded to the scene and came up on an older model red/maroon vehicle parked in the middle of the road. The headlight and tail lights were on, as well as the brake lights, and the vehicle was running. When I first pulled up behind the vehicle I could not see anybody inside. Once I made my approach, I noticed an older gentleman slumped over towards the passenger side. I watched the male for a few seconds to ensure he was breathing. Once I noticed he was breathing and seemed to be asleep, I returned to my unit and informed CenCom about the findings. I also informed them I was going to try and wake the subject up.

I returned to the vehicle and verbally tried waking the male. There was no response. I opened the door of the vehicle and attempted again. Still no response. I started banging on the roof of the vehicle, while trying verbally to wake the male. Finally, the male woke up in a startled state, looked at me and stated, "You don't have to be like that" and went right back to sleep. I continued with the process several times of trying to wake the male. Before he became fully awake, he would mumble, "Hold on" while still slumped to the right. He finally sat up in the seat and became fully awake. I identified myself again and asked if he was alright. He said he was. I could smell a strong odor of intoxicants coming from the vehicle. I asked the male how much he had had to drink. He said, "To much". I instructed the male to step out of the vehicle at that time. The male looked me in the eyes and stated very clearly, "Bye" and reached for the gear shift, as if to leave. I grabbed the male by the shirt and told him to get out of the vehicle. Soon as I started to pull, the shirt ripped and I lost my grip. I grabbed the male's right arm and began pulling while telling him to get out of the vehicle. He was refusing to comply and was pulling against me. I gained control of his left arm and started to pull against the B post of the vehicle to perform a straight arm bar take down, using the vehicle as leverage. The male was still pulling against me. I continued using the vehicle as leverage until he was partially out of the vehicle. Once his upper body was partially out, I grabbed his overalls on the back side with my left hand,

Appendix Z (*Cont.*)
PC Affidavit for Philpott's 2017 Felony Meth, DWI, etc.

while still maintaining control of his left arm. After I had a secure grip on his clothing with my left hand, I gained control of the lower part of his clothing with my right hand and removed him from the vehicle.

When the male was removed from the vehicle, he was placed on the ground. When the male landed on the ground, he hit his head on the road. After he was on the ground, I placed his right arm in a post position while his left arm was still under his body. I had my left knee between his shoulder blades and my right at his lower back to maintain control of his body. I instructed him to place his left arm behind his back. Once there, I controlled both hands and placed him in handcuffs. He was assisted to his feet and instructed to lean against the vehicle. I performed a search on the male. I search his immediate area of the vehicle and discovered a small bag of what appeared to be marijuana. He confirmed that it indeed was such, without being asked. Since there was a bump and small cut with little blood, I asked CenCom to call EMS to my location to ensure he was alright. The male did not want EMS to come and check him and said he could not afford it. I informed him they were going to come regardless. EMS arrived on scene and checked to male. He refused medical attention.

While speaking with male, finally identifying his as Darrell Philpott, I noticed his eyes were very blood shot, slurred speech, and an odor of intoxicants coming from his person. I asked him if he would take a PBT test. He said he would. Returned to my unit and retrieved my PBT instrument. The result of the PBT was .170. I informed Darrell he was under arrest for DWI and Possession of a Controlled Substance. A search of the vehicle was performed. He was transported to the jail for further testing. Dep. Chandler remained on scene for the tow service.

Once at the jail, during the search for the intake process, Dep. Deleon discovers a small orange baggie in one of the small pockets of his overalls. Dep. Deleon gave me the baggie. When I examined the baggie, I noticed it was a crystal like substance that resembled methamphetamine. Dep. Deleon performed a strip search of Darrell at that time. No other items were found. Next I read, and had Darrell follow along on his own sheet, the Implied Consent form. I had him initial and sign in all appropriate locations. When asked if he would take the test, he said and initialed he would. The result of the test was .117. Next I read him the second half of the Implied Consent, asking if he wanted a second test at his own expense. Darrell said he did not and initialed "No".

Darrell was booked in on the charges of DWI, No DL, Possession of a Controlled Substance (Meth), Possession of a Controlled Substance (Marijuana), Careless/ Prohibited Driving, and No Insurance. He was to be held for a bond hearing.

I used a field test kit to test the crystal like substance. When I broke the swab with the crystal substance on it, it immediately turned blue, which is a positive indication for methamphetamine. Both the baggies were placed into evidence and are being sent to ASCL to further testing.

Based on the nature of the crime, and the likelihood of conviction, the possible severity of the penalty that could be imposed, the state joins me in requesting that **Darrell Eugene Philpott**, be held for the offense of: **Possession of Controlled Substance (Meth), Possession Controlled Substance (Marijuana), DWI, No DL, No Insurance, Careless Prohibited Driving**

Appendix Z (Continued)

PC Affidavit for Philpott's 2017 Felony Meth, DWI, etc.

I conducted a criminal history check on **Darrell Eugene Philpott** which reflected:

1. **Criminal Mischief (no disposition)- BCSO**
2. **Possession w/ purpose to Deliver Controlled Substance (F)- BCSO (Guilty)**
3. **Fleeing- Sulphur Springs (Guilty)**
   DWI- Guilty
   Possession Controlled Substance- Dismissed

Based on the above and foregoing the State joins me in requesting Darrell Eugene Philpott be bound over on Probable Cause for committing the above listed crimes and that the bond be set in the amount of $ 5,000 .

I swear that the allegations contained herein are the truth, the whole truth, and nothing but the truth. Witness my hand this.

Deputy Justin Crane BC153
Benton County Sheriff's Office
1300 SW 14th Street
Bentonville AR 72712
Phone (479) 271-1008

STATE OF ARKANSAS
COUNTY OF BENTON

Subscribed and sworn to before me this ___6th___ day of ___October___, 2016

NOTARY PUBLIC

My Commission Expires: July 5, 2023

APPROVED: (Via Phone) **Tyler Hawkins**
DEPUTY PROSECUTING ATTORNEY

ROXANNE SUZETTE MAI
MY COMMISSION # 123974400
EXPIRES: July 5, 2023
Benton County

Appendix AA
Philpott's 2017 Arrest Warrant for Failing to Appear on 2016 Felony Meth, DWI, and Class VI Drug Charges

IN THE CIRCUIT COURT OF BENTON COUNTY, ARKANSAS

WARRANT

BENCH

CASE NO. CR 2016-1813-2

DEFENDANT INFORMATION:
DARRELL EUGENE PHILPOTT
W/M DOB: 2/16/1961

F02342017

THE STATE OF ARKANSAS:

TO ANY SHERIFF, CONSTABLE, CORONER, POLICEMAN OR MARSHAL OF THIS STATE:

YOU ARE COMMANDED FORTHWITH TO ARREST: DARRELL EUGENE PHILPOTT
LKA: 10650 SHADY LANE CR
GRAVETTE, AR 72736

AND BRING HIM BEFORE THE BENTON COUNTY CIRCUIT COURT TO ANSWER AN INFORMATION IN THAT COURT

AGAINST HIM FOR:
BY ORDER OF THE COURT FOR FAILURE TO APPEAR IN DIV II ON 1/9/2017

OC: POSSESSION OF CONTROLLED SUBSTANCE (CLASS D FELONY), POSSESSION OF CONTROLLED SUBSTANCE (CLASS A MISDEMEANOR), DRIVING WHILE INTOXICATED - FIRST OFFENSE (CLASS U MISDEMEANOR)

A FELONY, A MISDEMEANOR, OR IF COURT BE ADJOURNED FOR THE TERM THAT YOU DELIVER HIM TO THE

JAILER OF BENTON COUNTY, ARKANSAS

WITNESS MY HAND AND THE SEAL OF SAID COURT THIS 10TH DAY OF JANUARY , 2017.

BRENDA DESHIELDS, CIRCUIT CLERK

BY_____

STATE OF ARKANSAS – COUNTY OF BENTON) SS
I HEREBY CERTIFY THAT I HAVE THIS_____23_____ DAY OF __March__ , 20_17_

DULY SERVED THE WITHIN WARRANT BY ARRESTING THE WITHIN DEFENDANT.

_____SHERIFF

BY:_____D.S.

Appendix BB

Philpott's 1981 Pre-Sentencing Report

PRE-SENTENCE REPORT
Darrell Eugene Philpott

IDENTIFYING DATA

Darrell Eugene Philpott
Rt. 1, Box 13
Decatur, Ark.
DOB: 2-16 61
Place of birth: Gravette, Ark.
Social Security #: 430-29-7908
Present offense: Possession of a Controlled Substance with Intent to Deliver
Date of offense: 6-16-81
Date of arrest: 6-16-81
Arresting agencey: Benton Co. Sheriff/Decatur Police Dept.
Defense attorney: Stephen Sawyer

PRESENT OFFENSE:

As the court has previously heard testim9ny regarding the present offense at a
suppression hearing and on trial date, an outline of the offense is not given.

DEFENDANT'S VERSION OF OFFENSE

Philpott agrees to the official version of the offense as previously testified to.
Philpott states he and Meek had found the marijuana on some land owned by Peterson
Industries.near a pond where they frequently fished. Philpott denies growing the
marijuana, but admits pulling it up and attempting to dry it. Philpott also denies
any intent to sell any of the marijuana and stated he was putting it in plastic bags
only for purposes of dividing it up between himself and Meek. Philpott indicated
he planned only to smoke the marijuana for personal use.

PRIOR RECORD

Philpott has one prior felony conviction. On 6-8-81, Philpott pled guilty to charges
of Burglary and Theft of Property. Philpott was placed on three years probation
with no supervision conditioned upon payment of restitution, costs, and Public Defender fee of $1035.00. The present offense occurred eight days after the above
court appearance.

Philpott has also recorded several arrests for liquor and traffic violations. At
present, Philpott has three DWI charges pending in courts in Decatur and Siloam
Springs.

FAMILY HISTORY

Darrell Eugene Philpott was born 2-26 61 in Gravette, Ark. He is one of two children
born to the marraige of Harold and Gilda Philpott. Philpott's parents were divorced
when he was approximately three years of age. The divorce was due in part to excessive drinking on the part of Philpott's father. Philpott's father presently resides
in Maysville, Ark. and is employed by O'Brien Foods, Noel, Mo. Prior to this employment, Mr. Philpott was employed by Peterson Industries for approximately ten years.
Philpott did maintain relations with his father and frequently visited him. They
also shared some recreational activities such as fishing and hunting and apparently
have a good, ongoing relationship.

Appendix BB (Continued)
Philpott's 1981 Pre-Sentencing Report

Philpott's mother did not remarry until 1979 and was solely responsible for the up-bringing and maintenance of the family. Philpott's mother is presently employed by Franklin Electric Co., Siloam Springs. Mrs. Philpott married Marvin Wayne Shook in 1979 and as a result of that marraige, Philpott has three stepbrothers and two step-sisters. Philpott states he has a good relationship with the stepfather. The family resides outside of Decatur and Philpott occupies a trailer next door to his mother's residence. The trailer is owned by his mother and she provides the residence free of charge to Philpott.

Philpott's mother stated tha Philpott presented no unusual problems as a child and she is unsure of why he is involved in the present offense. She did state that Phil-pott did appear to lack ambition and gave up easily if confronted with problems. She believes that Philpott did have a drinking problem as evidenced by his DWI arrest but thinks he now has the problem under control. She also stated that Philpott is very scared about going to jail and realizes he has made some serious mistakes. The family appears to be able and willing to provide adequate moral and financial support for Philpott to help him sove his present problems.

MARITAL HISTORY

Philpott has never been married and has no dependents. It has been alleged, however, by Cathy Meek, sister of Philpott's co-defendant, that she is carrying his child. Cathy Meek is fifteen years of age.

EDUCATION

Darrell Philpott attended public schools in Decatur, Ark. through the eleventh grade. School records indicate that Philpott had a good attendance record and exhibited average performance through the eighth grade. After this period, Philpott's grades began to drop off until he was finally expelled from school over a dispute with a teacher.

School officials indicated Philpott's poor performance was due to poor attitude to-ward his studies. They believe Philpott was capable of doing the required work but chose to not participate of try to succeed. Philpott's mother stated that most of his problems at school were his own fault. After leaving the Decatur schools, Phil-pott attended the Alternative School in Siloam Springs for a short time. He did not graduate or receive his GED from that attendance.

EMPLOYMENT HISTORY

Since dropping out of school, Philpott has not maintained steady employment. He has worked for brief periods at Peterson Industries, O'Brien Foods, and Wal-Mart Distri-bution but usually quit because he did not like the work. For the most part, Phil-pott has worked at various odd jobs for his uncle, Dean Philpott. These jobs include hauling hay, other farm work, and masonry. At present, Philpott is helping his uncle part-time in his masonry business. Philpott stated he had not worked much because he had not needed to. Philpott has no occupational skills and has no real career ambition. He stated he would like to drive a truck or work in the construction industry in the future.

Appendix BB (Continued)
Philpott's 1981 Pre-Sentencing Report

MILITARY SERVICE

Philpott is presently a member of the National Guard unit in Siloam Springs. Philpott attended basic training at Ft. Sill, Okla. in field artillery. Philpott is in good standing with the unit and has approximately four years left to serve.

INTERESTS, LEISURE TIME ACTIVITIES

Philpott lists a number of diverse hobbies. For outdoor activity, he enjoys hunting, fishing, and horseback riding. For indoor activity, Philpott enjoys cooking and crocheting. Philpott also stated he liked "partying."

MENTAL AND PHYSICAL HEALTH

Philpott describes his health as good. He has not been hospitalized with the exception of a tonsillectomy as a child. Philpott has suffered no major illness or injury, is not being treated by a physician, or taking any medication.

Philpott describes his personality as shy and states he is uncomfortable around strangers. Philpott says he makes friends easily if he wants but is cautious in forming new relationships. He has nver been treated for any mental illness.

ALCOHOL AND DRUG ABUSE

Philpott stated he first began using marijuana at the age of 16. His usage is con fined to 1-2 joints per week. Philpott admits he has continued to smoke marijuana but does not believe his usage is a problem. Philpott also admits to using "speed" about 7-8 times while he was working nights.

Philpott stated he had previously used alcohol quite heavily drinking about 1-2 six-packs of beer daily and more on weekends. Philpott also stated he usually got drunk if he started drinking. Philpott stated that since his arrests for DWI, he had tried to control his drinking and had been partially successful. Philpott admits to the continued use of alcohol, but has limited his drinking to only about 2-3 times per month. Philpott believes that alcohol has been a problem in the past, but believes he has the problem under control.

FINANCIAL CONDITION

Philpott lists as assets a $65.00 monthly income from the National Guard and approximately $400.00 miscellaneous income from various odd jobs. He also owns a 1975 Chevrolet Monte Carlo valued at $1600.00.

Philpott lists liabilites as $101.83 car payment to GMAC, $63.00 monthly car insurance to Decatur State Bank, and $50.00 per month restitution to Benton Co. Circuit Court.

SUMMARY AND EVALUATION

Darrell Eugene Philpott is a 20-year old male facing charges of Sale of a Controlled Substance with Intent to Deliver. Philpott is making his second appearance in Benton Co. Circuit Court this year. Philpott was previously convicted of Burglary and Theft of Property on 6-8-81 and was placed on three years probation.

Appendix BB (Continued)
Philpott's 1981 Pre-Sentencing Report

Philpott was born in 1961 in Gravette, Ark. and has lived in the Decatur area all of his life. He is one of two children born to the marraige of Harold and Gilda Philpott. The marraige of the parents ended in divorce and Philpott was reared primarily by his mother. Philpott has had a continuing relationship with his father. There appears to have been adequate parental guidance and support during his formative years and the family is still quite concerned about his welfare.

Philpott attended public schools in Decatur through the eleventh grade before finally dropping out. There is evidence that Philpott had the ability to perform well, but failed to do so because of poor attitude. Philpott has received no other formal education or training.

Since leaving school, Philpott has not maintained steady employment. He has worked at a number of local industries bu usually quit because he did not like the work. Philpott has worked on and off for his uncle, Dean Philpott, for about 8 years and this has constituted the majority of his work experience. Philpott has no definite career ambitions.

Philpott is in good physical health and has suffered no major illness or injury. He appears to be stable mentally, but ther is ample evidence of substance abuse by Philpott - mainly alcohol and marijuana. If probation were granted, Philpott should be required to pursue alcohol treatment and counseling. There is no definite evidence that Philpott has been involved in the sale of marijuana or other drugs.

Philpott appears to realize he has made some serious mistakes and is quite apprehensive about the possibility of being sent to prison. Philpott does not think he will be involved in any further criminal behavior and believes that some type of punishment is justified.

RECOMMENDATION

Darrell Eugene Philpott appears to be a poor risk for probation. This consideration is based mainly on his previous conviction in this court, the number of misdemeanor arrests he has experienced, and his propensity for substance abuse. It is recommended that Philpott be sentenced to a moderate term in the Arkansas Department of Correction.

Respectfully submitted,

Eddie Cobb
District Parole Officer

Appendix CC
Tulsan WWII Hero advises Brad Pitt
Tulsa World, 22 October 2014

Tulsan WWII hero advises Brad Pitt, movie team making 'Fury'

By MICHAEL SMITH World Scene Writer   Oct 12, 2014

World War II veteran Paul Andert talks about consulting for the upcoming film "Fury" at his home in Tulsa. Andert and other veterans went to Hollywood in 2013 to advise the film's cast and producers on the reality of the conflict. MATT BARNARD/Tulsa World

Matt Barnard

Upon his arrival in Hollywood, Paul Andert could see how important his role would be as a consultant.

Brad Pitt and his producing partners were filming "Fury," an $80 million movie about World War II and the tanks that were used to drive into Germany and defeat the Nazis. They

Appendix CC (Continued)
Tulsan WWII Hero advises Brad Pitt

were making a film about the famed 2nd Armored Division, a group of 14,000 soldiers, of which only a handful are still alive.

Andert is one of those men.

That would be Technical Sgt. Paul Andert, a 91-year-old Tulsa man and a platoon sergeant during the invasions of North Africa and Sicily.

One of this country's most decorated soldiers, he was part of the D-Day landing at Normandy, and he fought in the Battle of the Bulge.

He arrived in Los Angeles in August 2013 along with three other 2nd Armored Division members to meet with Pitt, his co-stars and writer-director David Ayer. Their meeting was a four-hour swap of war stories and a military education.

"I could tell that they didn't know much about how things worked in an armored division. Like an actor, one of the tankers (soldiers inside the tank) asked me, 'How did you see, because I couldn't see anything in there?'" Andert remarked.

"I told them that of course you are partially blind inside the tank, and that's where my job as infantry came in: I was riding on top of the tank, telling those inside where the fire was coming from, saying 'We're taking fire from the left' or the right or from behind.

Appendix CC (Continued)
Tulsan WWII Hero advises Brad Pitt

"I would call them on the phone that was on the back of the center tank (of five tanks driving forward as a platoon of tanks). We spent 30 months going from Africa to Sicily to

Germany, and I probably spent half of that time on top of a tank."

In talking with Pitt and actors Shia LaBeouf, Logan Lerman, Michael Pena, and Jon Bernthal, was there any other immediate advice he offered the stars?

"They showed up, and some had ponytails," Andert recalled. "I told them that those had to go."

As a consultant, Andert said the "Fury" production team wanted his expertise "purely because there aren't many of us left." But when they fly him to Washington, D.C., next week for the film's Wednesday premiere, that will be about celebrating him for the hero that he has always been.

"We got them corrected on some things. We had to tell them that some of the cuss words they were using weren't right

because we weren't using some of those until after the war," Andert said.

"Later they recorded me on video, too, and during that we talked about many more things, like concentration camps and rescuing people from burning barns. ... The filmmakers

Appendix CC (Continued)
Tulsan WWII Hero advises Brad Pitt

said they wanted the real information, and I think it's time that we got down to what it was really like."

War is hell

Andert served with the 41st Armored Infantry Regiment, part of the 2nd Armored Division, serving between 1940 and 1945, from the ages of 17 to 22. He can confirm that war, for lack of any other appropriate term, is hell.

He also realizes how difficult it can be to portray such carnage on the big screen, but he's doing what he can to make sure that "Fury" is as accurate as possible. For many years, Andert showed off a German soldier's helmet he had brought home from the war. The helmet had belonged to the last man he had killed in Germany.

"When you were fighting, you had to be a savage," Andert said. "Then, when you stop, you have to become a human being again, and you wonder, 'How did I do that?' "You had to become two different people. You went a little nut. People ask, 'How did you do that?' and there's only one answer: We had to."

Andert served under Gen. George S. Patton and knew the man well from their 2nd Armored Division days. "Old blood and guts," Andert said, chuckling as he recalled Patton's Nickname and the man as a great leader. "It was his guts and our blood."

Appendix CC (Continued)
Tulsan WWII Hero advises Brad Pitt

Then there was his meeting with Gen. Dwight D. Eisenhower, as recalled by Andert.

Eisenhower: "You're a bit young to be a platoon sergeant, aren't you?"

Andert: "Yes, sir."

Eisenhower: "You lied about your age to get in, didn't you?"

Andert: "Yes, sir."

Andert received the Silver Star (the third-highest award for valor and gallantry an Army serviceman can receive) to go with his two Bronze Stars and pair of Purple Hearts after being injured twice. If you read Andert's book "Unless You Have Been There," you will find a tell-it-like-it-is account of his war experiences. He's considering writing another book. "The medals mean a lot to me, because they mean I was knocked off a couple of times," he said. "I was in a plane that crashed, a boat that sank, a truck that was blown up, and I was blinded by the flash of a cannon shell. "Another book could be on the 14 times that I should have been knocked off for good."

There are plenty of military veterans who rarely talk about their battle experiences, if at all. Andert talks to kids at elementary schools and church groups and many more, keeping a busy schedule after the death of his wife of 65 years

Appendix CC (Continued)
Tulsan WWII Hero advises Brad Pitt

and a couple of his children. "I feel like I have to talk. I don't know how a person can be a leader, and I don't know how you can expect to win a war if you don't know how it's done," he said.

"We haven't truly won a war since WWII," he declared, "and we can't be a nation of wimps."

Hollywood goes to war

When talking about war films, Andert has seen his share, and he often sees something that's not quite right. The best he's seen. "Pork Chop Hill," a 1959 Gregory Peck film based on a Korean War battle.

"Saving Private Ryan" was "very good at the beginning part, the landing on Normandy," said Andert, who was there. "But after that part, not so much." He hasn't seen "Fury" yet to give his review, but Andert said he has reason to trust Pitt.

At the conclusion of that 2013 meeting, while the other men hovered around Pitt asking for a multitude of photos to be signed, Andert sat down and made out a list of his own requests for photos and autographs. When his chance came to speak privately with Pitt, Andert gave him some of his books, and he asked for autographed photos to be sent later to about

a dozen people, most of them veteran's hospital nurses and those with local hospitals who have helped him for years.

Appendix CC (Continued)
Tulsan WWII Hero advises Brad Pitt

"Brad did it all. He sent those items to everyone I asked. To us veterans, he always signed, 'With respect,' and I respected that," Andert said. He motions across the room to an American eagle statuette. It's an item he has purchased multiple times and sent to some of his favorite people. He had one delivered to Hollywood. "I sent one to Brad, and I told him, 'This goes to a true patriot. This is my Academy Award to you.'"

Appendix DD
Turlington's Current Teaching License

OKLAHOMA STATE DEPARTMENT *of* EDUCAT

TEACHING CERTIFICATE

The State Board of Education certifies and authorizes

EDWIN H. TURLINGTON

to serve in the accredited schools of Oklahoma as indicated below.

Description	Level	Valid From	Valid To
PHYSICAL EDUCATION/HEALTH/SAFETY	PK-12	5/1/2015	6/30/2020
US HISTORY/OK HISTORY/GOVERNMENT/ECONOMICS	5-12	5/1/2015	6/30/2020
WORLD HISTORY/GEOGRAPHY	5-12	5/1/2015	6/30/2020
DRIVER/SAFETY EDUCATION	5-12	5/1/2015	6/30/2020

Appendix EE

Philpott's 1979 Minor in Possession Conviction

DECATUR POLICE DEPT.
RECORD OF ARREST

Name Darrell Eugene Philpott

Address Route 1 Decatur, AR

License FRC 131   Make 79 Bedford   Dr. Lic. 9039-6617

Date 8-16-79   Time 12:30   A.M. **P.M.**

Place of Arrest Hiway 102

Offense Failure to maintain Contrel of Motor Vehicle

Sex M Hair ___ Eyes ___ D.O.B. 2-16-61   Ht. 5'11 Wt. 125

Remarks: Ticket # 62596

(illegible handwriting) guilty f c-#5

Witnesses: _____

Arresting Officer Mc Bryde

DECATUR, ARKANSAS

DECATUR POLICE DEPT.
RECORD OF ARREST

Name Darrell Eugene Philpott

Address Decatur, AR

License _____ Make _____ Dr. Lic. 9039-6617

Date 8-16-79   Time 5'11"   A.M. P.M.

Place of Arrest 102 Hiway West

Offense Minor in Poss.

Sex M Hair ___ Eyes ___ D.O.B. 2-16-61   Ht. 5'11" Wt. 125

Remarks: Ticket # 62557

Witnesses: _____

Arresting Officer Petros

DECATUR, ARKANSAS

Appendix FF

Philpott's 2017 DWI Conviction

Defendant's Full Name: __Philpott, Darrell__

A.C.A. # of Offense/ Name of Offense+	S-64-419(a)(b)(5)(A) Possession of a Controlled Substance			Case #2016-1813-2

A.C.A. # of Original Charged Offense	ATN BTN0057982	Offense was ☐ Nolle Prossed ☐ Dismissed ☐ Acquitted
	Appeal from District Court ☐ Yes ☒ No	Probation/SIS Revocation+ ☐ Yes ☒ No

Offense Date 10/4/2016	Offense is ☐ Felony ☒ Misd. ☐ Viol.	Offense Classification ☐ Y ☒ A ☐ B ☐ C ☐ D ☐ U

Number of Counts: 1	Criminal History Score 0	Seriousness Level	Defendant ☐ Attempted ☐ Solicited ☐ Conspired to commit the offense

Presumptive Sentence ☐ Prison Sentence of _____ months ☐ Community Corrections Center ☐ Alternative Sanction

Defendant Sentence* (see Page 2) Imposed ☐ ADC ☐ Jud. Tran. ☐ County Jail	If probation or SIS accompanied by period of confinement, state time: 76 days or _____ months.
_____ months	Sentence was enhanced _____ months, pursuant to
Probation 12 months	A.C.A. §§_____
	Enhancement(s) is to run: ☐ Concurrent ☐ Consecutive.
SIS _____ months Other ☐ Life ☐ LWOP ☐ Death	Defendant was sentenced as a habitual offender, pursuant to A.C.A. §5-4-501, subsection ☐ (a) ☐ (b) ☐ (c) ☐ (d)

Victim Info# (See page 2) ☒ N/A [Multiple Victims ☐ Yes ☐ No]	Age	Sex ☐ Male ☐ Female	Race & Ethnicity ☐ White ☐ Black ☐ Asian ☐ Native American ☐ Pacific Islander ☐ Other ☐ Unknown ☐ Hispanic

Defendant voluntarily, intelligently, and knowingly entered a ☒ negotiated plea of ☒ guilty or ☐ nolo contendere. ☐ plea directly to the court of ☐ guilty or ☐ nolo contendere.	Defendant: ☐ was sentenced pursuant to ☐ §§16-93-301 et seq., or ☐ other §§. ☐ entered a plea and was sentenced by a jury. ☐ was found guilty by the court & sentenced by ☐ court ☐ jury. ☐ was found guilty at a jury trial & sentenced by ☐ court ☐ jury. ☐ was found guilty of lesser included offense by ☐ court ☐ jury.

Sentence is a Departure ☐ Yes ☐ No	Sentence Departure is ☐ Durational or ☐ Dispositional. If durational, state how many months above/below the presumptive sentence:

Departure Reason (See page 2 for a list of reasons) Aggravating # _____ or Mitigating # _____. For Agg. #16 or Mit. #10, or if departing from guidelines, please explain: _____	Sentence will run: ☐ Consecutive ☐ Concurrent to Offense # _____ or Case # _____

A.C.A. # of Offense/ Name of Offense+	5-65-103 Driving While Intoxicated - First Offense	Case # 2016-1813-2

A.C.A. # of Original Charged Offense	ATN BTN0057982	Offense was ☐ Nolle Prossed ☐ Dismissed ☐ Acquitted
	Appeal from District Court ☐ Yes ☒ No	Probation/SIS Revocation+ ☐ Yes ☒ No

Offense Date 10/4/2016	Offense is ☐ Felony ☒ Misd. ☐ Viol.	Offense Classification ☐ Y ☐ A ☐ B ☐ C ☐ D ☒ U

Number of Counts: 1	Criminal History Score 0	Seriousness Level	Defendant ☐ Attempted ☐ Solicited ☐ Conspired to commit the offense

Presumptive Sentence ☐ Prison Sentence of _____ months ☐ Community Corrections Center ☐ Alternative Sanction

Defendant Sentence* (see Page 2) Imposed ☐ ADC ☐ Jud. Tran. ☐ County Jail	If probation or SIS accompanied by period of confinement, state time: 76 days or _____ months.
_____ months	Sentence was enhanced _____ months, pursuant to
Probation 12 months	A.C.A. §§_____
	Enhancement(s) is to run: ☐ Concurrent ☐ Consecutive.
SIS _____ months Other ☐ Life ☐ LWOP ☐ Death	Defendant was sentenced as a habitual offender, pursuant to A.C.A. §5-4-501, subsection ☐ (a) ☐ (b) ☐ (c) ☐ (d)

Victim Info# (See page 2) ☒ N/A [Multiple Victims ☐ Yes ☐ No]	Age	Sex ☐ Male ☐ Female	Race & Ethnicity ☐ White ☐ Black ☐ Asian ☐ Native American ☐ Pacific Islander ☐ Other ☐ Unknown ☐ Hispanic

Defendant voluntarily, intelligently, and knowingly entered a ☒ negotiated plea of ☒ guilty or ☐ nolo contendere. ☐ plea directly to the court of ☐ guilty or ☐ nolo contendere.	Defendant: ☐ was sentenced pursuant to ☐ §§16-93-301 et seq., or ☐ other §§. ☐ entered a plea and was sentenced by a jury. ☐ was found guilty by the court & sentenced by ☐ court ☐ jury. ☐ was found guilty at a jury trial & sentenced by ☐ court ☐ jury. ☐ was found guilty of lesser included offense by ☐ court ☐ jury.

Sentence is a Departure ☐ Yes ☐ No	Sentence Departure is ☐ Durational or ☐ Dispositional. If durational, state how many months above/below the presumptive sentence:

Departure Reason (See page 2 for a list of reasons) Aggravating # _____ or Mitigating # _____. For Agg. #16 or Mit. #10, or if departing from guidelines, please explain: _____	Sentence will run: ☐ Consecutive ☐ Concurrent to Offense # _____ or Case # _____

Appendix GG

2018 Philpott Resisting Assaulting Medics, Threatening to Kill Deputy, Resisting Arrest, etc.[xlv]

INCIDENT REPORT

PAGE #	DATE	INCIDENT NUMBER	REPORTING OFFICER		CODE #	VICTIM NAME
4	07/21/2018	18-07-0352	Deputy Cedric Lampkin		5031	State, of Arkansas

NAME:	Last,	First,	Middle	SEX: ☐ (U) Unk. ☐ (M) Male ☐ (F) Female	AGE: ☐ (00) Unknown	RACE: ☐ (U) Unk. ☐ (W) White ☐ (B) Black ☐ (I) American Indian ☐ (A) Asian/Pacific Islander
RESIDENT ADDRESS:	Street	City	State	Zip	RESIDENT PHONE	EMPL. PHONE
DATE OF BIRTH	SSN	OCCUPATION		PLACE OF EMPLOYMENT		

NAME:	Last,	First,	Middle	SEX: ☐ (U) Unk. ☐ (M) Male ☐ (F) Female	AGE: ☐ (00) Unknown	RACE: ☐ (U) Unk. ☐ (W) White ☐ (B) Black ☐ (I) American Indian ☐ (A) Asian/Pacific Islander
RESIDENT ADDRESS:	Street	City	State	Zip	RESIDENT PHONE	EMPL. PHONE
DATE OF BIRTH	SSN	OCCUPATION		PLACE OF EMPLOYMENT		

NARRATIVE:

On Saturday, July 21, 2018, at 0017hrs while I Deputy Cedric Lampkin was on patrol, I was dispatched to a welfare call at 25682 W Hwy 72. Cencom advised me the RP stated there was a man laying down in the road. Cencom then stated the RP said he looked like he was drunk.

Once on scene, I observed a white male later identified as Darrell Philpott W/M DOB 2/16/1961 was laying on the side of W Hwy 72 with his legs in the westbound lane. When I approached Darrell, I could see a liquor bottle next to his head. I asked him was he ok and could he stand. He stated he was drunk and just wanted to go to jail. I noticed he had open cuts on his face do to him falling so I had Cencom send in the medics. While the medics was trying to put him in the ambulance he could not stand without help so they put him on the bed. Darrell continued to say take him to jail and wouldn't let the medics transport him do to his condition.

The medics advised me because of Darrell was trying to fight them they couldn't transport him. I advised Cencom and placed him under arrest after the medics cleared him. While placing handcuffs on Darrell began to resist me doing so. Darrell stated he was going to kill me for putting cuffs on him. When I placed Darrell in my unit he became more upset and said just kill me.

I advised Cencom I was in route to the jail and to notify them he was combative. While in route Darrell hit his head up against the windows of the unit and was trying to kick it out. Darrell continued making statements that he was going to hurt me and anyone else. When we arrived at the jail he was charged with 5-71-102 Public intox and 5- 54-102 obstruction governmental operations.

Darrell was then turned over to the intake deputy.

There are is audio and video recordings of this incident.

Appendix HH

1963 Nancy Kelly Basketball, Softball, Cheerleader, Band Majorette

The newly organized Afton Rebels, girls softball team, played Wyandotte here Tuesday night and won 16-15. Nancy Kelly was the winning pitcher.

The girls have a game scheduled at Wyandotte on August 9th. They will play the Miami Yankees here on Tuesday, August 13th; and on August 16th, the Wyandotte team will play here.

The Afton lineup lists Brenda Frost as catcher; Fredrea Gregath 1st base; Gloria Chandler, 2nd base; Brenda George, 3rd base; Martha King, shortstop; Mary Gibson, left field; Sandra Turner, center field; Brenda Kersey, right field. Sandra Moody and Gwen Hogan are also on the team; and Nancy Kelly, pitcher.

Appendix II
Preliminary Transcripts, pp. 31-32, 68-69,85
Philpott admits to possessing firearms as a felon

31

1	A	What happened?
2	Q	The shooting; you get shot in the leg.
3	A	April 14th.
4	Q	Of what year, sir?
5	A	2014.
6	Q	All right. And tell me where you were that morning.
7	A	That morning?
8	Q	Yeah.
9	A	I was deer hunting.
10	Q	And --
11	A	-- or I was hog hunting.
12	Q	Well, which one was it?
13	A	I was hog hunting.
14	Q	Because deer hunting would have been illegal in April,
15		I guess?
16	A	Yeah.
17	Q	Okay. So, you were hog hunting?
18	A	Yeah.
19	Q	Then you quit hog hunting at what time?
20	A	Oh, I don't know; 10:30, 11:00.
21	Q	Then where did you go?
22	A	To the house.
23	Q	All right. Did you go deer or hog hunting with
24		someone or by yourself?
25	A	With Jack Thomas.

Appendix II (*Cont.*)
Preliminary Transcripts, pp. 31-32, 68-69,85
Philpott admits to possessing firearms as a felon

32

```
1    Q    And you left the house -- this shooting incident --
2    well, let me back up. When did you go to cut wood?
3    A    About 4:00 in the afternoon
4    Q    So, had you just stayed at your house between the deer
5    or hog hunting and going to cut wood?
6    A    Yeah.
7    Q    All right. So, tell me what inspired -- what was the
8    reason for deciding to leave your home to go cut wood on
9    somebody else's land?
10   A    Because it was supposed to -- it had started drizzling
11   rain, and it was supposed to turn cold, and we heat with
12   wood.
13   Q    All right. You say 'we heat with wood'. Who is 'we'?
14   A    Me and Jack Thomas and his family.
15   Q    You all live together there --
16   A    -- I stay with them; yes.
17   Q    All right. So, when you say you were at your home,
18   you were at Jack Thomas' home?
19   A    Yeah.
20   Q    And who else was there?
21   A    At Jack's?
22   Q    Yeah.
23   A    Him and his wife and me, and then Steve come along.
24   Q    What's her name?
25   A    Debbie Thomas.
```

Appendix II (*Cont.*)

Preliminary Transcripts, pp. 31-32, 68-69, 85

Philpott admits to possessing firearms as a felon

68

1 A   Yeah.

2 Q   And it was your right leg?

3 A   Yeah.

4 Q   All right. That's where you believe the shot entered?

5 A   I know that's where it entered. I don't believe. I

6 know.

7 Q   Well, that's where you say it entered; right?

8 A   That is where it entered.

9 Q   All right. In front of you is Exhibit 7 and Exhibit

10 8?

11 A   Correct.

12 Q   Exhibit 7 is the back, right side of your leg where

13 you say it entered, right?

14 A   Right.

15 Q   And Exhibit 8 is the front of the leg where you

16 believe it exited, right?

17 A   Yes.

18 Q   What's your experience with guns?

19 A   I've been around them all my life.

20 Q   Did you have a gun that day?

21 A   No.

22 Q   What were you hunting with?

23 A   I wasn't hunting. I was cutting wood.

24 Q   Well, you were hunting that day.

25 A   Yeah; earlier that day.

Appendix II (*Cont.*)

Preliminary Transcripts, pp. 31-32, 68-69,85

Philpott admits to possessing firearms as a felon

69

1   Q   Well, what were you hunting with?

2   A   A rifle.

3   Q   Are you allowed to have a rifle as a convicted felon?

4   A   Yeah.

5   Q   Says who?

6   MR. LELECAS   I'm going to object, your Honor;

7   relevance.

8   THE WITNESS: Says me. It was under Act 378.

9   It's not supposed to be on my record.

10   MR. CONNOR: All right. That helps me --

11   THE COURT: That does it.

12   MR. CONNOR: I had a reason for going there.

13   Q   [By Mr. Connor] So, your drug case in Arkansas was an

14   Act 378 case; is that what you're telling us?

15   A   Yeah.

16   Q   All right. Thank you. Now, tell me about -- are you

17   pretty knowledgeable about guns?

18   A   Yes, I think so.

19   Q   Now, granted, it's hard to see in those photos -- I'm

20   sure you had a much better look, in person, than the

21   photos, so tell me, the larger of the two holes, would you

22   agree, is on the back right side of your leg and the

23   smaller hole is on the front?

24   A   Well, they're about the same.

25   Q   You sure?

Appendix II (*Cont.*)

Preliminary Transcripts, pp. 31-32, 68-69, 85

Philpott admits to possessing firearms as a felon

85

1   administered any pain medication by the hospital?

2   A   I don't believe I was.

3   Q   Now, you said you were hunting hogs earlier that day?

4   A   Yeah.

5   Q   Did you take any hog that day?

6   A   No.

7   Q   What kind of rifle was it?

8   A   A .308 Savage.

9   Q   How long were you out hunting for before you stopped?

10   A   About four years -- four or five hours.

11   Q   Mr. Connor was, initially, asking quite a few

12   questions about your conversations with Shorty Rainey and

13   Michael Rainey, and you indicated that it happened in

14   November, is that correct?

15   A   Yeah; around November.

16   Q   And that's the November preceding the April shooting,

17   correct?

18   A   Yes.

19   Q   And you said Jack was with you at the time?

20   A   Yes.

21   Q   Approximately, prior to April 14th, how many times did

22   you go to this location to cut wood?

23   A   Eight, 10, 12; several times.

24   Q   Did you always cut wood with the same chainsaw?

25   A   Yeah, pretty much.

Appendix JJ
1999 Philpott Affidavit of Abuse

Felon Philpott grabs a gun, assaults a woman and her daughter

(2) Existence of IMMEDIATE DANGER to your person, property or members
of your household.
(State in detail the date and location of most recent acts of conduct by
defendant giving specific acts and circumstances of alleged abuse.)

9-25-99 at 24284 Cherokee Rd Sentry, Came home
drunk, when asked by visitor not to hold her baby when
drunk, he left + came back 30 minutes later in a rage, cussing
kicking animals + telling us he could do anything he wants
too. He told me not to come close to him cause he didn't
know what he would do to me, then started laughing (a very
dimented laugh) He kicked the bedroom + broke it, kicked
the post on the porch, causing it to come loose. The window
in the front door was cracked + he slammed it shut + broke
it out the rest of the way. He lunged at my 21 yr old
Daughter when she told him that that was our house
+ not to distroy it, I between them + he pushed me
out of the way + told me he would knock my head off. Then
we (Daughter + I) left.

AFFIDAVIT OF DOMESTIC ABUSE

(To be used if Temporary Order is requested) 1999 Oct -7 AM 9 53

I, the undersigned, state under oath that the following facts are true and correct
to the best of my knowledge and belief.

SUE HODGES
CIRCUIT CLERK AND RECORDER
BENTON COUNTY, ARK.

(1) Previous history of domestic violence between petitioner and respondent
including verbal threats, harassment and physical abuse.

I had an order of protection on him before
for threatening me + threatening to burn my
house down. Put his fist through the gun case
to get a gun, when we were having a fight

Appendix JJ (*Cont.*)

14 October 1999 Philpott Assault Docket

Felon Philpott grabs a gun, assaults a woman and her daughter

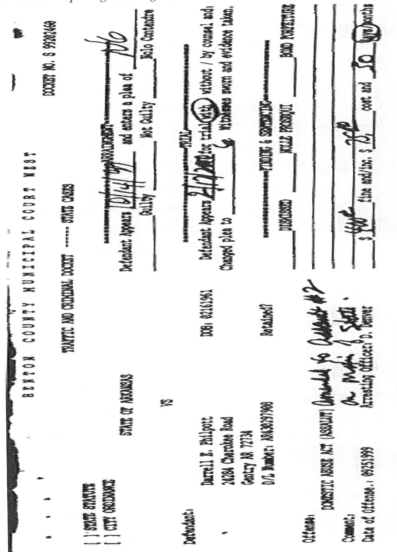

Appendix JJ (*Cont.*)
14 October 1999 Protective Order Against Philpott
for Woman and her Teenage Children

IN THE CHANCERY COURT OF BENTON COUNTY, ARKANSAS

FILED

Kelli K. ▮▮▮▮▮
PETITIONER
SS# 432-31-9260

'99 OCT 14 AM 10 24

SUE HODGES
CLERK AND RECORDER
BENTON COUNTY, ARK.

Petitioner's Home Address:
24284 Cherokee Rd.
Gentry, AR

Petitioner's Work Address:
Gentry Public Schools

No. E 99-1727-1

Darrell E. Philpott
RESPONDENT
SS#

Respondent's Home Address:

Respondent's Work Address:
Jason Black Elec.
Maysville, OK

ORDER OF PROTECTION

Now on this 14th day of October, 1999, being the date previously set for hearing the above named petitioner personally appeared and gave sworn testimony to sustain a finding existence of domestic abuse as defined by Act 266 of 1991 Section 2(a) committed by the respondent as to the victims, Kelli ▮▮▮▮▮, Patricia ▮▮▮▮▮ and Matt ▮▮▮▮▮. Respondent also personally appeared.

IT IS THEREFORE ORDERED, ADJUDGED AND DECREED BY THIS COURT, that

(a) The respondent is ordered and directed to remove himself/herself and to remain away from the premises of the dwelling or residence of Kelli K. ▮▮▮▮▮
at 24284 Cherokee Road, Gentry, Arkansas pending further order of this Court.

(b) The respondent is ordered and directed to have no physical contact with or harass victims, Kelli ▮▮▮▮▮, Patricia ▮▮▮▮▮ and Matt ▮▮▮▮▮.

(c) Based on the affidavit of facts filed with this Court under oath, the petitioner shall refrain from initiating any contacts with or harass respondent and to remain separate and apart until this Order of Protection is vacated or be subject to a

Appendix KK

Philpott's 28 year Witness Protection Program Begins

Philpott's Violation is Dismissed

GRDA LAKE PATROL
OKLAHOMA UNIFORM VIOLATIONS COMPLAINT

Crm 91-355 — Docket No. _____ Page N _____

In The Distric _____

State of Oklahoma ss. Judicial District _____
County of DELAWARE

COMPLAINT - INFORMATION OLP W **10467**
the undersigned, being duly sworn, upon his oath deposes and says that:

on or about (date) 8/18/91 at (time) 3:40 AM at or near (location) CAREY BAY

County number 21 — East / North

within the county and state aforesaid: AFP ☐

Name: PHILPOTT, DARRELL E.
last / first / middle / zip code

Address: PO BX 484

City: GENTRY State: ARK

Birthday (Mo., Da., Yr.) 2/16/61 height 5'11" weight 145 race Cauc sex M op. ☒ Cc. ☐ Mc. ☐ Other ☐

DL No: 430-29-7908 Year 91 State: ARK
Operate ☐ Park ☐

Employer: PETERSON INDUS Did Unlawfully:

Make EBKO Year ___ Style Blu/Alum Color Reg No. AR9742B0 State ___ Year 92

and did then and there commit the following offense:

☐ Failure to properly equip vessel with: 3
(specify) 7

☐ Reckless Operation

☐ Failure to have vessel currently registered 2
☐ Failure to have motor properly muffled

Other violation __Improper Safety Equip__
__LIFE JACKETS - NONE__
(specify) 4207-F

The undersigned further states that he has just and reasonable grounds to believe, and does believe, that the person named above committed the offense herein set forth, contrary to law

Sworn to and subscribed before me, this 19 day of Aug 19 91 — signature M C WELLS Troop'r

Rachel H. con Clerk II
name and title — Badge No. 27 Dist. No. ___
exp 3-1-95 Aug 30 day of Sept 19 91 at 1:30 P M

Court Appearance: _____

Address of Court: Jay, OK

without admitting guilt, I promise to appear in said court at said time & place:

Signature: X Darrell E Philpott

WATER CONDITIONS PD P1 FATAL
☐ ☐ ☐

Weather Conditions: clear / cloudy / darkness
☒ Calm ☐ Rough
☐ Choppy ☐ Very Rough
☐ Strong Current

☐ Hit By Boat Or Propeller
☐ Fire Or Explosion (Fuel)
☐ Fire Or Explosion (Not Fuel)

TYPE OF ACCIDENT
☐ Grounding
☐ Capsizing
☐ Falls Overboard
☐ Collision With Vessel
☐ Collisions With Fixed Object
☐ Collision With Floating Object

☐ Burns ☐ Falls in Boat
☐ Flooding ☐ Sinking
☐ Other (Specify Below)

Other Vessels present: ☐ cross ☐ on coming ☐ same direction

Area of Water: ☐ Swimming ☐ Fishing ☐ Marina ☐ Dam OPEN LAKE
Other _____ Specify

BOND POSTED: _____ CASH: $ _____ DL _____ BOND CARD NO. _____

OLP W 10467

Appendix KK (*Cont.*)
Philpott's 28 year Witness Protection Program Begins
Philpott Jumps Bail and a Warrant is Issued for his Arrest

001669

ALIAS

BENCH WARRANT

MISDEMEANOR OR BAILABLE FELONY
IN THE DISTRICT COURT

STATE OF OKLAHOMA,)
COUNTY OF DELAWARE.)

THE STATE OF OKLAHOMA,

Plaintiff,

-vs-

No. CRM-91-955

DARRELL E. PHILPOTT,
DOB: 2/16/61
LAST KNOWN ADDRESS: P. O. BOX 484, GENTRY, AR
Defendant.

THE STATE OF OKLAHOMA:

To any Sheriff, Constable, Marshal or Policeman in this State, GREETINGS:

WHEREAS, an Information having been filed charging DARRELL E. PHILPOTT, with the crime of IMPROPER SAFETY EQUIPMENT, NO LIFEJACKETS.

You are hereby commanded forthwith to arrest the above named DARRELL E. PHILPOTT (between the hours of 6:00 a.m. and 10:00 p.m. or at any time in a public place) for failure to appear for arraignment on the 30th day of September, 1991, and bring him before the District Court to answer said charge or if the Court has adjourned the term that you deliver him into the custody of the Sheriff of Delaware County to be detained by said Sheriff until the further order of the Court.

Given under my hand and the seal of said Court, this __1__ day of October, 1991.

By Order of Court:

Bond: 100.00

Sam C. Fullerton
Judge of the District Court

Appendix KK (*Cont.*)
Philpott's 28 year Witness Protection Program Begins
6 Years Later Philpott's Charges are Dismissed at Cost to State

001810

202   1810

IN THE DISTRICT COURT OF DELAWARE COUNTY, STATE OF OKLAHOMA
97 MAR 12

COURT MINUTE

CRIMINAL MISCELLANEOUS

DATE: _____   CASE NO. CM-91-955

JUDGE: _____   COURT REPORTER: _____

STATE OF OKLAHOMA vs. _____Darrell Philpot_____

_____STATE IS PRESENT BY ASST. D.A. OF DELAWARE CO._____

_____DEFENDANT IS PRESENT IN PERSON ___PRESENT BY ATTY. _____

Dismiss Cost to State

Appendix KK (*Cont.*)
Philpott's 28 year Witness Protection Program Begins
6 Days After Philpott's Arrest Warrant is Dismissed

FILED
IMAGE 203   001668
1668-1669

IN THE DISTRICT COURT OF DELAWARE COUNTY 91 MAR 17 PM 1:27

STATE OF OKLAHOMA

JUDY E.
COURT CLERK

BY

W A R R A N T   R E C A L L   N O T I C E

CASE NUMBER: _CRM 91-955_

DEFENDANTS: _Darrell Philpott_

_____

_____

_____

DATE WARRANT WAS ISSUED: _10-1-91_

TO: COUNTY SHERIFF:

You are hereby directed to immediately recall the warrant in this case which was issued on the above date.

JUDY E. LARMON
Court Clerk

BY: _____
Deputy

Original filed and copy taken to Delaware County Sheriff this _14_ day of _March_, 1997

Appendix KK (*Cont.*)

Philpott's 28 year Witness Protection Program Begins
5 Days After Philpott's 6 Year Old Warrant is Dismissed

MF 1458
203

3-14-97
KP

001458

97 MAR 17 PM 1:44

IN THE DISTRICT COURT OF DELAWARE COUNTY

STATE OF OKLAHOMA

W A R R A N T   R E C A L L   N O T I C E

CASE NUMBER: CRM 91-955

DEFENDANTS: Darrell Philpot

DATE WARRANT WAS ISSUED: 10-1-91

TO: COUNTY SHERIFF:

You are hereby directed to immediately recall the warrant in this case which was issued on the above date.

JUDY E. LARMON
Court Clerk

BY: _____
Deputy

Original filed and copy taken to Delaware County Sheriff this 14 day of March, 1997

Appendix LL
Philpott Fleeing From Arrest
Philpott flees from Arkansas Deputies to Delaware County

FILED '415

Bonded Out (Date & Time): _____

State of Oklahoma

By: _____ APR 18 2001

13th Judicial District

Charge(s) M-01-339 _____

Delaware County

CAROLINE M. WEAVER
DELAWARE CO. COURT CLERK

PROBABLE CAUSE AFFIDAVIT

Comes now the undersigned Affiant, and states under Oath or Affirmation that the following information and facts are correct to the best of the Affiant's knowledge and belief:

Name of Person Arrested: Darrell F. Philpott _____ Date of Birth: 2-16-61

Date of Arrest: 4-14-01 _____ Time of Arrest: 2120 (a.m.)/p.m.

Show facts upon which probable cause for arrest was based: On above date + time A/O was asked to assist Benton County Deputies on a pursuit that they had stopped by Southeland Farms 1 mile west of maysville in Delaware County. Upon Arrival A/O asked mr. Philpott how many beers he had to which he stated two. A/O @ this time observed a strong odor of alcoholic beverages about his breath and presence. A/O then placed Mr. Philpott under arrest for P.I. and transported him to the SO. where he was booked (Use reverse side or attach another page if necessary) and lodged.

Anticipated Charge(s): Public Intox.

Place of Detention: Delaware County Jail

Date and Time of Detention: 4-14-01 @ 2300 hrs

_____ #4
Affiant (Arresting Officer)

Subscribed and sworn to before me

this 14 day of April, 2001

My Commision Expires:

2/07/05

_____
Notary Public/Judge

PROBABLE CAUSE DETERMINATION

I, _____, Judge of the District Court, reviewed the above and foregoing Probable Cause Affidavit on the 16 day of April, 1998/___, at A-D. a.m./p.m., and make the following findings and Order pursuant to Gerstein v. Pugh 420 U.S. 103 (1975), and County of Riverside v. McLaughlin (1991) U.S. Lexis 2528):

☑ The above and foregoing Affidavit contains sufficient facts showing probable cause to detain the Arrestee to await further proceedings

☐ The Court sets an Appearance Bond in the amount of $ public writ -170°

☐ The Court denies bond at this time.

_____
Judge

Appendix MM
The Rape Of Delaware County
By William Norman Grigg

May 24, 2012

In Oklahoma's Delaware County, Sheriff's deputies were too busy figuratively raping motorists in the <u>village of Bernice</u> to supervise guards who were literally raping inmates in the county jail. As a result, the County Commission has put the screws to the entire county in the form of an 18 percent sales tax increase in order to pay the victims a $13.5 million settlement.

<u>Bernice</u>, which has a population of about 600, is bisected by Highway 85A. For the past quarter-century, the town has been one of the most notorious speed traps in the Midwest. Until recently, the town didn't have a police department; instead, it contracted with the Delaware County Commission, paying $5500 a month to rent sheriff's deputies to write speeding tickets and other citations.

A recent investigation conducted by Oklahoma State Auditor and Inspector Gary A. Jones discovered that since 1977, the municipal government had never published its ordinances as required by state law — which meant that its schedule of fines and court fees was invalid: The trustees never published the ordinances, as required by state law.

Appendix MM (Cont.)
The Rape Of Delaware County

"Any ordinances (other than those pertaining to the appropriation of money) that are not published within 15 days of their passage are not in force," notes the <u>audit</u>. As a result, "the municipal court should not have collected fines of more than $50. The court has over-collected approximately $106,308 in fines through the end of June 2011"; in addition, the court also "over-collected" nearly $8,000 in court costs. The auditor directed the Bernice Town Board to reimburse those who had been subjected to illegal fines (in one instance, a motorist was given a ticket for $545). More importantly, from the perspective of those higher up in the tax-feeding chain, the auditor slammed the Town Board for withholding a cut of ticket revenue and court fees from the Oklahoma State Bureau of Investigation and state Council on Law Enforcement Education and Training.

In response to the audit, David E. Jones, the bar-certified sophist retained as Bernice's town attorney, weaved a seamless web of persiflage, insisting that even though the cabal that employs him "did not follow the strict technical requires for publication [of the traffic ordinance], the public clearly had constructive notice of the existence of the Bernice Penal Code...."

Jones's claim, rendered in less opaque language, was that the town's status as a well-known speed trap constituted

Appendix MM (Cont.)
The Rape Of Delaware County

legal "notice" of the practice. Buttressed with this spurious and self-serving assessment, the town's trustees voted on May 14 not to grant refunds to victims of the illegal ticket scheme, thereby laying permanent claim to more than $100,000 in illegally collected revenue.

Like nearly all official business conducted in Bernice, the May 14 vote took place in a meeting that was closed to the public, a practice typical of the cabal's serial violations of the Open Meeting Act. The audit described habitual violations of that statute, each of which is a crime punishable by a year in the county jail and a fine of up to $500.

Until recently, the Town Board — which conducts nearly all significant business in "executive session" — had forbidden citizens to participate in monthly town meetings. Subsequent to the audit, that policy was modified to permit three minutes to citizens who wish to speak, which is not to say that the Board will allow anything that is said to have any measurable effect on its decisions.

"The atmosphere in a Town Board Meeting is meant to intimidate and silence people," commented Bernice resident Steve Miller, who lives with his 72-year-old mother in Bernice, in an interview with Pro Libertate. "When you go to a town meeting in Grove, which isn't far from here, there are no policemen, no security cameras. There is a U.S. flag, an

Appendix MM (Cont.)
The Rape Of Delaware County

Oklahoma State Flag, microphones set up for each Council member and for the citizens who wish to participate. Here in Bernice, however, there are always armed and uniformed officers present, security cameras — and no mike for public comments. It's like going into a jail — or walking into a den of thieves."

Miller, a consulting engineer by profession, is the civic-minded resident whose petition drive resulted in the state audit. His involvement grew out of the harassment suffered by his mother, Mary Zapf.

Starting in May 2010, Miller and his mother noticed that Delaware County Sheriff's Deputies "began patrolling our property daily," Miller recalled to Pro Libertate. "Our property is surrounded by three public streets, and I saw these deputies slowly driving by constantly. I started taking their pictures and even got one of them to talk to me briefly. I asked him why they were keeping our property under surveillance; his reply was, 'Because the mayor told me to.'"

With Miller's help, Mrs. Zapf was doing some construction and renovation on their property. This included modifying a driveway that had been used as a short-cut by motorists seeking to avoid a nearby intersection.

On May 4 of that year, Mayor Bill Raven visited Zapf to tell her that there was an unspecified "problem" with her

Appendix MM (Cont.)
The Rape Of Delaware County

landscaping project, and to ask her to "hold off until the town could get some things together." Mrs. Zapf offered to have the mayor discuss the renovation with the contractor, who was on-site; Raven declined that invitation, insisting that he didn't want to start a "fight."

The following day, Raven and the Town Board decided to take "emergency" action to deal with supposed "zoning violations" on Zapf's property. That matter, in typical fashion, was discussed in "executive session" during the May 10 Board Meeting. When it emerged from its secretive huddle the Board informed Zapf that no action would be taken, because she had agreed to "hold off" on further construction.

After waiting for nearly a month to hear from the mayor and the board, Mrs. Zapf sent them a letter announcing that she intended to resume work on her property. The improvements were finished on June 4th. Five days later, the Town Board sued her for "trespassing" by allowing alterations on her own driveway.

"The material basis of their claim was that they had an easement on the driveway because at some unspecified point in the past they had plowed it during the wintertime," Miller observes. "We went through one of the biggest snowstorms in Oklahoma history a few years ago, and they never sent a plow."

Appendix MM (Cont.)
The Rape Of Delaware County

Shortly after being informed of the town's lawsuit against her, Mrs. Zapf visited the town clerk's office to request the agendas for the upcoming meetings of the Bernice trustees and the Zoning Board — matters in which she had an obvious and urgent interest. Town Clerk Connie King, ever the dutiful public servant, reacted to this eminently reasonable request by slamming the door in Mrs. Zapf's face. That prompted the long-suffering widow to exclaim that the clerk was being a "stupid witch" — an epithet several orders of magnitude milder than what might normally be employed in a situation of that kind.

On the basis of that remark, Mrs. Zapf received a citation on July 20 for "disturbing the peace." Although the only "witness" to Zapf's supposed offense was the officious personage on the other side the door she had slammed, a police report was filed — two months after the incident — by two deputies who were not present when it occurred. The fine listed on the summons was $195 — an amount well in excess of the $85 prescribed in the fine and bond schedule.

"I knew the trespass lawsuit was a malicious attempt by the mayor to seize land, as there were no town residents ... listed as plaintiffs," <u>Miller explained in his letter to the state auditor</u>. "The harassment by the deputy sheriffs was an abuse of power by the mayor, and an attempt to intimidate

Appendix MM (Cont.)
The Rape Of Delaware County

and coerce my mother into a submissive position. The disturbing the peace accusation was false and intended to scare her away from obtaining public records. The police summons was another attempt by the town to intimidate a citizen. The fine was not only unfounded, it seemed excessive, so I began my own investigation."

With the analytical discipline of a trained engineer, Miller examined the city's penal codes and Delaware County Records to find out if this grotesque over-charge was a vindictive anomaly, or part of a larger pattern. What he discovered — and the independent state audit confirmed — was that the town had been in violation of state statutes "for approximately 25 years."

Publication of the audit was greeted by the Bernice Town Board with what one participant in a rare public meeting described as "smirks and laughs." By that time, however, the Delaware County Commission had cancelled its contract to provide deputy sheriffs for traffic enforcement. This was done not because of developments in Bernice, but rather because of "potential liability issues" arising from <u>a $13.5 million settlement reached with victims of sexual abuse by deputies in the County Jail.</u>

Complaints from female inmates at the Delaware County Jail began to accumulate in March 2008, many of them

Appendix MM (Cont.)
The Rape Of Delaware County

involving a part-time transport deputy named Bill Sanders, Sr. Sanders, recalled the Tulsa World, "would often take female inmates to 'appointments' without reporting his departing mileage and time.... It was during many of these transports that inmates say they were assaulted by Sanders and forced to perform sex acts."

Key elements of the accusations were confirmed by a former county dispatcher, who also described how the former jail administrator, Lonnie Hunter, would "shake boxes of cigarettes at the inmates to encourage them to flash their breasts at him." (Two dispatchers eventually filed sexual harassment lawsuits of their own.) Some of the inmates testified that both Sanders and Hunter would exchange cigarettes and other coveted goods for sex. When confronted with a particularly intransigent inmate, Sanders would simply assault her in the serene confidence that he would never be held accountable.

"Now you said you wouldn't tell, and even if you did nobody would believe you, because you're just a drug addict," he told one victim during a trip to the emergency room. "Who are you compared to me?"

Sanders — who died at age 63 of "natural causes" in November 2008, just after being fired and just before the lawsuit was filed — was a part-time deputy who had no formal

Appendix MM (Cont.)
The Rape Of Delaware County

training and no personnel file on record. When deposed for the lawsuit, Hunter, Sanders's supervisor, insisted that he was not responsible for the crimes committed against helpless inmates: "My responsibility is to the last locked door. After that, it's up to the transport officer."

The OSBI gave Sheriff Jay Blackfox a detailed report describing the sexual abuse suffered by more than a dozen women by staff under his authority. In his deposition, Sheriff Blackfox insisted that he wasn't "aware" of what was happening in his jail, because he had only read "part" of the OSBI's report owing to his busy schedule.

Blackfox was dismissed by County Commission at roughly the same time the Commission ended its traffic enforcement contract with Bernice. This left the Bernice Town Council with the perceived need to hire a police chief and create its own police force to patrol a town with a population of fewer than 600 people. It settled on a "gypsy cop" named <u>Daniel Travis Lowe</u>, who had just been fired from his job as police chief of Burden, Kansas — another town of roughly 600 people.

At the time he was hired by Bernice, Lowe <u>was still subject to a "diversion program" growing out of a domestic violence incident involving his ex-wife, who was Burden's Town Clerk</u>.

Appendix MM (Cont.)
The Rape Of Delaware County

The terms of that agreement specified that the charge would be dismissed if Lowe refrain from criminal behavior for one year. Unfortunately, this refers only to unlicensed criminal behavior; becoming chief enforcer for Bernice's ruling clique wouldn't qualify. News of Lowe's background provoked understandable controversy, which led to another Town Meeting where the Board — acting in "executive session," of course — ratified its decision.

"There is something oddly appropriate about the selection of this guy to be the chief of police," Steve Miller commented to Pro Libertate. "This is entirely typical of the way things operate in this county." In fact, the institutionalized sexual abuse and related corruption that has festered in Delaware County is hardly atypical of Oklahoma as a whole.

Over the past eight years, tax victims in three Oklahoma counties have been forced to pay more than $24 million to settle lawsuits arising from the routine sexual abuse of female inmates. Two former sheriffs — Melvin Holly of Latimer County, and Mike Burgess of Custer County — have been given prison terms of 25 and 79 years, respectively, for sexual assaults on incarcerated women.

Holly told one of his victims, a 19-year-old girl, that if she ever disclosed what happened she would "end up dead somewhere, floating face-down in a river."

Appendix MM (Cont.)
The Rape Of Delaware County

Burgess used his position on the Custer County Drug Court to create <u>what was described as a "sex slave ring."</u> He told one woman who rebuffed his advances that if she didn't submit to him she would "not ever be able to see her children until after they had grown up." Another woman who resisted was placed in lockdown, denied her medications, and forced to eat food that induced rectal bleeding.

Sales and property taxes were increased to pay the settlements arising from lawsuits filed by the victims. Next January, residents of Delaware County will suffer an 18 percent sales tax increase; all purchases will be taxed at 9.3 percent for seventeen years. The $13.5 million settlement is an amount <u>three times larger than the county budget</u> — and more than the construction price of the jail where the sexual assaults occurred.

County Tax Assessor Leon Hurt, whose name is one of God's little Dickensian jokes, points out that most of the people with whom he deals "are barely making it <u>on their own income</u>. For them to see this extra impact ... could be the last straw."

Oklahoma is a state in which piety has curdled into punitive sanctimony, which explains why it has <u>some of the most stupid and vicious drug laws in the English-speaking world</u> — and, in <u>per capita</u> terms, <u>the largest female prison populations on the planet</u>. Thanks to the wise and perceptive people in the state legislature, however, residents can take comfort in this thought: If their <u>mother, sister</u>, or daughter <u>commits a trivial drug offense in Oklahoma</u>, she may be caged by the government and be pitilessly molested or even raped by her jailers, but <u>at least she won't be forced to wear a burqa</u>.

Appendix NN
Lance's Letters to DELCO Law Enforcement and related Court Records

District Attorney Kenny Wright
13th Judicial District
102 East Central, Suite 301
Miami, OK 74354

28 March 2017

Delaware County Sherriff Harlan Moore
327 S 5th Street
Jay, Ok 74346

Grove Police Chief Mark Morris
13 E 3rd Street
Grove, OK 74344

Gentlemen,

1. **Richard ███ of Grove Oklahoma took my car hauler and refuses to return it.** On Friday, 17 March of this year, I reported my car hauler (valued at $2500) stolen by Richard ██████. I reported the theft (by telephone) to Detective Hendricks of Delaware County Sherriff's Office. I provided Detective Hendricks a copy of my trailer title, so the serial number can be verified on the trailer. The trailer was (and probably still is) at ██████'s house in Grove.

I tried to resolve this peacefully with ██████. I offered (through Deputy Hendricks) that if ██████ would simply take my trailer to the Grove bowling alley, we would have a third party (██████'s own son in law, who lives by the bowling alley) assist with transferring my stolen trailer back to my brother, Ed Turlington, Jr. My brother has my permission to keep my trailer. Deputy Hendricks called ██████, and ██████ **refused to return my trailer**, even after being informed by law enforcement that I reported it as stolen, and he does not have my permission to have it.

Deputy Hendricks informed me that ██████ **acknowledged possession** of my trailer, but ██████ said he would only return my trailer in exchange for a trailer that ██████ left at my brother Ed's place (██████ referred to this second trailer as "his" trailer, as if ██████ were the owner). ██████ did in fact leave a trailer on my brother's property at 68901 East 370 Road, Jay Oklahoma.

However, ██████ failed to mention to Deputy Hendricks that the other trailer is NOT ██████'s property. The trailer that ██████ left at my brother's property belongs to a Mr. John R███ of Bartlesville. ██████ brought Mr. R███'s trailer from Bartlesville to Ed's place, and tried to sell it to Ed. Once my brother figured out who the trailer belonged to, he contacted Mr. R███ and made arrangements to return that trailer to Bartlesville.

2. **Background**: Both Ed and Mr. R███ have been paying ██████ for work on their homes, and ██████'s story is that he was just using the trailers for that work. ██████ has not finished

Appendix NN *(Cont.)*
Lance's Letters

the work at either home, despite receiving thousands upon thousands of dollars to do so. My family has paid ▮▮▮ around $18,000 for the work he has still not completed.

I understand that ▮▮▮ is telling a different story, and his claiming he had permission to take both trailers, etc. After refusing to return my trailer, ▮▮▮ now claims that he was asked by my brother to put a $165 winch on my trailer, and that he won't return the trailer until he gets paid $165. My brother flatly denies either giving ▮▮▮ to take my trailer or asking him to work on it. I have to believe that any winch Rich tries to sell is stolen anyway. No matter what story ▮▮▮ comes up with next, this much is certain: **a. he still has my trailer, b. he was informed by law enforcement that he does not my permission to have it, and c. he still refuses to return it.** If this were a big misunderstanding (which I do not believe), an honest man would have returned the trailer as soon as the Deputy told him he does not have my permission to have it (as evidenced by the fact that I reported it stolen).

I am happy to testify and provide sworn statements as necessary, but I have no interest in any further negotiation with a thief to try to convince him to give my property back. Any misunderstanding ▮▮▮ claims to have with Ed or Mr. R▮▮ or anyone else has no bearing on my stolen trailer. If he claims he put a winch on it, he can take it off. I would expect any property ▮▮▮ has to barter with is stolen anyway. I don't want the winch; I want my trailer and charges filed.

3. **Credibility**: As a former prosecutor, I can sympathize with law enforcement's task of weighing credibility in any issue with conflicting stories, so I offer you the following for your assessment:

   a. I am a member of the Oklahoma Bar (since 2003), Oklahoma Bar Association # 19959. *See attached certificate of good standing.* As an officer of the court, I would never make a false statement to law enforcement (or to anyone else). I would not jeopardize my law license over a $2,500 trailer.

   b. I am an active duty Army Lieutenant Colonel (Promotable). I will be promoted to Colonel on 1 May 2017. As a Soldier and an Officer I would never lie to any government agency, or to anyone else. I would not jeopardize my military career over a $2,500 trailer.

   c. I am a Staff Judge Advocate, currently serving at Fort Eustis, Virginia (but my roots and family are back in Oklahoma). *See attached orders.* I would not lie to the court, to law enforcement, or to anyone else, and if I did, I would lose the faith and confidence of the Army JAG Corps, and I would likely be relieved of my position. I would mislead you over a $2,500 trailer, or anything else.

   d. Rich ▮▮▮, on the other hand, is a known thief and liar. Based on the public record, I respectfully ask you to consider and verify the following:

Appendix NN *(Cont.)*

Lance's Letters

1) Rich ███████ is currently on probation for felony "**False Declaration of Ownership in Pawn**" under 59 OS 1512(C) (2). **Arrested 24 March 2015 by** Officer Ray Harvey, Grove P.D.

2) ███████ was **arrested 10 December 2014** for felony Larceny of Farm Equipment by Deputy Corbey Christian, Delaware County Sherriff's Office. It was for **stealing from his own mother.**

3) Judge Denney ruled on December 18 2012 against ███████ and ███████ construction in civil court for relief more than $10,000.

4) Judge Haney ruled on 29 April 2010 against ███████ and his son Rich ███████ in civil court for relief more than $10000.

5) ███████ swindled my mother, Nancy Turlington, of Miami, OK out of (at least) $11000 in the past year for work he has not completed. My mother is a retired school teacher (Afton) and school principal (Fort Gibson and Sapulpa), a lifelong member of local churches, and a politically active and respected member of the community. I would love to put her on the stand, compared to Rich ███████

6) While I firmly believe that ███████ engages in fraudulent charging practices and other business misdealings, ███████ unfinished work (and subsequent debt) to my mother, my brother, and Mr. R███████ can be addressed in civil court. That is a separate issue from my stolen trailer.

4. **Sources.** As I am out of state, I received most of my leads and information from my brother Ed. Ed is a former Military Policeman and is currently certified as a private investigator. He inquired around Grove, and most of the leads were provided by Rich's own (former) friends, acquaintances and family, many of whom Rich has swindled. Several were happy to tell Ed about Rich's criminal past, but are afraid to go on the record against Rich. Rich is allegedly a drug addict who has lost most of his teeth to his drug addiction. Again, there is no need to verify the rumors, because there is already a legal record of theft and fraud or bad business debts. If you want more information about any of the above you may contact Ed at (███████).

5. To avoid any confusion, all references to Ed Turlington above are referring to my brother, Ed Turlington Jr. Many people in the area also know my father, Ed Turlington Sr, as he is a former Principal at Grove and Colcord, and a former Superintendent at Afton and Oaks, OK.

6. Finally, I have to tell you that you should expect tall tales and stories from Rich ███████, as he is prolific liar. He will be the tragic victim, once again, in a great big misunderstanding, if you hear him out. But, **he has already stated that he will keep my trailer** until Ed gives him another one, or pays money for the winch I didn't ask for. Rich should take such claims to a civil proceeding, unless he is afraid to lie under oath. The only relevant facts about the **theft of my trailer** is that Rich ███████ took it, he admits he has it, he was informed by law enforcement that he does not have my permission to have it, and yet he still insists that he

Appendix NN *(Cont.)*
Lance's Letters

will just keep it anyway until he gets more money or property from third parties. **None of his stories even claim that he has my permission to have my trailer,** which is the criminal matter at hand, and sole issue I ask you to engage in. I have no interest in negotiating further with the man that stole my trailer. I want to press charges.

7. Respectfully, please acknowledge this letter and advise me of the status of my stolen property report. I will be taking my family on a spring break trip from April 1 through April 8, but I will be available at my cell phone, below. Thank you for your attention on this matter.

Sincerely,

██████████

Lance B. Turlington,
Lieutenant Colonel (Promotable)
Staff Judge Advocate
(██) ██-██ (office)
(██) ██-██ (cell)

Appendix NN *(Cont.)*
Lance's Letters

PROBABLE CAUSE AFFIDAVIT FOR ARREST WARRANT

Comes now the undersigned Affiant, and states upon Oath or Affirmation that the following information and facts are correct to the best of the Affiant's knowledge and belief. The undersigned believes that probable cause exists for the detention of the below named ARRESTEE for the below listed crimes committed on the below listed date, in Delaware County, State Of Oklahoma.

Subject Name	███ RICHARD ███		
SSN	562295673	DOB	███

Sex	Male	Race	White
Hair		Eye	
Ethnicity		Build	
HGT	0 Ft. 0 In.	WGT	0 lbs.

Address	███
City	Grove
State	Oklahoma 74344

Date Of Arrest   Time Of Arrest
Arrest Location
Arrest City
Offense Location LAKE ROAD 8
Offense City

Offense(s) Committed / Anticipated Charge(s)
> 1. 21 O.S. § 1720 • Larceny of an automobile, motor vehicle, aircraft, construction equipment or farm equipment

Facts & Circumstance that support probable cause to arrest the above named person are
> 1. On 10/20/2014 at approx. 09:30 hours I Deputy Christian Corbey of the Delaware County Sheriffs Office was handed a statement from Lt. Stanley in reference to a ███ needing a report made for a stolen Kubota Tractor.

Appendix NN *(Cont.)*

Lance's Letters

Facts & Circumstance that support probable cause to arrest the above named person are

2. I made contact with ███ who stated that her son Richard ██████ sold her Kubota Tractor. ███ stated that one of Richards friends ██ told her that Richard tried to sell him the tractor but he told him no and now it is no where to be found.

3. ███ said that the last time she saw the tractor was about two weeks ago. From my understanding contact with Richard has been attempted several times by Deputies and each time Richard has been uncooperative or not answered his door or phone.

4. ███ described the tractor to be a **Orange Kubota tractor serial Number L2000T3526034913 Model Number LB400A10504.**

5. ███ stated that her son Richard did not have permission to take her tractor nor did he have permission to sell her tractor. ███ said that her son is not working and is on meth so she believes he stole it to be able to provide for his drug use. ███ also stated that she believes Richards girlfriend ██████ knows that he took it and is helping him. To my knowledge contact has not been made with ███ at this time.

I will be entering the Kubota Tractor into NCIC and I am requesting a warrant be issued for the anticipated charges of.

Count 1. Larceny theft of motor vehicle

Count 2. Obstruction

At this time nothing further

End of report

AFCF: No ☑ / Yes ☐   Times (1) ☐ (2) ☐ or ____

Upon oath, I declare that the above information is true and correct to the best of my knowledge and belief.
Officer's Name   CHRISTIAN, , CORBEY L   **Badge No.** D 18

(Signature of Affiant)

Appendix OO
*Turlington Schools a Career DELCO Deputy in Police Rescue
Tactics "Delco Shitshow" Facebook Group, 2019*

to get there as fast as possible with your lights on. Unless
there's a tactical reason for not having them on.

Like · Reply · 1d

 R[████████] And if you have an "intruder" or someone
prying on grandma's window, I'm going to do 90+ with lights
and sirens and cut them 3 miles out while keeping the pace.
Even further away if it's out in the boonies because sound
carries.

Like · Reply · 1d

 D[████████] I'm not worried about them speeding I'm
worried about them almost running me over no I would not
want you to kill an innocent man on a motorcycle that has a
family............. to get to another accident what kind of oxy
f****** moron is at

Like · Reply · 1d · Edited

D[████████] The f****** point is very simple here folks if
you're going to drive at high rates of speed don't f****** run
somebody over ... I mean this is the biggest crock of s*** and
hypocrisy I've ever heard of oh well if it was your kid you'd
want us to speed yeah ...don't want to run somebody over
Jesus Christ I can't even wrap my head around. Some of
y'all's way of thinking

Like · Reply · 1d · Edited

Edwin Hardee Turlington ▶ R[████████] in that situation
you would leave lights going and the siren going.

The objective is not to catch the burglar. The objective is to
protect the grandma.

You leave your lights on you leave your siren on
You make as much noise as possible from as far as way as
possible to let the Intruder know as soon as possible that the
good guys are coming.

There's a much better chance that as soon as the bad guys
hear the siren and see the lights those drop what they're
doing and run like hell.

Are you in law enforcement and where did you get your
training on tactical response? Not being smart aleck here just
curious

*DCSO has experienced a near 400% turnover rate during Sheriff
Moore's 2 terms and he rarely replaces Deputies with locals. The
above Deputy is one of Moore's many City Boys.*

Appendix PP
2012 Tulsa World Article on 13ᵗʰ Judicial District
Murders and Mysterious Deaths

NEWS LOCAL

Grand Shadows: Lake's history filled with crime, corruption

Lake's history filled with crime, corruption

CARY ASPINWALL World Staff Writer   Jul 29, 2012

GRAND LAKE O' THE CHEROKEES - Politicians headed to prison on corruption convictions usually slink out of town or get sent packing by angry constituents.

Back in 1982, Delaware County Commissioner H.B. Richie got a party.

Before he reported to federal prison for taking kickbacks, locals threw him a hog fry gala in a show of gratitude. His parting words: "I regret getting caught, but I don't regret a hell of a lot of what I done."

"If you are going to do anything, don't get caught."

Grand Lake is massive in terms of miles of shoreline and impact: It stretches serpentine-like through Ottawa, Delaware, and Mayes counties.

Waterfront homes sell for $500,000 into the millions, making it a haven for well-to-do retirees. The lake itself is a playground for many of the state's affluent. But in the hills and valleys that surround it, there are shadows of darker stories - part of a history of crime and corruption that lurk behind the hard-fought progress and placid lake life.

Women and men "go missing," several deaths that might have been homicides are ruled suicides - and sometimes those charged with upholding the law have been on the wrong side of it, landing in jail, on trial or resigning.

Some locals grumble about the recent half-cent sales tax increase to pay for Delaware County's $13.5 million settlement in a federal civil rights suit, for sexual assault and mistreatment of female inmates at the county jail. Fifteen women allege they were groped, sexually assaulted and raped while in custody in 2008. They said they told jail managers and then-Sheriff Jay Blackfox about what was happening, but nothing was done. Blackfox resigned in 2011 and denied any wrongdoing.

Rick Littlefield, a former deputy, and state representative, took over as interim sheriff in the wake of the scandal. He focused on cleaning house: Video cameras were installed to monitor jail conditions, policies changed and deputies swept the jail for contraband. "We made lots of changes," he said. "We would frequently hear: 'Well, that's the way we've always done it.' Well, the way we've always done it cost us $13.5 million."

He said he never hesitated when county commissioners asked him to step in. But he'll likely let the winner of the Aug. 28 Democratic runoff between Harlan Moore and Mike Wilkerson take office as sheriff as early as he's ready, he said.

"I hope to leave it a little better than when we came in," he said.

He knew the challenges of upholding the law from his days as a young deputy. Also, his dad was sheriff in the 1970s. Each era brings a new scourge. Once, it was bootlegging; now it's meth.

"The lake brings a different group of people," he said.

The Rainbow Chasers

The dam was a dream when this place was still Indian Territory, before statehood. The Neosho and Spring rivers flowed from the north and merged into the Grand River, but the potential local visionary Henry Holderman saw was electric.

Dam the rivers and bring hydroelectric power to the Cherokee Nation and residents of northeastern Oklahoma's lush, rolling hills.

A group of men known as "The Rainbow Chasers" lobbied to make Holderman's dream happen, going so far as to stop President Franklin Delano Roosevelt's train as it passed through nearby Vinita to garner support. A giant sign shouted their enthusiasm: "Let's build the Grand River Dam!"

They won: The Works Progress Administration granted funding in 1937, and workers earning about $1 per hour and living in tents poured concrete 24 hours a day until the Pensacola Dam's 51 massive arches were complete.

The towns of Disney and Langley on either side of the dam boomed "from the dam activity of the day and from big spenders in their dance halls and taverns that sprung up overnight," according to "Heritage of the Hills," a local history book.

By summer 1940, Grand Lake was full. But progress didn't come without obstacles or controversy. Entire towns were lost in the lake, cemeteries and burial sites were relocated. Thirteen men died building the dam.

Shortly before it was completed, Gov. Red Phillips sent the state militia to halt progress on the dam because of a dispute over road funding. It took a restraining order to stop the governor's interference. Phillips claimed that engineers "went down like a thief in the night and closed the gates."

Kin folk and captains

Some 250 well-wishers showed up for H.B. Richie's prison send-off hog fry back in 1982, according to news reports.

Those who attended argued Richie - who died in 1997 - was a well-intentioned "victim of circumstances" who kept the roads graded.

Kelly Hampton has lived in Delaware County most of his life, and he and Richie taught school together.

"He was from a good family," Hampton said. "He's kin to half the county."

Hampton's parents settled in Zena around the time of statehood. He worked for years as a teacher, principal and school superintendent throughout the county and his wife teaches Cherokee language and culture in Grove. "We know what everybody's doing out here - but we read the Tulsa World to see who got caught," Hampton said.

"Families here go way back," he said.

"People coming in from Kansas and other places, they don't know what to think of us. We're kind of a breed of our own," he said. "All of Delaware County is kind of a unique place. You could probably write a book or movie on it."

Darrell Mastic works as a financial adviser in Grove and is a former high school football coach. He's lived there since the mid-1990s but started coming to visit when his in-laws moved there in the 1980s, before the town had a single stoplight. The lake attracts development and diversity, he said. "You've got people here who've never left the county versus people who are captains of industry," he said. "And they walk in the door and you can't tell who's who because it's the lake - everybody wears shorts and flip-flops."

Murder and mayhem

Eddie Wyant is the district attorney for District 13, covering Delaware and Ottawa counties, where the bulk of Grand Lake resides. "Every district's got its cases," he said.

Of the two counties in District 13, Ottawa has the higher crime rate, according to 2010 OSBI statistics. Ottawa had a crime index rate of approximately 25.8 crimes per 1,000 residents versus Delaware's rate of 18.5.

By comparison, Tulsa County has nearly twice the crime rate of either, with 49.5 crimes per 1,000 residents in 2010.

Wyant's district is bordered by Kansas, Missouri, and Arkansas, which often adds challenges to solving and prosecuting crimes, he said.

A high-profile, tri-state crime was Wyant's first major at-bat as a young prosecutor.

Shannon and Joseph Agofsky were arrested and charged with kidnapping banker Dan Short from his Arkansas home in the middle of the night Oct. 5, 1989, driving him to the State Bank of Noel in Missouri and forcing him to open the vault so they could steal $70,000. Short's hands and feet were bound with duct tape, he was taped to an antique chair weighted with chains and concrete blocks and he was tossed from the Cowskin Bridge into Grand Lake's Elk Cove. He drowned, and his body was found five days later.

From Elk Cove in Oklahoma, the lake narrows eastward into Missouri's Elk River, flowing past Noel, a tiny town where Short was loved. He emceed the Christmas parade and provided radio commentary and newspaper columns on local sporting events.

Wyant was a senior in college when Short was kidnapped and drowned. By the time Wyant graduated from law school and became a prosecutor in the 13th District in 1997, he was arguing the state's case against the Agofsky brothers. It took more than two years for authorities to arrest anyone. The murder trial stretched on for the better part of the decade as the Agofsky brothers changed attorneys, argued for venue changes, and challenged the validity of judges and evidence.

Both men received life sentences in federal prison for the bank robbery, but only Shannon Agofsky was convicted of Short's murder. Joseph Agofsky's murder portion of the trial ended in mistrial. In 2004, Shannon Agofsky was convicted of killing a fellow prison inmate and is now on death row at the U.S. Penitentiary in Terre Haute, Ind.

A bitter feud

Before the jail civil rights lawsuit, before million-dollar mansions dotted the lakeshore, before Grove got its first stoplight and before Delaware County constituents wished commissioner Richie farewell for prison, there was a battle for the courthouse itself. Grove, being the largest, most established city, assumed it would remain the county seat. Citizens further south felt that was too far to travel for county business and hired surveyors to find the county's geographical center.

In 1908, they circulated petitions, got an election and - to the surprise of everyone in Grove - team Jay won. And Grove then appealed to the Supreme Court to stop it. "It was really a bitter feud," said Jackie Coatney, curator of the Delaware County Historical Society. "Grove felt that they had been cheated. They really didn't think it was a serious election so few turned out to vote." It got ugly. Jay continued with courthouse construction as the legal battle raged.

Meanwhile, a Joplin, Mo., man named William Creekmore decided to build his own courthouse north of Jay and furtively moved all the court records from Grove into his courthouse in the middle of a January night in 1912.

The governor got involved and sent the militia to move the court records to the Jay courthouse. But the dispute continued, with the records being sent back to Grove until the courthouse dispute could be resolved. Again, the governor sent the militia. This time, the Delaware County sheriff assembled his own ragtag band of troops to counter the state's forces. They dug 4-foot trenches and erected barricades around both courthouses. No men were killed, and the Jay courthouse emerged victorious and housed the records - until a mysterious fire burned it down in 1913. They rebuilt it, and it burned down again in 1941.

It was a man named Claude "Jay" Washbourne Jr. who donated the land that became the town and the victor of the courthouse battles, hence the name - except even that is a matter of local dispute. Coatney said whenever she writes a story about how the town got its name, she has to include multiple versions to avoid re-igniting old family feuds. "You just don't want to hurt anybody's feelings in the telling of a story," she said.

Mysterious deaths in Delaware County

Phillip Porter

Porter was found dead Jan. 12 in his small motor home northwest of Sailboat Bridge on Grand Lake. His throat was slashed 1-inch deep, 4 inches across, severing his jugular vein. His death was initially ruled a suicide, until family members and the Tulsa World began to ask questions about the lack of evidence. No suicide note was left in the camper smeared with blood, no weapon was found near his body and his family said the 56-year-old had no history of depression. The OSBI launched a homicide investigation into his death shortly after. No one has been arrested or charged in connection with Porter's death.

Edie King

King's body was found hanged Oct. 17, 2008. When she died, King possessed a letter detailing sexual abuse of prisoners in the Delaware County jail - before the lawsuit was filed or any of the allegations had become public record. Days after she missed a meeting to discuss the letter with an attorney working on the inmate's lawsuit, her body was found in a horse tack barn a few hundred feet from her trailer home. Her death was ruled a suicide. Her relatives have said they don't believe she was suicidal.

Joann Ellis

Ellis went missing in 1998, but her body wasn't found until 2003, when her skeletal remains were found in a submerged car near Pensacola Dam on Grand Lake. Ellis, a 48-year-old mother of four, was last seen as she pulled out of her parents' driveway in 1998. Investigators found clothing, jewelry and identification belonging to Ellis in the car. The car's front windows were down when it went into the water and the speedometer was stuck on 45 mph. The death was ruled a suicide, but family members said they did not believe Ellis was suicidal. Ellis' sister said she suspected foul play because Joann allegedly owed money to drug dealers.

District 13: Land of law enforcement scandals

In 1972, Delaware County Sheriff Loyd Rosell appeared before a federal grand jury and denied that he was the target of a bribe attempt by the operators of the Mr. Yuk Club in Grove.

Later on in that case, Ottawa County District Attorney Frank Grayson was convicted of conspiring with Kansas City mob ties to establish gambling and prostitution within his jurisdiction of Grand Lake.

In 1980, Sheriff Rosell was accused of profiting from lease-purchase deals on county patrol cars, using the county's phones to conduct personal business and using his position of authority to force a prisoner to sell him land. He was acquitted, but a grand jury urged that he be forced out of office. He chose not to seek re-election.

In 1989, Ottawa County Sheriff Therl Whittle was charged with embezzlement and misconduct in office. In 1993, nearly a year after he left office, he was charged with lying to a grand jury about evidence in a 1987 murder case. He was acquitted in both cases.

Whittle had replaced the previous sheriff, Bob Sills, who resigned while under a grand jury investigation for allegedly mistreating prisoners and other misconduct.

In 1988, former District Attorney David Thompson resigned and later pleaded guilty to charges of marijuana possession.

In 1997, former Ottawa County Sheriff James Ed Walker pleaded guilty to aiding and abetting an illegal gambling business. He was first charged in 1996 on a 12-count indictment, but a lengthy trial resulted in acquittal on several counts and a mistrial declared on several others. When a federal judge sentenced him to 24 months in prison, Walker said: "I'm sorry that I pleaded guilty."

In 2004, Delaware County Sheriff Lenden Woodruff apologized and resigned when he was convicted of DUI while driving his personal vehicle, for which the county paid him a monthly stipend.

Historical background

"Heritage of the Hills" is a history of Delaware County and the communities surrounding Grand Lake, published by the Delaware County Historical Society. Copies are available for $60 and can be ordered by calling 918-253-4345. Historical anecdotes for this story also came from archives of the Tulsa World, Tulsa Tribune, Associated Press and Grand River Dam Authority. GRDA offers free tours of the Pensacola Dam during the summer. Call 918-782-4726 for more information.

Crime Statistics 2010

Here's a look at the crime rate in northeast Oklahoma counties. The data reflect the Crime Index Rate among eight categories of crimes, per 1,000 population.

Craig.............................18.25

Delaware 18.46

Adair 18.67

Mayes 21.57

Cherokee 22.24

Ottawa 25.81

Tulsa 49.52

State 38.68

Crimes Reported in 2010

Crime	Delaware County	Ottawa County
Murder	2	0
Rape	20	11
Robbery	2	8
Felonious Assault	69	60
Breaking and Entering	233	197
Larceny	395	514
Vehicle theft	42	31
Total	**763**	**821**

World news researcher Hilary Pittman and Enterprise Editor Ziva Branstetter contributed to this story.

CHRONOLOGY

PHILPOTT:	TURLINGTON:
16 FEB 1979 Becomes a legal adult; his remarkable public criminal records begins exactly 6 months later **16 AUG 1979** **ARRESTED** for **Minor in Possession** and **Failure to Maintain Control** in Decatur, Arkansas. **09 FEB 1981** **ARRESTED** for **DWI** (.18 Blood Alcohol Concentration [BAC], 225% the legal limit for DWI) in Decatur, Arkansas. **24 APR 1981** **ARRESTED** for **DWI** (.12 BAC, 150% of the legal limit for DWI) in Decatur, Arkansas.) **08 JUN 1981** **CONVICTED and SENTENCED for FELONY** 3 years' probation for Burglary and Theft in Benton County, Arkansas on the condition he possess no firearms and commits no offense punishable by prison.	 *1979. Lance, Eddie, Ed sr, Country life before meth addicts took over*  *1984 Spelunking trip to Twin Caves and Jack Squirrel's cave.*[xlvi] *Ed jr, sleeveless on left end, Ed sr back row on right end (moustache)*  *Shani Green muddy after caves*

PHILPOTT:	TURLINGTON:
16 JUN 1981 <u>**Arrested for Possession with Intent to Deliver**</u>	**NOV 1987:** Enlists in Florida National Guard
	AUG 1988: Activated to Miami Beach to participate in US Customs drug interdiction operations.
23 SEP 1981 <u>**PRE SENTENCE REPORT**</u> Parole officer submits his recommendation to the court, noting that Philpott's current drug felony occurred EIGHT days after his convictions for felony burglary and felony theft.	**NOV 1988:** Enlists in Army with 82d Airborne Division in his contract.
	DEC 1988: Graduates Airborne school, assigned to 82nd Airborne Division.
	FEB- MAR 1989: Attended US Army Jungle Operations Training Center at in Panama. Learned Jungle Survival and Jungle Warfare, including Jungle Navigation and Tracking, Water Survival, Mine and Boobytrap Identification and Deployment, Waterborne Operations (small boat drills, Riverine Reconnaissance and Demolitions) and small unit Jungle Operations (Recon, Raid and Ambush)
23 SEP 1981 <u>**CONVICTED for FELONY**</u> **Possession Controlled Substance w/ Intent** in violation of probation	
31 OCT 1981 <u>**Sentenced**</u> **for violation of felony probation.**	
22 JAN 1982 <u>**PAROLED**</u> for <u>**Possession Controlled Substance w/ Intent**</u> by Arkansas Dept. of Corrections	**1991-** assigned to US European Command Europe at Patch Barracks, Germany. There he protected a 4 star General, his family and visiting dignitaries as part of the Command Security Detachment.

PHILPOTT:	TURLINGTON:
(CONT.):	1991- assigned to US European Command Europe at Patch Barracks, Germany. There he protected a 4 star General, his family and visiting dignitaries as part of the Command Security Detachment.
26 NOV 1982 **ARRESTED for VIOLA-TION OF PAROLE** in Decatur, Arkansas by Decatur PD for possessing a half gallon of whiskey and a firearm after being stopped by Decatur officers who observed PHILPOTT in a public family disturbance	
	1992 Honorably discharged from Army, assigned to 12th Special Forces Reserves in Tulsa.
20 SEP 1991 **ARREST by GRDA**	**JAN 93** Turlington's childhood friend Dean Bridges introduces him to Shodai Gary Dill. After interviewing with Dill, Turlington begins classes in Jeet Kune Do and Bushido Kempo.
30 SEP 1991 **FAILURE TO APPEAR for GRDA** / **BENCH WARRANT for AR-REST** issued	**1993** US Army Reserves Special Forces transfers to National Guard component and Tulsa unit closes. Turlington transfers to A Co. 1/279th Infantry Battalion where childhood friend Dean Bridges was his squad leader. Several years later, Bridges would serve as Turlington's platoon sergeant in C. Co. in Claremore.
28 FEB 1997 **ASSAULTS wife** in front of 10 & 12-year-old children and threatens to burn down their house according to domestic abuse affidavit.	
12 MAR 1997 **PROTECTION ORDER** E 97-404-2 (Benton County, Arkansas) issued to wife and three children for ONE YEAR against PHILPOTT for *assaulting* them and *threatening* to burn	 *Jungle Patrol*

PHILPOTT: (CONT.):	TURLINGTON:

PHILPOTT:
(CONT.):

their house. Violation is punishable by imprisonment.

14 MAR 1997
Delaware County cancels Arrest Warrant and dismisses charges *at cost to State*

14 OCT 1997
Additional PROTEC-TION ORDER
E 99-1721-1 (Benton County, Arkansas) issued for Philpot's ex-wife and two children.

25 SEP 1999
ARRESTED FOR *DO-MESTIC BATTERY*
(amended to **Assault**) in Gentry, Arkansas.

THREATENS and AS-SAULTS ex-wife in response to her not letting him hold a baby while drunk "...**in a rage, cussing, kicking animals and telling us** *he could do anything he wants*". Philpott, forbidden to possess firearms as a felon, grabs a gun and threatens to burn down her house. (Ch.5)

TURLINGTON:

Glastonbury, England, 2001

Ed, Joe, David,
Strasbourg Health Club, 2001

PHILPOTT:	TURLINGTON:
(CONT.): **12 FEB 2000 CONVICTED of ASSAULT** **26 FEB 2000 ARRESTED for POS- SESSION OF INSTRU- MENT OF A CRIME AND POSSESSION OF A CONTROLLED SUB- STANCE** **19 APR 2000 CONVICTED POSSES- SION OF CONTROLLED SUBSTANCE** **19 APR 2000 CONVICTED POSSES- SION OF INSTRUMENT OF A CRIME** **06 MAY 2000 FAILURE TO APPEAR, BENCH WARRANT 2000414 ISSUED.** **19 APR 2000 CONVICTED POSSES- SION OF INSTRUMENT OF A CRIME** **06 MAY 2000 ARRESTED on WAR- RANT 2000414 for CONTEMPT OF COURT.**	 *Ed and Lisa, Strasbourg, 2001*  *Uncle Ed with Anna, February 2003*

PHILPOTT:	TURLINGTON:
14 APR 2001 ARRESTED FOR DWI and FLEEING FROM POLICE in Benton County	**February – March 2004** Turlington attends US Army Watercraft Operator school, trained in seamanship: firefighting, water survival, and water rescue.
18 APR 2001 (filed) **ARRESTED FOR PUBLIC INTOXICATION** in Delaware County, Oklahoma – Incarcerated 2 days, posted bail	**March 2004**- graduates Watercraft Operator school, awarded 88K Military Occupational Specialty (MOS), and is assigned to USAV New Orleans.
25 APR 2001 Failed to Appear, Arrest Warrant issued for 18 APR 2001 Public Intoxication,	
26 APR 2001 CONVICTED FOR 18 APR 2001 PUBLIC INTOXICATION	
23 AUG 2001 ARRESTED FOR PUBLIC INTOXICATION (again) in Delaware County, Oklahoma – Incarcerated 2 days	
	USAV New Orleans, 2004
18 SEP 2001 CONVICTED OF 23 AUG 2001 PUBLIC INTOXICATION	**Summer 2004** , sails from Tampa Bay to Puerto Rico and back, awarded "Jethro" sea name by crew.

PHILPOTT:	TURLINGTON:
17 JAN 2002 <u>**CONVICTED for OS-SESSION OF A CON-TROLLED SUBSTANCE.AND FLEEING FROM PO-LICE**</u> **17 JUL 2009** <u>**ARRESTED for Pursu-ing/Tak-ing/Killed/Possessed Or Disposed Of Wild-life Illegally in McDon-ald County, Missouri**</u> **10 SEP 2009** <u>**FAILED TO APPEAR FOR 17 JULY 09 POACHING ARREST / CRIMINAL SUMMONS 09-CRSU-2229 ISSUED**</u> McDonald County, Mis-souri **24 SEP 2009** <u>**ARRESTED for DWI**</u> by Missouri Highway Pa-trol Troop D Spring-fiel**d.** **21 OCT 2009** <u>**FAILED TO APPEAR / ARREST WARRANT 09-MCFTA-739 IS-SUED FOR POACHING.**</u> McDonald County, Mis-souri.	**4 JUL 2008**, marries Julie Kristine Hoss at Tulsa **Fall 2008**- Attends US Army Civil Affairs School, learns civil-military procedures within the civil population including :coordi-nating the integration of Civil Affairs plan-ning integration with conventional and special operations, restoring government operations and services normally provided by host nations, and coordinating the reset-tlement of dislocated civilian. Awarded 38B MOS 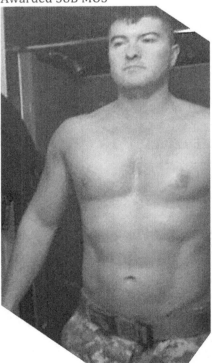 Ed, 40 year old, Civil Affairs School, 2008

PHILPOTT:	TURLINGTON:
04 NOV 2009 <u>FAILED TO APPEAR / ARREST WARRANT 09-MCFTA-780 IS-SUED FOR DWI,</u> <u>McDonald County, Missouri.</u> **10 JAN 2010** <u>FAILS TO APPEAR, ARREST WARRANT ISSUED;</u> **Philpott goes into hiding.** **14 APR 2014** <u>Commits aggravated assault against disabled veteran while trespassing and is protected by DCSO</u> **8 DEC 2015** District Attorney Kenny Wright and Prosecutor Nic Lelecas allow Philpott to come into court, with multiple warrants for his arrest, commit multiple perjuries while testifying against Turlington, and leave a free man.	**May 2009**- Turlington's firstborn, Edwin "Hardee" Turlington III, born in Paris, Texas.[xlvii] **June 2010** – Edwin. Lance and Julie Turlington certified as Jeet Kune Do instructors by Shodai Gary Dill **September 2011** – Birth of Turlington's second son, Hoss Britton Turlington in Tulsa, Oklahoma.[xlviii] **27 AUG 2013** Inducted into Sons of American Revolution with brother Lance under their 7th great grandfather, Alexander Fullerton, National # 188457.[xlix]  **14 APR 2014** Shoots an attacking violent felon he caught trespassing. Turlington reports it to authorities, but they protect Philpott and arrest Turlington. **17 APR 2014** Local former prosecutor Winston Connor says he can "take care of " the charges for $10,000. Turlington retains him without a contract. Over the upcoming weeks, Turlington emails Connor proof of withheld and altered evidence as well as Philpott's extensive criminal past. **August 2014** – Birth of Turlington's first daughter, Audrey Maxine Turlington, in Joplin, Missouri.[l]

PHILPOTT:	TURLINGTON:
04 OCT 2016 ARRESTED FOR FELONY Possession of a Controlled Substance SCHED I,II (METH & COCAINE). Possession of a Controlled Substance SCHED VI, DWI, No DL, No Insurance, and Careless Prohibited Driving by Benton County Deputy Justin Crane. Crane found PHILPOTT passed out in his car, in the middle of the road with the engine running. Crane finds a *baggie of meth* in PHILPOTT's overalls. **10 JAN 2017 FAILS TO APPEAR for 2016 FELONY CHARGES, ARREST WARRANT ISSUED** **25 FEB 2017 ARRESTED in Missouri FOR FAILURE TO APPEAR ON DWI CHARGE FOR DWI, Possession of a controlled Substance, (Meth), Operating Vehicle in a Careless Manner- Involving an Accident, and Failing to Secure Child, and Wildlife Crimes**	**8 DEC 2015** Turlington's preliminary hearing takes place, long after the Speedy Trial review should have begun. Connor fails to mention that the Prosecution's star witness (Philpott) has warrants for his arrest, or that he had warrants for his arrest when he attacked Turlington. Connor fails to impeach the Philpott on any of the many reasons given in Chapter 4. Connor fails to address Philpott's previous multiple perjuries. Connor questions Philpott's use of firearms as a felon, however, both Connor and Prosecutor Nic Lelecas accept Philpott's legal opinion that it was allowed. Lelecas tries multiple times to enter a falsehood into the court records. **March 2016** Turlington's 3rd son, John Duke Kelly Turlington is born in Joplin, Missouri. Duke is named after his 3rd Great Grandfather, Missouri Partisan Ranger and Quantrill Bushwhacker, John Duke Kelly (p, 61 and throughout Ch. 6) **15 MAY 2017** – Turlington retires from Oklahoma's 45th Infantry Brigade after serving over 20 years in the Active Army, US Army Reserves, and Florida National Guard and Oklahoma National Guard. **3 JAN 2018** Writes Connor requesting an accounting of his $10000 retainer. Connor responds by stating he would need another $10,000 to $20,000 to continue representing Turlington. **17 Sep 2018:** Complains to Oklahoma Bar about Connor for refusing to account for his $10,000 retainer (among other things).

PHILPOTT:	TURLINGTON:
22 MAR 2017 **CONVICTED for 2009 Missouri DWI** **23 MAR 2017** **SERVED ARREST WARRANT FOR 2016 AR FELONY** **7 June 2017** **Philpott convicted for Meth Felony, DWI and Schedule VI drugs** **21 JUL 2018** **ARESTED for Public Intoxication and Obstruction of a Governmental Operation** Benton County, Arkansas Deputy Cedric Lampkin finds Philpott passed out drunk in road. Philpott resists arrest, assaults medics, calls Lampkin "nigger" repeatedly and threatens to kill him repeatedly. VIDEO **08 OCT 2018** **FAILS TO APPEAR / BENCH WARRANT** 51052018 ISSUED FOR HIS ARREST for 21 JUL 28 Crimes	**14 Nov 2018**: In response to Turlington's Bar Complaint , Connor tells lies to the Bar that, if true, would violate the Attorney Client privilege. Among other lies, Connor tells the Bar his agreed upon representation would be limited to the preliminary trial. Remember, Connor continued to make appearances in Turlington's case for over three years after the Preliminary Trial. **12 May 2019** – Turlington warns on social media he would "would post "true and accurate, documented and very embarrassing videos" of the prosecution team if his case wasn't "dropped soon". **1 July 2919**- DA Kenny Wright motions to dismiss Turlington's case, deceiving the public one last time in the process. **25 December 2019** – Turlington finishes writing "The Most Dangerous Man and The Rape of Delaware County" about his false arrest and the collusion between the Delaware County, Oklahoma District Attorney's Office, and the Delaware County Sheriff's Office. He registers the copyright. In the following weeks, print, electronic, and audio versions are published. **21 May 2020** - Turlington publishes video about leading Sheriff Candidate and Harlan Moore protégé move-in Tracy Shaw. www.rapeofdelco.com/shaw.htm **30 June 2020**- Shaw fails to make the primary runoff election for Sheriff. .

PHILPOTT:	TURLINGTON:
01 JUL 2019 DA Kenny Wright mis-leads public when mo-tioning court to drop charges **28 June 2020-** Okla-homa Highway Patrol Aaron Gibe pulls Phil-pott over at 9:10 PM for driving without work-ing lights and without a license plate. Philpott had a partially drunk bottle of vodka between the front seats. Phil-pott's driver's license had been suspended and the vehicle he was driving hadn't been tagged in over 3 years Gibe arrested him. **13 July 2020-** Prosecutor Nic Lelecas arranges for Judge Barry Denney to release Philpott *on his personal recognizance*. **Summer 2020-** Philpott moves back to his cousin Jack Thomas' house down the road from Turlington in Delaware County as a protected criminal.	**31 March 2021-** Turlington files a federal lawsuit against 23 Delaware County Government agencies and officials for False Arrest, Prosecutorial Misconduct, Retaliation, Conspiracy, and violations of the Americans with Disabilities Act.

Postscript

One of the challenges in writing this book was choosing which Delaware County scandals to include. Two days after completing the book, and minutes before sending it to the publisher, the above jailhouse torture scandal broke the news here.

Some law enforcement officers don't treat people in custody like humans. This is more common when they don't identify with the people in their custody as real people; their neighbors and their neighbors' family members. When the detainee is "other", it is easier to dehumanize them. This is just another reason why it is better to elect our own people to these positions of power.

David Sergeant, instructs and certifies all the local law enforcement in the use of tasers. David told me that, due to the well-known track record of the Delaware County Sheriff's Office, he actually makes law enforcement officers from that agency sign special legal waivers in *addition* to the standard waivers all students sign.

◢ Former DelCo detention officers charged in taser case

By Chloe Goff • cgoff@grovesun.com
Posted Jan 27, 2020 at 12 00 PM
Updated Jan 27, 2020 at 12 28 PM

JAY, Okla. - Charges have been filed against two former
Delaware County jail detention officers and roommates for
incidents that allegedly occurred at the jail.

District Attorney Kenny Wright filed the charges against
Charles Hayes and Shelly Mayberry Thursday. Hayes, 37, is
charged with seven counts of assault and battery with a dangerous weapon, while Mayberry, 45, is
charged with two counts of assault and battery with a dangerous weapon.

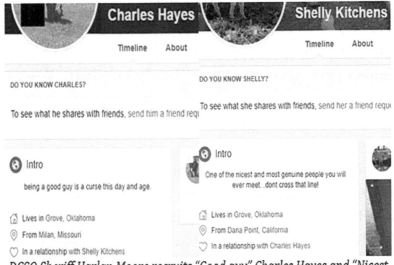

*DCSO Sheriff Harlan Moore recruits "Good guy" Charles Hayes and "Nicest
and Genuine" girl Shelly Kitchens (Shelly Mayberry in the above news
article) aren't from around here. These torturers aren't even Okies.*

Post Postscript

There were four candidates for Sheriff in the 2020 election. Three were raised here, and the fourth, Tracy Shaw, was Sheriff Harlan Moore's Undersheriff and protégé. Similar to how his boss had to lie about his beliefs in order to be elected, Tracy Shaw convinced Don Spencer, president of the Oklahoma 2nd Amendment Association and author of Oklahoma's gun laws, that he was pro-gun. Spencer backed Shaw's candidacy. On 21 May 2020, I published a video about Shaw – who was leading the polls at the time (largely in part to his masquerading as a pro gun candidate). It was seen by thousands of local voters. I called Don about Shaw and sent him the video. The OK2A immediately revoked their backing of Shaw.

Shaw failed the primary election. The video is available at www.rapeofdelco.com/shaw.htm/   .

On 31 March I filed a federal lawsuit against 22 Delaware County defendants for False Arrest, Retaliation, Conspiracy, Prosecutorial Misconduct, and Violations of the Americans with Disabilities Act.

SUBJECT INDEX

PERSON INDEX

ABOUT THE AUTHOR

Ed "Hoss" Turlington retired from the military in 2017, having served in capacities ranging from Infantryman in Oklahoma's 45th Infantry Brigade, Civil Affairs specialist, 82nd Airborne Division Paratrooper, deckhand on an oceangoing vessel, to Military Police patrol officer in Germany and, later, at the joint US European Command where he protected a 4-star general and his family and visiting dignitaries from bodily injury and invasion of privacy and the VIP living quarters and working quarters against sabotage, riot, and espionage. Turlington is an expert in the usage of numerous firearms to include shotguns, submachine guns, machine guns, pistols, and revolvers. He has intensive training and experience in the areas surrounding physical security and special expertise relative to VIP security and International Terrorism Surveillance.

Hoss lives with his wife Julie and their children, Hardee, Hoss, Audrey Maxine, and Duke, 4, and their Turkish Boz Shepherd, Duchess, 4 miles from the borders of Missouri, Arkansas, and Oklahoma where they raise St. Croix sheep. Hoss and Julie are licensed Oklahoma teachers. Hoss homeschools their children and runs the farm with his sons. Julie teaches High School Biology in Miami. Both Hoss and Julie are certified Jeet Kune Do instructors under 1st Generation practitioner Shodai Gary Dill. He volunteers his spare time researching and exposing criminals for victims in his community and does what he can to fight the rampant and systematic abuse of police and prosecutorial discretion. When he is not fighting crime or working on his farm, Hoss enjoys making wine, working out, forging knives, and taking his family to the swimming hole walking distance from his home.

NOTES

[i] Sam sr, moved to Miami, Indian Territory to practice law in 1898. When the 13th Judicial District was formed, Sam was elected the first presiding Judge. Sam served as president of the Angus association from 1925 to 1929, and again in 1937 and 1938. He was a 32° Freemason and Past Master of the Miami lodge. His son, Sam jr, developed his father's farm into one of the world's leading Aberdeen-Angus ranches. Sam jr was a freemason. Sam III graduated from Princeton where he played football. Afterwards he served in the Army. He was an associate Delaware County judge from 1974 to 1976 when the Governor appointed as 13th Judicial District judge. He was repeatedly re-elected until his retired in 1998. Sam was a 32° Freemason in the Miami lodge and a Shriner. He called my mother to his office in the 60s, told her a story of the murder of their mutual relative and the subsequent lynching and gave her a copy of the lynching article.

See http://www.rapeofdelco.com/labanfullerton.htm for details. See endnote xiv. Sam sr's Grandfather, John McCune Fullerton was the first permanent white settler in the Southwest Octant of Missouri.

[ii] Miami native (and former Marine) David Anderson ran against Wyant for DA in 2002. David won in Ottawa County, but because of the large population of retirees on Grand Lake in Delaware County who, like Wyant, are not from here, David lost the overall election to the disgusting, undisciplined outsider.

[iii] John L Rotramel & Mary Ronald > Martin Rotramel & Alice Bullock Leon Rotramel > Ronald Leon Rotramel

Documentation at www.rapeofdelco.com/Rotramel.htm

[iv] Documentation at www.rapeofdelco.com/shotpouch.htm

[v] Leroy Summerfield > Levi Summerfield & Annie Lee Cornshucker > Leach Ridge Summerfield & Mary Kingfisher > Joseph Summerfield & Wahlea Ah-se-ni Documentation at
www.rapeofdelco.com/Summerfield.htm

[vi] Polson Cemetery is in Delaware County, two miles west of South West City and two miles north of Hoss Turlington's Bee and Goat Farm. It is named for Dr. William D. Polson and the Polson Family. In addition to the Polsons, the cemetery includes the Ridges, Bells, Washbournes, and Adairs. Confederate Brigadier General and Cherokee Chief Stand Watie is buried there. Dr. Polson was a Freemason.

[vii] Julie > Kurt David Hoss & Kay Cooley > Ralph Haland Hoss & Fern Burdine > Ralph Wynne Hoss & Winifred Price > Thomas Washington Price & Minnie Katherine Burke > Peter Pressler Burke & Winnifred White Smythe

[viii] Their father, native Tennessean James Burke, fought in the War of 1812 under General Claiborne and pioneered Arkansas and Texas after that war.

[ix] Julie > Kurt David Hoss & Kay Cooley > Ralph Haland Hoss & Fern Burdine > Ralph Wynne Hoss & Winifred Price > Thomas Washington Price & Minnie Katherine Burke > Henry Emery Price & Martha Almira Renick

[x] Kennedy, W., 1893, History of Texas together with a biographical history of Milam, Williamson, Bastrop, Travis, Lee and Burleson Counties, The Lewis Publishing Company, Chicago, p. 489 and
www.rapeofdelco.com/texashistory2.pdf

[xi] Edwin jr > Edwin Hardee Turlington sr & Nancy Lynn Kelly > Robert Leroy Kelly & Myrle Maxine Simmons > William Thomas Kelly & Emma Gertrude Baugher > John Duke Kelly & Muta Angeline Davis

[xii] *History of Vernon County, Missouri: Written and Compiled from the Most Authentic Official and Private Sources, including a History of Its Townships, Towns and Villages, Together with a Condensed History of Missouri ; a Reliable and Detailed History of Vernon County--its Pioneer Record, Resources, Biographical Sketches of Prominent Citizens ; General and Local Statistics of Great Value ; Incidents and Reminiscences. Illustrated* (St. Louis: Brown &, 1887). Online at www.rapeofdelco.com/vernonhistory.pdf

[xiii] Fredrea Gregath Cook, *Afton (Indian Territory – Oklahoma) Some Early History* (Wyandotte: Gregath Company, 2016): 115-116

xiv When Capt. Heinrich Adam Herrmann Jr was born in 1700, in Mannheim, Mannheim, Mannheim, Baden-Württemberg, Germany, his father, Johann Michael Harman, was 30 and his mother, Anna Becker, was 54. He married Louisa Katrina Mathias on 8 October 1723, in Mannheim, Mannheim, Baden-Württemberg, Germany. They were the parents of at least 13 sons and 8 daughters. He lived in Harman, Tazewell, Virginia, United States in 1760. He died on 24 January 1767, in Augusta, Virginia, British Colonial America, at the age of 67, and was buried in Toms Creek, Wise, Virginia, United States...

Captain Heinrich Adam Herrmann (Harmon) jr & Louisa Katrina Mathias > Daniel Harman & Anna Bughsen > Henry Harman & Polly Day > Adam Harman & Nancy Swango > Phineas Albion Baugher & Jessian Harmon > William Kelly & Emma Gertrude Baugher > Robert Leroy Kelly & Myrle Maxine Simmons > Edwin Hardee Turlington sr and Nancy Lynn Kelly > Edwin jr

xvNancy's brothers Captain Henry Chapman Swango and Private Stephen served in Company E, 2nd Battalion Kentucky Mounted Rifles. Henry transferred to and commanded Company I until he died action at Mt. Sterling, Kentucky on June 8, 1864. His nephew (Harrison's son) Captain David Franklin Swango assumed command. Nancy's brother George Washington Swango and Samuel Swango served in Company D, 5th Kentucky Cavalry.

Harrison's son William H. served as an officer in Company E, 10th (Diamond's) Kentucky Cavalry. Harrison's son James Calvin (J.C.) served Nancy's brother George and Samuel served in Company D, 5th Kentucky Cavalry. The 2nd Battalion, Kentucky Mounted Rifles, the 5th Kentucky Cavalry, and the 10th (Diamond's) Kentucky Cavalry were all General John Hunt Morgan's Raiders.

Nancy's father "Little Abe" Swango served in the War of 1812 at Detroit in Captain Henry Daniel's Company and Captain Johnson Magowen's Company, both of the 28th Infantry Regiment of Kentucky. Little Abe was with General Jackson at the Battle of New Orleans and honorably discharged at Ft Shelby 30 Apr 1814.

Little Abe's Grandfather, Abraham Schwangau / Swango signed a lease with future president George Washington for property in Frederick County, Virginia. The lease called for "building of buildings, clearing of land, setting fruit trees" according to a plan laid out by Washington. (Source: Frederick County, Virginia Deed Book Series, Volume 4, Deed Books 12, 13, 14, 1767-1771, by Amelia C. Gilreath, Willow Bend Books, Westminster, Maryland, 2001, page 86.) Washington considered Germans the best farmers so discriminated for them in hiring. Abraham migrated to what is now Red River, Powell County, Kentucky about 1785.

Abraham Swango & Ailsie Pyles > Samuel Swango & Elizabeth Johnston O'Banion > Abraham Swango & Deborah Auglin Ogden > Adam H Harman & Nancy Swango > Phineas Albion Baugher & Jessian Harman > William Kelly & Emma Gertrude Baugher >Robert Leroy Kelly & Myrle Maxine Simmons > Edwin Hardee Turlington sr & Nancy Lynn Kelly > Edwin Hardee Turlington jr

[xvi] Paul's Grandfather, Paul Reinart Andert, emigrated from Breslau, Silesia, Germany to Missouri in 1883. Andert's father, Charles Joseph Pierre Andert, served in France in World War I. He married Paul's mother, Frenchwoman Marie Clotilde Anne Alophonsine neé Gergaud, at Temple De Bretagne after the war. Andert's older brother, Charles, served in the Navy in WWII, and his younger brothers Joseph and Pierre, served in the National Guard during peacetime.

[xvii] Sergeant Charles Everett Turlington, Company E, 11th Florida Infantry C.S.A. & Margaret Jane Henry > Charles Edwin Turlington & Christiana Frances Roberts > Robert Edwin Turlington & Annie Lee Townsend > Richard Edwin Turlington & Theresa Genice (Teresa Janice) Hardee > Edwin Hardee Turlington sr & Nancy Lynn Kelly > Edwin jr

Captain Robert Augustus Hardee, Company H (Brooks County Rifles), 9th Georgia Infantry Regiment & Emma Provida Willard > Robert George Hardee & Clarissa Maskery Kitching > Richard Edwin Turlington and Theresa Genice Hardee ... ibid

Captain Lot Townsend, Company H (Wise Yankee Catchers), 50th Georgia Infantry & Lamenda Lawson > Thomas Oscar Townsend & > Annie Lee Townsend ... ibid

>Sergeant James Gary Roberts, Company B (Marianna Dragoons), 15th Florida Cavalry Regiment and Mary Jackson > Charles Edwin Turlington & Christiana Frances Roberts ...ibid

Private Levi Stephens, Company A, 36th Regiment, Georgia Infantry, (Broyle's) & Rebecca Tyler > David Louis Ezell & Sarah Ann Stephens > Thomas Oscar Townsend & Cynthia V Ezell ... ibid

Private David Ezell, Companies I and J, 6th Florida Infantry and Sarah Ann Stephens ...ibid Revolutionary Ancestors include Southey Turlington, William Bachelor Denmark (DAR A031796), Bartholomew Burns (DAR A018157), Townsend, Joseph Register (DAR A002461) W Samuel Jackson Townsend (DAR A115723) Hugh O'pry, Stephen Costin (DAR A026349), Ed belongs to the sons of Confederate Veterans and the Sons of the American Revolution

He is descended from the below Jamestowne colonists.

Captain Thomas Harwood & Ann Bray > *Major Humphrey Harwood & Ann Needler* > Matthew Jones II & Martha Harwood, Francis Jones I and Mary Ridley > Francis Jones II & Elizabeth Huckabee > William Jones & Elizabeth Cosby > Thomas Jones & Martha Denmark > Thomas Edward Hardee & Gracy Ann Jones > Robert Augustus Hardee & Theresa Genice Hardee > Edwin Hardee Turlington sr

Burgess Peter Ridley & Mary Elizabeth Thorpe > Captain Nathaniel Ridley & Elizabeth Day > Francis Jones I & Mary Ridley ...ibid.

None of Ed Turlington sr's ancestors have ever resided above the Dixon-Mason line. Documentation at Turlingtons.org and www.rapeofdelco.com/edturlington.htm

[xviii] John's great grandfather, James Maher, immigrated to Indian Territory from Ireland and married Cherokee Elvira Lovett in 1884. John's 2nd great grandfather, Thomas Alexander Cathey, fought for the Confederacy in Company H, 28th Regiment, Louisiana Infantry.

[xix] Dean Bridges > David Ait & Sarah Bridges > Albert Ait & Mabel Huffman > James Huffman & Fannie Davis > Solomon K. Huffman & Mary Elizabeth Bland

Dean Bridges > David Ait & Sarah Bridges > Albert Ait & Mabel Huffman > James Huffman & Fannie Davis > Solomon K. Huffman & Mary Elizabeth Bland Documentation available at
www.rapeofdelco.com/dean.htm

[xx] *Thomason, Denton. "Cherokee Restaurant Prides Itself on Great Tasting Southern Comfort Classics." Vinita Daily Journal Online. Vinita Daily Journal, December 19, 2019.*
https://www.etypeservices.com/SWF/LocalUser/Vinita1//Magazine64491/Full/index.aspx?II=264491#12/z.

[xxi] Although I hadn't heard from Sergeant 30 years, when another cop asked David what he thought about my arrest for shooting Philpott, David answered that he grew up with me in Afton, his family was friends with mine, and that if I shot someone, they deserved it. David currently works as a full time police sergeant at Commerce, Oklahoma and for the Wyandotte Nation. He is on the President's honor roll at Northeastern State University in Tahlequah where he is pursuing a Master's degree in Police Science. David has blackbelts in Hwa Rang Do, Tae Koshi Do and Tae Kwon Do, and took Bushido Kempo for a year from Professor Gary Dill. He is a former State heavyweight sparring champion for Arkansas and Missouri and in September 2018 was inducted into the United States Martial Arts Hall of Fame. David's brother, Steve is also a multiple blackbelt and former Oklahoma State heavyweight sparring champion.

David is married to Rick Littlefield's (p.200) niece, Shannon (nee Littlefield). David's 4th Great Grandfather, Young Abercrombie, moved to Benton County, Arkansas after serving the Confederacy in Company G, 52nd Georgia Infantry Regiment. After serving in the Infantry in Campbell County, Georgia, Young's brother David served under Stand Watie in Co. A, 1st Cherokee Mounted Volunteers. David's 2nd Great Grandfather, John Hall, a former Tennessee Confederate, moved to McDonald County, Missouri after the war. David is a patriot and a friend. David > Gerald Lee Sergeant & Helen Irene Hall > Estle Ira Hall & Irene Abercrombie > John Edward Hall & Ina Ellen Dean > John Randolph Hall & Jennie Christenberry

(see above) ...Estle Ira Hall & Irene Abercrombie > Benjamin Abercrombie & Laura Thomas > Young Andrew Abercrombie & Easter Stalcup > Young Samuel Abercrombie & Lucy Ann Montgomery

Documentation available at www.rapeofdelco.com/sergeant.htm

[xxii] Gordon's great grandfather, Denis Carlin, fought for the Confederacy in Capt. Barr's Independent Co. (Blakesley Guards, Yellowjacket Battalion), Louisiana Infantry. Denis' grandfather, Italian Giuseppe Vincenzo (Joseph Vincent) Carlin, was a Revolutionary War veteran. Giuseppe was a Spanish subject in the Colony of Louisiana and served as a Sergeant in the Attakapas Post militia. After Spain declared war against England in 1779, Joseph took part in the Battle of Baton Rouge under Governor-General Bernardo de Gálvez. Joseph was the first white man to occupy Orange Island (now Jefferson island) in the Louisiana Delta. Governor Esteban Miró granted Joseph 25 arpents of coast 40 arpents deep for his military service. Thomas Carlin, son of Confederate Denis, moved the Carlins to Texas during the 19 oil boom.

Gordon > Gordon Earl Carlin sr & Susan Stout > Dewey Carlin & Mayme Howell > Thomas Evis Carlin & Nancy Crowson > *Denis Peter Carlin* & Amelia Mendoza > Ursin Carlin & Arsese Verret > Dionysius Denis Carlin & Suzanne Labatrie > Giuseppe Vincenzo Carlin & Francoise L Ange Carterouge Genealogical and historical documentation is available at www.rapeofdelco.com/carlin.htm

xxiii Local attorney Jason Smith told me that perhaps another strategy may have been to not object the second time the prosecutor tried to enter a falsehood into the record, but to wait for prosecution to rest its case, then move for dismissal upon grounds of the alleged victim's misidentification of the shooter.

Jason is a is a 5th generation Missourian. His 5th great grandfather, Virginian John Wesley Surface, moved to Missouri after serving as a Partisan Ranger in Company H, 37th Battalion, Virginia Cavalry (Dunn's Battalion). John Wesley's father served in Company E, 54th Virginia Infantry Regiment. Jason > Charles Surface & Joyce Coleman > Hubert Surface & Hazel Ulmer > Charles Surface & Myrtle Jones > John Jacob Surface & Margaret Allen > John Wesley Surface & Mary List Documentation at www.rapeofdelco.com/jason.htm

xxiv McCormick, Charles Tilford., John William. Strong, and Kenneth S. Broun. *McCormick on Evidence*. St. Paul, MN: West, 1999.

xxv Chronology, P, and online version with links to documentation and police videos.

xxvi Since I shot his cousin, Jack has been a guest in my home, and I have been a guest in his. The first scoped rifle Hardee shot was Jack's. When I asked Jack about the Tulsa World article that stated Sheriff Moore told reporters that Jack "instructed" Philpott and Barrett "set a small, controlled fire, to burn trash on the property," Jack said it wasn't true. Jack said he wasn't in charge of them, had never instructed either of them to do *anything*, and he wasn't with them on the property that day, so he had no way of knowing what they were doing or weren't doing, or even where they were. Jack also told me he didn't allow methamphetamines in his home, which would explain why Philpott went to my property (that he thought was foreclosed) to manufacture meth.

Jack's second great grandfather was a Confederate in North Carolina's A. Company, 21st Infantry Regiment. Jack Thomas > Jack Thomas sr & Betty Jo Van Horn > Charles Van Horn & Mary Kelley > Charles Van Horn & Mary Wilda Hughes > James Hughes & Martha Cornell. Jack flies the Battle Flag at his place.

[xxvii] Grisham is the son of an Arkansas construction worker and the 2nd great grandson of Andrew Jackson Gresham, who fought in the 1st Tennessee Cavalry Regiment. A. J. Gresham's father, Moses, fought in Davis' Battalion, Metcalfe's Regiment, West Tennessee Militia during the War of 1812. Moses' father, Virginian George Gresham was a Cavalry Captain in Georgia during the Revolutionary War.

John > John Grisham sr & Wanda Skidmore > Bluford M. Grisham & Mable Yates > George Washington Grisham & Amanda Patterson > Andrew Jackson Grisham & Gilla Olive > George Gresham & Elizabeth Watts

[xxviii] David was born and raised in Miami and is the descendant of Indian Territory pioneers from both his mother's and father's families. David's great grandparents, Tennesseans Lucas Anderson and Ada Cook moved to Indian Territory in what is now Sequoyah county, in the late 1800s. Lucas' father, Archibald, was a Confederate sergeant in Co. F, 25th Regiment, Tennessee Infantry. David's mother is Carolyn Sue neé Sumpter. Her great grandfather, John William Sumter, was a Confederate soldier in Co. F, 39th North Carolina Infantry Regiment. John and his wife, Jane moved to Cherokee Nation, Indian Territory with David's great grandfather, John Elisha in the late 1800s.

David > Riley Anderson & Carolyn Sumter > Fred Anderson & Lenora Young > Lucas Anderson & Ada Mae Cook.

David > Riley Anderson & Carolyn Sumpter > Clarence Sumpter & Cecil Margaret Cooper > John Elisha Sumter & Eliza Jane Coppinger > John William Sumter & Malinda Jane Stockton.

Documentation available at:

www.rapeofdelco.com/anderson.htm

David has used a firearm in self-defense, twice, in the past two years. David also participated in the police manhunt for Clint James, a suspect in the murder of Texan Amanda Thacker. David is a Patriot and a friend.

[xxix] Kaylea M. Hutson-Miller, "More Emerges about Charges against Connor," Grand Lake News (Grove Sun, January 24, 2019),

https://www.grandlakenews.com/news/20190124/more-emerges-about-charges-against-connor)

xxx Pander, v. To pimp; to cater to the gratification of the lust of another. To entice or procure a female, by promises, threats, fraud, or artifice, to enter any place in which prostitution is practiced, for the purpose of prostitution... –Henry Campbell Black and Joseph R. Nolan, *Black's Law Dictionary: Definitions of the Terms and Phrases of American and English Jurisprudence, Ancient and Modern* (St. Paul, MN: West Pub., 1996).

xxxi Solicitation. ...Thus "solicitation of prostitution" is the asking or urging a person to engage in prostitution. – Ibid.

xxxii Hardison graduated High School from Afton. He is descended from at least six Indian Territory and Oklahoma Territory pioneers, including his 2nd great grandfather, Arthur Hardison. Arthur was born in 1895 at Indian City, Oklahoma Territory, to Kentuckians Samuel Hardison and Lydia Johnson.

xxxiii 5 OK Stat § 5-2 Attorney's Oath: Upon being permitted to practice as attorneys and counselors at law, they shall, in open court, take the following oath: You do solemnly swear that you will support, protect and defend the Constitution of the United States, and the Constitution of the State of Oklahoma; **that you will do no falsehood or consent that any be done in court, and if you know of any you will give knowledge thereof to the judges** of the court, or some one of them, that it may be reformed...

xxxiv Rick is the son of Jarvis Littlefield and Joann Bilbo of Robert Lee, Texas. They moved to Afton the year Rick was born, where they farmed and raised coon dogs. Jarvis sat on the Grove School Board for 13 years as his 5 children attended. Jarvis was a police officer in neighboring Ottawa, Adair and Benton Counties, and was Delaware County Sheriff. Rick's little brother, Randy, was an Oklahoma Highway Patrol. Randy died in the line of duty on Oklahoma State Highway 20, which is now designated as Randy Littlefield Memorial Highway. It runs from Jay Oklahoma up to the Missouri state line, straddling Oklahoma and Arkansas in the southern half and Oklahoma and Missouri in the northern half, through South West City, Missouri.

The town of Robert Lee, Texas is named after the Confederate General.

[xxxv] Steve Martin's 2nd great grandfather, Captain Ephraim Martin Adair and both Ephraim's brothers, James Adair and Quartermaster George Washington Adair, rode in Company G, Cherokee Mounted Rifle regiment.

Steve's 2nd great grandfather Hamilton Martin was a Confederate Infantryman in Arkansas' 45th Militia Regiment and his 3rd great grandfather, Tennessean Dr. George Washington Currey, was a surgeon in the Confederate Army. 25 Adairs are listed in Watie's unit roster. Documentation at www.rapeofdelco.com/stevemartin.htm

[xxxvi] I posted this to my Facebook page and several Facebook groups dedicated to local events on 12 May 2019. My promise to post "true and accurate, documented and very embarrassing videos" of the prosecution team if my case wasn't "dropped soon" worked. Less than two months later, and over five years after my false arrest and the misery it caused me and my family, the Authorities decided to drop the case against me. A case they never really had.

[xxxvii] Hendrick's grandfather, Martin Hendricks served in the US Army. The Hendricks emigrated here from Russia in the 1880s.

[xxxviii] Josh Shaddon is a direct descendant of Indian Territory pioneer Doctor Robert Shaddon. Joshua Randall Shaddon > Frank Shaddon & Charlene Bass > Edgar Shaddon & Rosie Pruitt > John Turner Shaddon & Dona Mathis > Dr. Robert Shaddon and Amanda Jane Ivey. Documentation at www.rapeofdelco.com/joshshaddon.htm

[xxxix] I later learned that Gerald Sergeant and Duane Thomas had sued Rohman after he ripped them off. Sergeant and Thomas coached at Afton High School when my father was Superintendent there. Gerald was a golden gloves boxing champion. Sergeant's sons Steve and David went to school with Lance and me. See footnote xx

[xl] Bohannan's grandparents, Dennis Bohannan and Minnie Woolbright were Talihina, Indian Territory Choctaws. Dennis was born in Poteau and Minnie in Kully Chaha. Dennis' grandfather William moved his family from Choctaw, Mosholetubbe District, Mississippi to Indian Territory in the early 1850s and died in 1855.

Talihina is Choctaw *Tully Hina*. It means *Iron Road* (Rail Road). Choctaw is named after the Choctaw tribe of Muskogee Indians. Poteau is French for *post*. In the late 1700s there were French outposts along what is now known as the Poteau River in Oklahoma. Kully Chaha is Choctaw for *high spring*. Mosholetubbe was a Chief of the North Eastern District of the Choctaw Nation. This district included all of what is now Mississippi and parts of Georgia (including Quitman, the home of my second great grandfather Captain Robert Augustus Hardee, Company Commander of Brooks County Rifles.

"Mosholetubbe" is Choctaw for *Determined to Kill.*

[xli] I have left names of Rohmans' girlfriend and sister out of this book out of pity. The "men" in their lives failed them.

[xlii] Of the time Philpott **was not** wanted by police, Philpott he spent 3 months and 20 days in Missouri and Arkansas jails. The remaining 305 days he was on Judge Karren's probation, living in his car, and committing god knows what crimes until Deputy Lampkin arrested him. (Appendix)

Philpott's arrest warrant for his 2009 Poaching charge was served on 25 February 2017. During that time, Philpott jumped bail on his 2016 felony arrest for Meth, DUI (Arkansas' version of Oklahoma's and Missouri's DWI) and schedule XI drugs. On January 10, 2017 Benton County issued an arrest warrant for Philpott failing to appear.

On 22 March 2017, Philpott pled Guilty to his 2009 DWI and four 2009 charges (including the poaching charge) were dismissed. Judge LePage sentenced Philpott to *25 days in jail.* (Appendix E) The following day, Benton County Deputy Steimer served the Arkansas warrant. Philpott remained in custody while waiting for trial.

We don't know the specifics of the deals Philpott made with Prosecutor, but we know he made at least three. According to the Sentencing Order, Philpott negotiated a guilty plea for each charge. The Order also rates Philpott, the serial drunk driver and drug criminal, a "0" on "Criminal History Score" for each crime. This is just another of Philpott's actual crimes are not reflected in his RAP sheet because he always makes deals with the Prosecution.

On 7 June 2017, the judge found Philpott guilty of felony Possession of a Controlled Substance (Meth), Possession of a Controlled Substance (Schedule XI drugs), and drunk driving. Philpott was sentenced to *76 days* in jail for each of the drug charges and no jail for the DWI. The 76 days were to run concurrently. The judge gave Philpott 60 months' probation for the felony meth conviction, 12 months' probation for the Schedule XI drug conviction, and 12 months' probation for the Drunk Driving conviction. **Then the judge gave Philpott credit for 76 days' time served.** So once again, Philpott walked out of a court house a free man; free to commit more crime, which of course he of course did.

On 17 July 2018, Arkansas Deputy Lampkin arrested Philpott for "Public Intoxication" and "Obstruction of a Governmental Operation" after finding him passed out drunk in the middle of the road. Philpott assaulted responding medics, threatened to murder Lampkin repeatedly, and called him a "fucking nigger" (Lampkin is African American). Philpott absconded as usual and on 8 October 2019 Benton County issues Warrant 51052018 for his arrest. As of this writing (25 December 2019) Philpott is wanted by Arkansas authorities. If you add the time Philpott has spent either incarcerated, wanted by police, or on probation, and add that to just one his Oklahoma absconding that lasted most of the 90s (Appendix KK), that totals. To put that in perspective, that is enough time for a person to start Kindergarten, graduate High School and earn a Ph.D.

xliii I later learned the schizoid had murdered the sister of one of my childhood friends. I can't help but wonder if the Sheriff didn't move me from my Army veteran cellmate to the murderer, hoping I would extract jailhouse justice on the murderer so he would have a chance to legally arrest me.

xliv 22 OK Stat § 22-181 **Delay in taking before magistrate not permitted:** The defendant must, in all cases, be taken before the magistrate without unnecessary delay.

The US Supreme Court decided in County of Riverside v. McLaughlin, 500 U.S. 44 (1991), that the burden should be on the government to demonstrate reasonable cause for delay following arrest but concluded that a twenty-four hour deadline sufficiently balanced the competing concerns. Oklahoma Courts have interpreted that to mean, "a delay of more than 48 hours is presumptively unreasonable." and cited Gerstein v. Pugh (another Supreme Court decision) to explain, "...the rationale behind the requirement for a prompt hearing is to prevent an onerous oppression - Black v. State, 1994 OK CR 4, 871 P.2d 35

xlv Police Video of Philpott threatening (4 times) to murder Deputy Lampkin, repeatedly calling him a "f*cking nigger" (Lampkin is African American), etc. is at RapeOfDelco.com/philpott2018.mp4

xlvi Jack Squirrel was one of Stand Watie's Cherokee Braves in Company A with Joseph Summerfield. (see page 39)

xlvii Hardee is Ed sr's mother's maiden name. It is also the surname of her grandfather, Robert Augustus Hardee. R.A. commanded "Brooks County Rifles", Co. H, 9th Georgia Infantry Regiment and pioneered early Florida after the war. He was the previous owner of what is now Cocoa, where he served as State Representative. His nephew, Cary Hardee, was the 23rd Governor of Florida. R.A. settled in what is now Sebastian, where his son Robert built what is now the City Dock.

xlviii Hoss is mother's virgin name and Britton is his Uncle Lance's middle name.

[xlix] Ed, Lance > Edwin Hardee Turlington sr & Nancy Lynn Kelly > Robert Leroy Kelly & Myrle Maxine Simmons > James Henry Simmons & Mabel Frances Mann > Charles Taylor Mann & Olive Abigail Abbott > Pinkney Tell Mann & Mary Catherine Kay Fullerton > Laban Taylor Fullerton & Margaret Mary Potts > John McCune Fullerton & Ann Rawls Fort > Thomas Elder Fullerton & Isabella McCune > Alexander Fullerton & Mary Jane Sharp

Samuel Clyde Fullerton III & Priscilla Haigh Cook > Samuel Clyde Fullerton II & Barbara Swihart > Samuel Clyde Fullerton sr & Minnie Lillian Beck > Josiah David Fullerton & Sarah > John McCune Fullerton & Ann Rawls Fort ...ibid.
Documentation at www.rapeofdelco.com/alexanderfullerton.htm

[1] Audrey is the middle name of her mother's maternal grandmother. Maxine is the middle name of her father's maternal grandmother.

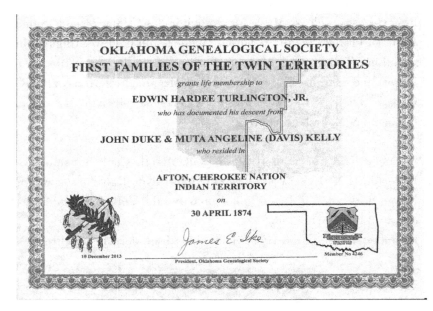

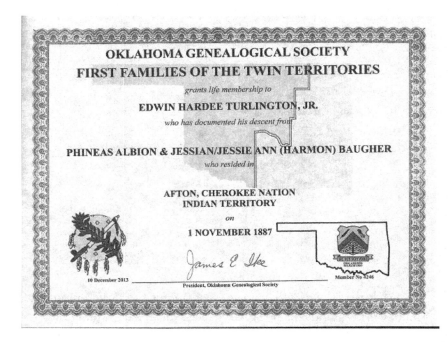

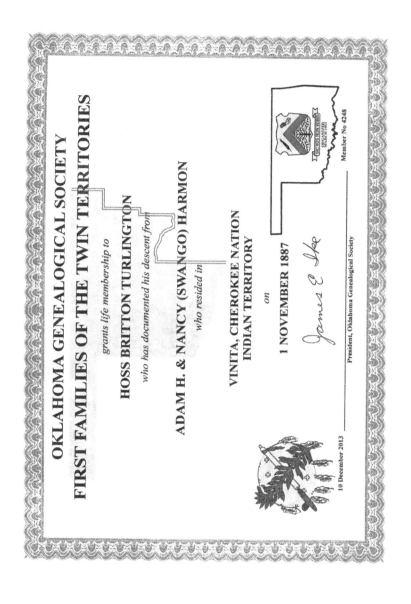

OKLAHOMA GENEALOGICAL SOCIETY

FIRST FAMILIES OF THE TWIN TERRITORIES

grants life membership to

HOSS BRITTON TURLINGTON

who has documented his descent from

ADAM H. & NANCY (SWANGO) HARMON

who resided in

VINITA, CHEROKEE NATION
INDIAN TERRITORY

on

1 NOVEMBER 1887

President, Oklahoma Genealogical Society

10 December 2013

Member No 4248

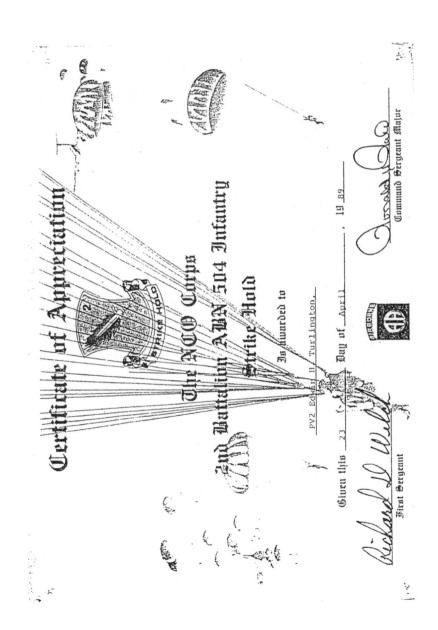

Certificate of Appreciation

The NCO Corps

2nd Battalion ABN 504 Infantry

Strike Hold

Is Awarded to

PV2 Edwin H. Turlington,

Given this 23 Day of April, 19 89

Richard D. Webb
First Sergeant

Command Sergeant Major